SOCIAL CHANGE, DEVELOPMENT AND DEPENDENCY

Modernity, Colonialism and the Development of the West

TONY SPYBEY

Polity Press

First published in 1992 by Polity Press in association with Blackwell Publishers

Editorial office:
Polity Press
65 Bridge Street
Cambridge CB2 1UR, UK

Marketing and production:
Blackwell Publishers
108 Cowley Road
Oxford OX4 1JF, UK

3 Cambridge Center
Cambridge
Massachusetts 02142, USA

ISBN 0 7456 0729 2
ISBN 0 7456 0730 6 (pbk)

A CIP catalogue record for this book is available from the British Library and the Library of Congress.

Typeset in $10\frac{1}{2}$ on 12 pt Times
by Times Graphics, Singapore
Printed in Great Britain by Billing and Sons, Worcester

This book is printed on acid-free paper.

Contents

Figures

Acknowledgements

I should like to thank Dave Dawson, my colleague at Plymouth, for his patient reading of early drafts and helpful comments; Jenny Des Fountain for helping me over some of my extravagances with the English language; Tony Giddens for his constructive criticism, encouragement and helpful suggestions; Colin Rallings and Michael Thrasher, good friends and colleagues, for their advice in my final editing; Andrew Webster for his comments on the complete manuscript; and Stewart Clegg and Winton Higgins for some earlier collaboration which contributed to chapter 11. Responsibility for what appears in the final version, of course, remains entirely with me.

A Note on Terminology

There are a number of terms to describe the former European colonies and Hamsa Alavi and Teodor Shanin have described this admirably, as follows:

> Something must be said about the way that the terminology developed. An earlier label, 'backward societies', informed a colonial vision. With decolonization, the term 'emergent nations' came into use, expressing a 'Western' ethnocentric outlook, as if those newly independent nations had no history and no past. The term soon gave way to the expression 'underdeveloped societies', naturally interpreted within the 'moderniza-tion' paradigm as meaning those countries that were 'still underdevel-oped', but on their way, in time, to join those already 'developed', once the right medicine was applied. As the postcolonial societies began to take their place in international forums, and as 'developmentalist' projects got under way, those ideas found expression in the more flattering and optimistic alternative term, 'developing societies'. This word-producing industry is not yet at a standstill. More recently, the term 'less developed societies' or 'LDCs' has been gaining ground in the vocabulary of developmentalism. (1982: 2)

I shall normally use the term, Third World countries, except when it is useful to emphasize a Western perception, as in the case of 'developing countries' or the term 'emergent nations', to emphasize the manner of the constitutional process of independence from colonialism.

Abbreviations and Acronyms

AID	(United States) Agency for International Development
BP	British Petroleum (Company)
CMEA (Comecon)	Council for Mutual Economic Assistance (USSR and its allies)
D–Day	Allied invasion of Nazi-occupied Europe, Normandy, 4 June 1944
EC (formerly EEC)	European Community (formerly European Economic Community)
ECLA	(United Nations) Economic Commission for Latin America
EFTA	European Free Trade Association (originally countries not in EEC)
EPZ	Export processing zone (free trade zone)
ESAF	Enhanced structural adjustment facility (of the IMF)
GATT	General Agreement on Tariffs and Trade (substitute for ITO)
Group of 77	Economic grouping of 77 Third World countries (since increased in number)
G7 countries	Grouping of the seven largest economies in the world
IBRD (World Bank)	International Bank for Reconstruction and Development (specialized UN agency), known widely as the World Bank
ICP	Industrial Cooperation Programme (of UNFAO)

ILO	(United Nations) International Labour Organization
IMF	International Monetary Fund (specialized UN agency).
ISI	Import substitution industrialization (in Third World countries)
ITO	International Trade Organization (putative, 1948)
KGB	Secret police of the Soviet Union
LDC	Less developed country
MITI	(Japanese) Ministry of International Trade and Industry
NATO	North Atlantic Treaty Organization (the post-war Western allies)
NGO	Non-government organization (voluntary aid agency)
NIC	Newly industrializing country
OAU	Organization for African Unity
ODA	(UK) Overseas Development Administration
OECD	Organization for Economic Co-operation and Development (grouping of the major industrialized countries)
OEEC	Organization for European Economic Co-operation (forerunner of OECD)
OPEC	Organization of Petroleum Exporting Countries
SAF	Structural adjustment facility (of the IMF)
SDR	Special drawing rights (of the IMF)
SILIC	Severely indebted low income country (World Bank category)
SIMIC	Severely indebted medium income country (World Bank category)
SPD	Sozialdemokratische Partei Deutschland (German Social Democratic Party)
TNC	Trans-national corporation (multi-national company)
VOC	Vereenigde Oost-Indische Compagnie (Dutch East India Company)
UDI	Unilateral declaration of independence (in Rhodesia, 1965)
UN(O)	United Nations (Organization)
UNCTAD	United Nations Commission for Trade and Development

UNESCO	United Nations Educational, Scientific and Cultural Organization
UNFAO	United Nations Food and Agriculture Organization
UNICEF	United Nations International Children's Emergency Fund
UNIDO	United Nations Industrial Development Organization

Introduction

For a long time I have been concerned that the sociology of development has become too compartmentalized in its deep obsession with the modernization theory–dependency theory debate. Modernization theory proposes that societal development can take place in the Third World through the application of capitalist economic mechanisms, whilst according to dependency theory the very structure of the capitalist world-economy prevents more equitable development. Any review of established sociology of development texts will reveal the extent to which this controversy has a prime place. As many of these texts confirm quite explicitly, the modernization–dependency debate mirrors the broader debate in sociology between ideas with structural-functionalist origins and various forms of Marxist critique. The work generated by such a debate is both necessary and valuable to the discipline, but the exchange can go on for too long.

Over the last few years I have been fortunate in having the opportunity to develop my own approach to the teaching of a second-year degree course on social change and development. This is the result partially of some five years spent working in the Third World, as well as subsequent visits and a general passion for poking around the ancient civilizations both at first hand and in literature. In the course which I teach, modernization theory and dependency theory have not been neglected, but I have sought to broaden the curriculum. I have included a more comprehensive approach to the historical and geographical aspects of the development of Western civilization in terms of the pervasive influence of its institutions upon the rest of the world. In this I have emphasized the development of the Western state as a model for societal organization, the politico-military dimensions to the development of a nation-state system and the importance of cultural exchanges and the trading of commodities in a global economic system. This is consistent with existing world-system theory, but it is possible to go deeper into the formation and constitution of the European states and their colonial activities in order to gain a better understanding of 'development issues'. Nation-states are a feature of Western culture that serve to distinguish it from other civilizations consisting typically of fluctuating and rather inconsistent empires in which the aim is to combine both political and economic institutions in one constitutional hierarchy. Europe and the West has consistently comprised separate states rendered increasingly interdependent by a capitalist world-economy which, according to dependency theory, has been the medium of development for Western states and of underdevelopment for other parts of the world. Yet more recently, East Asia and parts of Latin America have displayed a propensity for development which, in East Asia particularly, shows signs of challenging the West's economic supremacy. More recently still, the sweeping changes in Eastern Europe involving the dismantling of state socialism and the adoption of the market economy present a new range of possibilities. I interpret all of this as requiring a re-examination of the terms development and dependency in all their dimensions.

I have approached the study of social change and the sociology of development in a way that takes account of contemporary developments in social theory. I agree with Stuart Corbridge (1990) that existing non-Marxist development studies suffer from economism and determinism as much as the classical Marxist and neo-Marxist varieties (cf. Booth 1985), as I will argue in chapter 2. But I believe that Anthony Giddens's structuration theory offers the best way forward for sociology, drawing as it does from critiques of structural–functionalism, historical materialism and various phenomenological contributions to social theory. Structuration theory offers not only a conceptual framework for interpreting the institutional aspects of society in terms of social interaction but also a sense of time and space in societal change which lends itself particularly to the sociology of development. Western society consists of institutions built up through social interactions within that society and with other societies over the past millennium. In their global context, these developments incorporate the proper subject matter of the sociology of development, that is, the imposition of Western institutions on other societies mainly for the benefit of the West, or at least with little consideration for the interests of those other societies. The concept of the duality of structure in structuration theory posits that every instance of social interaction is at the same time the reproduction of social institutions. Structuration theory is useful in the study of social change precisely because of its emphasis on the reproduction of social institutions. There is only an abstract existence for social institutions other than in the immediate nexus of action at a passing moment in time. Social institutions extend the structure of social actions through time and space. All social interaction takes place in terms of the unacknowledged conditions presented by existing social institutions and in turn gives rise to unanticipated consequences in the further reproduction of those institutions. The crucial intermediary in this process is human agency in social interaction. Social change is not evolutionary, as the 'logic of industrialism' in the structural–functionalist approach or the principle of historical materialism in the Marxist critique would suggest. Rather, social change is subject to outcomes determined by the aggregate effects of human agency and not guaranteed by any evolutionary principle. Against the hopes for continuous advancement that have been a feature of Western civilization are counter-factual outcomes. For instance, in terms of political institutions, liberal democracy can lead to totalitarianism as it did in Germany during the 1930s. In terms of economic institutions the development of technology has led to nuclear weapons, while mass consumption in social institutions has raised grave concern about the depletion of resources – both of which have the potential capacity for massive global damage.

Social development in terms of structuration theory

In the terms of structuration theory, a case of significant societal development is provided by the city-states which were created, amidst a hinterland of rural tribal society, to form the earliest civilizations. But the important point is that city-states should not be seen as superseding tribal society, as evolutionary theories portray. City-states existed in a form of interdependence with tribal society, albeit on an unequal basis. Interdependencies and inequalities such as these are the essence of societal development and, therefore, are the proper subject matter for the sociology of development. Modern class (capitalist) society is the result of five or so centuries of Western civilization, during which time interdependent but unequal relationships were established between Western society and other forms of society across the world. There was never an enduring unified political framework in this process. Instead, the nation-state system and the capitalist world economy were developed historically as global systems by Europeans who, through the exploration of the oceans, also created a global communication system. Contributions to Western civilization were derived from classical times via Christianity and the always tentative

Holy Roman Empire and developed through medieval kingdoms, Renaissance city-states and the absolutist states of the Reformation and Counter-Reformation. This has culminated in what will be described here as the inter-societal system of the modern industrial period involving the co-existence of Western societies based upon liberal democracy, state socialist societies and developing societies of the Third World. The colonial and post-colonial relationships between European countries and other parts of the world have been reproduced as part of this process in the form of social, political and economic institutions and the results need to be unfolded and disentangled in any adequate sociology of development.

However, the future outcome of such historical developments must remain uncertain and a suitable subject for continuing scrutiny with reference to the historical and comparative dimensions. The economic rise of East Asia, the resurgence of Islam in the Middle East and the political developments in Eastern Europe all represent more recent changes to the global systems of information (communication), nation-states, world-economy and military order. The outcome is certainly not reducible to fixed theories, either of evolutionary modernization or of Marxist economic dependency, although contributions from these areas do remain useful. In the light of these considerations I have produced a book targeted primarily at second-year undergraduates, but which hopefully will make accessible to many others too a non-compartmentalized sociology of development drawing widely from historical and comparative materials and underpinned by the non-evolutionary conceptual framework of structuration theory.

Part I presents an appraisal of structural–functionalism and historical materialism as opposing major theoretical influences on the study of social change and an argument for their ultimate rejection as discrete paradigms for sociology (chapter 1). This is followed by an equally critical review of their equivalents in the sociology of development, modernization theory and dependency theory (chapter 2). These form a lead-in to the introduction of my proposal for the adoption of structuration theory which is presented as the most suitable framework for broadening the sociology of development. Through the concept of inter-societal systems, which articulates interdependencies and inequalities between societies, the sociology of development becomes more sensitive to the varieties of societal change that have taken place historically and continue to take place throughout the world (chapter 3).

Part II contains the historical evidence for my proposal and I present the formation of Western culture and institutions in their social, political and economic context (chapter 4), with particular emphasis on Western society as a state system (chapter 5) and on colonial episodes as the implanting of Western institutions around the globe (chapter 6). The rise of Western civilization is the most significant factor in the concept of modernization, the dependency critique and their transcending through structuration theory. It is in Western culture that the terms of the debate have been defined and by the same token it is Western culture that provides the model for development however it is conceptualized. Other cultures and civilizations have been considered inferior in terms of Western preconceptions of progress, thus rendering the concept of development ethnocentric. This must not be allowed to mask the need for a more adequate analysis of both the benefits and the drawbacks of Western culture compared with other cultures. A conceptual framework which can adequately accommodate the interrelationships and interdependencies between different types of society in a non-evolutionary yet constructive fashion would appear to represent the most promising way forward for the sociology of development.

Part III emphasizes the importance of the two world wars as watersheds in the more recent development of Western civilization, particularly in terms of Western plans for post-war reconstruction after the Second World War (chapter 7). The establishment of the United Nations and the Bretton Woods financial arrangements as global institutions for social, political and economic development are seen as confirmation of the nation-state system and the capitalist world-economy. The UN is a forum for nation-states whilst the World Bank and the International Monetary Fund are its agencies of regulation and surveillance in the capitalist world-economy which is otherwise dominated by the operations of transnational corporations. These measures, together with the end of colonialism in its constitutional form, are related to the formalization of modernization theory as official policy and as a cornerstone of Western ideology in the face the contemporaneous creation of the NATO–Warsaw pact global military order. This raises the issue of state socialism as an alternative pathway of development (chapter 8) and by implication an alternative model for post-colonial 'emergent nations'. Moreover, the identification of the post-colonial Third World and its earmarking for development involved counterfactually the recognition of economic dependency, underdevelopment and 'neo-colonialism' which points to the need for analysis of state formation, development aid and the status of Third World societies as reservoirs of disposable labour (chapter 9).

Part IV looks at the world towards the end of the twentieth century after the West has faced crises and self-doubt but maintained intact its model of liberal democratic capitalism (chapter 10). However, changing global conditions are examined particularly in terms of late industrialization in Japan and other parts of East Asia. This includes an examination of the suggestion that vestiges of Confucian philosophy in societies of the 'China periphery type' have presented them with authoritarian and orderly social and industrial structures which are especially productive in the capitalist world-economy (chapter 11). The resurgence of Islam is also examined as a long-term rival both to Christianity and Western society (chapter 12), especially in the light of its contemporary grip on Middle East oil which is of course the most strategic of the world's energy reserves, given present levels of consumption in the West and in East Asia.

The book concludes with a re-examination of the sociology of development and its concepts of development and dependency in the light of the historical and comparative materials introduced in outline above and presented in the ensuing chapters. This involves a further review of the possibilities offered by structuration theory and the concept of inter-societal systems as means to the more adequate study of societal change.

Part I

CONCEPTS OF SOCIAL CHANGE

1

Opposing Influences in Sociology: Historical Materialism and Structural–Functionalism

Out of nineteenth-century reflections upon the development of Western industrial society, sociology became an academic discipline based, ostensibly, upon the secular, modernist notion that it is human beings who create society. However, the centrality of human agency is not always apparent from the conceptual frameworks that sociologists have used to explain social change. In classical sociology it is possible to perceive two basic patterns in which the transition to industrialization is viewed. Firstly, there is the dichotomous contrast between 'modern', industrialized society and earlier forms which are referred to collectively as 'traditional'. Examples of this are Emile Durkheim's distinction between 'organic' and 'mechanical' forms of social solidarity and division of labour, or Max Weber's distinction between 'rational–legal' and 'traditional' forms of social action and authority structure. Secondly, there is the evolutionary approach derived from natural science, in which industrial society is seen as the latest stage in a process of societal evolution. Examples of this are Auguste Comte's sequence of 'theological', 'metaphysical' and 'scientific' theorizing in society and Spencer's sociology as 'the study of evolution in its most complex form' (1873: 385); but also included must be Karl Marx's revolutionary 'materialist conception of history' because of its sequential epochs of 'ancient', 'feudal' and 'capitalist' production relationships. The major synthesis of these approaches in the mid twentieth century is represented by structural–functionalism as inspired by the work of Talcott Parsons. This emphasizes the traditional–modern dichotomy through 'pattern variables' (see figure 1 and evolutionary change through the differentiation, adaptation and integration of social institutions. Exceptionally, Marx's work has remained a separate and critical influence but at its core is historical material-

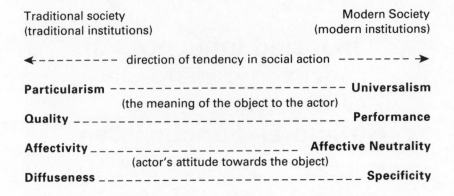

Figure 1 Parsons's pattern variables in social action related to traditional and modern social institutions

ism, a theory of social change in which each epoch produces class conflict resulting in the revolutionary transformation of the social structure.

During recent decades, therefore, structural–functionalism, the 'orthodox consensus' of sociology, has been confronted by historical materialism, the 'radical alternative' (cf. Atkinson 1971; Hoogvelt 1978, 1982; Etzioni-Halevy 1981; Strasser and Randall 1981). In both schools of thought, however, it is possible to discern a deterministic strain which has human society progressing, in terms of structural–functionalism, according to a relentless 'logic of industrialism', or, in terms of historical materialism, towards an inevitable socialist revolution. In neither case is human agency really allowed a decisive role because the form of future society is preordained, respectively, as universal industrialism or socialism. In each situation there is an ethnocentric element, too, reflecting sociology's origins as part of a nineteenth-century, European world-view which interpreted Western civilization as the culmination of human progress.

The impression is very different when the interpretation of Western progress and the time scale of events are fundamentally changed. Consider, for instance, the following alternative perspective from the environmentalist organization, Greenpeace:

Planet Earth is 4,600 million years old. If we condense this inconceivable time-span into an understandable context, we can liken Earth to a person of 46 years of age. Nothing is known about the first seven years of this person's life, and whilst only scattered information exists about

the middle span, we know that only at the age of 42 did the Earth begin
to flower. Dinosaurs and the great reptiles did not appear until one year
ago, when the planet was 45. Mammals arrived only eight months ago;
in the middle of last week man-like apes evolved into ape-like men, and
at the weekend the last ice-age enveloped the Earth. Modern man has
been around for four hours. During the last hour, man discovered
agriculture. The industrial revolution began a minute ago. During those
sixty seconds of biological time, modern man has made a rubbish tip of
Paradise. He has multiplied his numbers to plague proportions, caused
the extinction of 500 species of animals, ransacked the planet for fuels
and now stands like a brutish infant, gloating over this meteoric rise to
ascendancy, on the brink of a war to end all wars and of effectively
destroying this oasis of life in the solar system. (Greenpeace pamphlet:
Against All Odds 1989, reproduced by kind permission of Greenpeace
Ltd)

In place of classical sociology's emphasis on the emergence of modern
society, here modernity is set within the life of the planet and its
damaging effects assessed. The environmentally destructive power of
industrialized society is highlighted rather than its capacity to increase
standards of living. This puts a completely different interpretation on
the notion of progress in modernity. According to Eva Etzioni-
Halevy's (1981: 26–31) review of social change, in classical sociology
'modernity' was regarded with ambivalence and a critical role was
envisaged for the discipline. Yet the most influential sociological
theories of social change have involved a fundamentally optimistic
view of the future. The structural–functionalist approach bases such
optimism upon industrial development (industrialism) whilst the
Marxist critique bases it upon socialism. Each has a formula for
explaining and predicting social change.
    I am certainly not advocating here that sociology adopts the analogy
of the human lifecycle as in the extract from the Greenpeace pamphlet
and I include it only as a stark contrast with mainstream sociological
concepts of human societal development. What I do want to argue is
that a different overall time and space perspective and, therefore, a
different approach to social change is required in sociology, and
especially in the sociology of development. The sociological perspective needs to be expanded beyond the parameters of Western,
industrial, capitalist society to accommodate dimensions traditionally
covered by archaeology, anthropology, history, human geography and
philosophy. Above all, this should not be done in a way that orders
previous eras of human society into a simplistic framework which has
them 'evolving' into modernity. Nor should we resort exclusively to
the alternative notion of the diffusion of ideas and techniques between
societies, since social change is the ingenious work of flesh and blood

human beings and can be related to endogenous and exogenous influences. Furthermore, we must avoid the automatic assumption that processes of social change will necessarily be in a form beneficial to human society. Sociological concepts should emphasize the importance of human agency and the power of human beings in society and in the environment to take the course of social change in a variety of directions, good and bad, productive and destructive of human society and of the planet.

The environmentalist analogy described above, emphasizing the changes of the last 'sixty seconds of biological time' and their consequences, might, in fact, be taken as a justification for sociology. The discipline grew up with a focus precisely on those Western, capitalist, industrial developments which have created fears of environmental destruction. An understanding of environmental damage needs a complementary awareness of the underlying social developments which give rise to it. But a similar argument might also be used to point up some of the limitations of existing sociological theories of social change. They have tended to be abstract and ahistorical, without adequate time and space dimensions. I propose, therefore, to review structural-functionalism and historical materialism in the light of what I regard as key shortcomings.

The evolutionary viewpoint and 'Eurocentrism'

Concern about the negative effects of modernity, such as the alienation of the individual and the growing power of the state, was central to classical sociology, and yet the optimistic theme of 'social evolutionism' played a highly influential part in the foundations of social theory. This should not surprise us much, however, if we recall that sociology, as a distinct and separate discipline, was created during the nineteenth century when optimism about the power of human beings over their environment was at its height. Science became translated into technology on an unprecedented scale and pace, and there seemed no limits to what human beings could analyse, explain and, above all, rationalize. This philosophy is known as 'positivisim' and sociology was intended by its originator, Comte, to be the ultimate positivist science, capable of explaining the workings of society itself. Positivism embraces not only the evolution of scientific explanation, through the physical and natural sciences to social science, but also the implication of social evolution to a stage at which such explanation is possible. Charles Darwins *The Origin of the Species* of 1859 obviously provided the inspiration for evolutionary theories of society, and 'social Darwinism' became the term for the development of such ideas. However, this had been thoroughly discredited by the middle of the twentieth century, suggesting as it did the superiority of Western civilization and implicitly justifying attitudes such as racism.

Nevertheless, the evolutionary principle persists in a number of forms. In Marxist theory it is discernible as historical materialism in terms of the principles set out in the Preface to *A Contribution to the Critique of Political Economy*. Here, humanity is seen as passing successively through epochs of 'ancient', 'feudal' and 'capitalist' social relations in order to achieve the emancipation of 'socialist' and, ultimately, 'communist' society. In Frederick Engels's perception, Marx had discovered a 'scientific' theory of history. As such, it is the most rigid of evolutionary theories, albeit with the biological analogy of social Darwinism replaced by a sequential concept of social conflict giving rise to revolutionary change. The principle of historical materialism has, of course, been adapted in a variety of forms to justify social and political movements aimed at the apparently inevitable overthrow of capitalist society in favour of socialist society.

By contrast, the evolutionary principle appears more straightforwardly in structural–functionalism as a constant process of social development and the maintenance of equilibrium, involving the differentiation, adaptation and integration of social institutions. In ideological terms, this emphasis on the maintenance of social equilibrium constitutes the direct opposite of the revolutionary ethos in historical materialism. Parson's evolutionary framework was at one point simplified into a threefold sequence. Written language is seen as the crucial factor in the transition from 'primitive' to 'intermediate' society, and the setting up of legal systems has a similar significance in the transition from 'intermediate' to 'modern' society. The intermediate category is also divided up into 'archaic societies', 'historic intermediate societies' and 'seed-bed societies', the latter encompassing examples singled out for their culturally innovative features.

An alternative and clearer evolutionary model, drawn up on structural–functionalist principles, may be found in Gerhard and Jean Lenski's introductory textbook on sociology, *Human Societies* (1978). In the three editions up to 1978 the author claimed to be suffusing the structural–functionalist approach with an evolutionary dimension. His evolutionary framework begins with 'hunter–gatherer society', which is superseded by 'horticultural society' as cereals and animal herds become exploited. Following this is 'agrarian society' as the adoption of the plough, natural fertilizers and the practice of agriculture proper become widespread. Finally, 'industrial society', with all its productive power, completes the sequence, although capitalism forms only the most subsidiary of features in this interpretation. Nevertheless, at this point a similarity between historical materialism and structural–functionalism may be perceived. Although they are based upon very different beliefs about the relative importance of capitalism and industrialism, they share a common dependence upon the economy as the motor of social change.

Structural–functionalism as inspired by Parsons is, moreover, the sociological version of systems theory. A model of society is abstracted from time and space in the pursuit of universal laws, and society is seen as a self-regulating system, normally in a state of equilibrium. With social institutions operating as the functional mechanisms within the system, their condition may be judged by reference to 'pattern variables' (see figure 1). These are indicators of the form of social interactions within a society and, above all, they serve to distinguish the 'traditional' form from the 'modern'. Associated with the pattern variables is a familiar distinction derived from classical sociology and emphasized empirically by McLelland (1973). In traditional society the individual's status is normally 'ascribed' at birth and remains fixed whereas in the modern form it may be 'achieved' through mechanisms of 'social mobility'. As the diagram suggests, these concepts may be interpreted as a set of continua against which might be measured the level of 'modernization' in specific examples of society. In a similar vein, the work of Neil Smelser (1959) may be taken as an example of the principles of structural–functionalism applied to the archetypal case of the British Industrial Revolution. This was intended to produce a sequence of those changes in social institutions which Smelser saw as fundamental to that revolution. This form of historical interpretation can also be seen in Walt Rostow's work, *The Stages of Economic Growth* (1960), which sets out principles, also derived from the Industrial Revolution, in order to construct a universal model of the modernization process. In this work, which is subtitled *A Non-communist Manifesto*, structural–functionalist principles emerge fully as a prescription for the modernization of all societies including those regarded as 'backward' or 'developing'. At the same time the ideological dimension is clear. Rostow's work reflects its Cold War origins and the Western preference for universal modernization to extend capitalism as a safeguard against the apparent danger of the spread of communism. The connection between structural–functionalism and modernization theory in the Cold War context will be taken up further in chapter 7. For the moment, I want to proceed with comparison and criticism of historical materialism and structural–functionalism in order to shed further light on the conceptualization of social change in sociology.

Determinism in structural–functionalism and historical materialism

The basic distinction between structural–functionalism and historical materialism is that the former involves a gradual process of change, stimulated by increasing industrialization and accommodated by the differentiation, adaptation and integration of social institutions, whilst the latter posits a sequence of revolutionary changes. Nevertheless, there is a strong element of determinism in each theory. Under the terms of historical materialism, societies *must* pass through the epochs of ancient, feudal and capitalist society, each with its respective 'relations of production': 'master and slave'; 'lord and serf'; 'capitalist and worker'. When the 'relations of production' of an epoch cease to be appropriate for its technologically advancing 'forces of production', a major contradiction is created in the social structure and revolutionary change is regarded as inevitable. For this reason, historical materialism is sometimes referred to in terms of 'technological determinism'. The form of the contradiction which produces revolutionary change is, however, fully explained by Marx only for capitalist society, in which 'private appropriation' from the production process is seen as contradictory to the 'socialized' organization of production.

In structural–functionalism, by contrast, the emphasis is on industrialism rather than capitalism, as an inexorable process of modernization, involving what Clark Kerr et al. (1960) have succinctly referred to as the 'logic of industrialism'. In what came to be known as the 'convergence thesis', this represents a process by which all societies, whether capitalist or socialist, are seen as converging towards the same industrialist model. There are, in fact, a range of views pursuing a similar general theme in diminishing the role of capitalism and emphasizing that of industrialism. Ralf Dahrendorf (1959) sought to identify a 'post-capitalist society' in the class structure of twentieth-century industrialism, whilst Daniel Bell predicted the onset of global political convergence, *The End of Ideology* (1960), through processes of technological industrialism. Peter L. Berger, pursuing the same debate into the 1980s, eschewed this diminishing of the term capitalism and renewed the case in *The Capitalist Revolution: fifty propositions about prosperity, equality and liberty* (1987).

Further condemnation of evolutionary and deterministic theories of social change takes the form of the argument that they are 'Eurocentrist'. This is derived from the tendency in sociology and elsewhere for Western industrial–capitalist society to be equated unproblematically with the culmination of human progress to date. Perspectives which

see industrialism or capitalism as high points in a process of
evolutionary change do, however, involve either the devaluation of
alternative examples of societal development or the distorting of them
in order that they should fit conveniently into overarching theory. A
good example of this is the treatment of 'Asiatic society' in historical
materialism. Marx considered that this was a cul de sac of development whereby the societies 'of the East' suffered stagnation because of
their rigid and despotic form of leadership. This effectively prevented
the formation of social classes which, as the articulation of a basic
contradiction in the relations of production, would have otherwise led
to revolutionary social change. Although Marx accepts that the first
signs of civilization may be perceived in Asia, he maintains that this
example remained frozen in time whilst the full flowering of social
development was achieved in the West. Karl Wittfogel (1957) tried to
refine this view in terms of the requirements for large-scale irrigation
projects in agriculture and their stifling effects on social development.
However, writers such as Francesca Bray (1986) have argued that
these concepts represent a misunderstanding of development in the
East. In comparing change in that part of the world with the rise of
capitalist industrialization in the West, the rate of progress has, not
surprisingly, appeared slow. The dynamic of change and its pace are
very different, and, as a consequence, a model so 'Eurocentric' as
historical materialism is incapable of picking it up. Equally, she argues
that theorists of structural–functionalism or modernization, in prefer-
ring 'to think of Asia as following basically the same path as Europe,
but less successfully and less rapidly', have made more or less the same
mistake. 'Both of these methods are essentially negative, the one
denying the occurrence of any significant change, the other obscuring
the specificity of non-European societies' (Bray 1986: 1). Similarly, the
most effective criticism of Smelser's or Rostow's theoretical framework have highlighted their apparent insistence that the basic incentives and development of the British industrial revolution might be
recreated in all parts of the world.

'Economism' and functionalism

The appraisal and criticism of historical materialism and structural–
functionalism may be continued on the basis of their economistic bias.
The crucial mechanisms and dynamics of change in these influential
theories of social change are located exclusively in the economic
institutions of human societies. This implies a neglect of other
institutions, in particular, the politico-military institutions associated
with the wielding of power and authority. The corollary of this is that

economic institutions are given prominence because they are regarded as functional for the progress of social change. A connection so tautological is, however, a clear indication of both economistic and functionalist bias in the theories. The proposal that a single type of social institution alone can be seen as functional for change is one that must be treated with suspicion.

In the historical materialist perspective the dynamics of social change are the relations of production. Taking up the generic principle that human beings in all types of society must engage in production from their environment in order to survive, the social arrangements that they make for this (i.e. the relations of production) are necessary and unavoidable to all members of society. This proposal accommodates a potential and fundamental inequality in social relations, derived from the appropriation of ownership of the means of production and leading to the creation of class conflict. The political consequences of this, however, are relegated to a position of dependence upon economic developments. The assumption is that all societies will maximize their productive capacity in response to what Western economists have referred to as the principle of 'scarcity'. But there are instances of societies that have chosen, i.e. made a socio-political decision, not to respond in this way. For example, Marshall Sahlins (1972) refers to hunter–gatherer societies as the 'first affluent societies' because of their ability to keep their needs and demands within their limited productive capacity. Taking a broader view, it is surely demonstrable that some of the most significant turning points of history have been decided in politico-military terms. However long-term the perspective, it is difficult to ignore the significance of political decisions taken contrary to the principle of economic growth, as for example in the fighting of costly wars. This kind of argument is pursued in a broad historical perspective by such sociologists as Anthony Giddens (1981, 1985), John A. Hall (1986) and Michael Mann (1986).

In fact, if historical materialism were capable of explaining the direction of social change in the long term, irrespective of politico-military outcomes, then it follows that it must be subject to a similar kind of equilibrium principle to that which is central to structural-functionalism. For an epoch relentlessly to develop towards the point when revolutionary change is imminent, there must be a sense in which historical progress is self-regulating. Those social institutions which in terms of structural–functionalism maintain the social system in a state of equilibrium, have their equivalent in terms of historical materialism. The development of the relations of production is apparently 'functional' for society in order to bring it to a certain stage of technological development. At that point these relations become outdated and in conflict with new forces of production, thus placing

society on the point of revolutionary change. In both structural–
functionalism and historical materialism, therefore, social institutions
have a function that is consistent with a particular perspective of social
change. This is not to say that historical materialism and structural–
functionalism are alike as theories, but rather that they are prey to
similar conceptual problems.

Under the principles of structural–functionalism, the maintenance
of the social system is vested in the notions that its normal state is
equilibrium and that of its members, consensus. Power is something
derived exclusively from the institutions of society. Parsons defined
political institutions broadly as all decision-making processes in
society and likened power to money in economic institutions, i.e. as
something transferable and exchangeable – the 'zero-sum' concept of
power. The economic system is quite obviously the model which
Parsons used for his conceptualization of the political system and the
economistic bias is, therefore, quite evident. In more general terms,
structural–functionalism emphasizes the logic of industrialism and its
potential for economic growth in the progressive differentiation of
social structure.

Reflections

We have seen how, in terms of the principles of structural–
functionalism, social change takes place through a continuous process
of evolution involving the adaptation of social institutions, and the
normal state of society is one of equilibrium and consensus. All social
institutions are seen in some way as functional for society, and power
is available to people through the roles they play in functional social
institutions. This model of power in a political system is, however,
taken from the circulation of money in the economic system and,
overall, society is seen as developing due to the progress of industrialism. The continuing role of capitalism is discounted and becomes
reformulated as post-capitalism, or as ideological convergence through
the logic of industrialism.

In terms of the principles of historical materialism, social change
takes place through a series of historical epochs involving the
evolution of societal forms. The relations of production in any epoch
are at first seen as functional for the reproduction of society. Later, at
a certain stage of development determined by the forces of production,
they cease to be so, and the resulting contradiction leads to revolutionary social change. The relations of production are, however,
economic institutions to which political institutions are subordinate.

In both these theoretical frameworks there is a bias towards econo-mistic concepts.

Ultimately, criticism of these theories of social change must be concerned with their chronic under-representation of the capacity for human actors to make a difference even in regular social practices amongst the structure of social institutions. Such institutions are both enabling and constraining for human beings in the complexities of daily life. As Thomas Hobbes observed, human beings give up part of their individual freedom in return for the advantages of being part of the collective, but this does not entail a slavish adherence to collective norms. Rather, it enables individuals to achieve more than they would merely as individuals. Yet, both structural–functionalism and historical materialism seek to lay out a broad blueprint for the course of social change. They do so in such a way that the actions of human beings appear to be merely reactions to the pattern of history and social structure, rather than contributions to the making of them. It is easy to see the attraction of attempting to discover universal principles of societal development. The problem lies in escaping the consequence that such principles, once determined, fix the aggregate outcome of human interaction, even for interactions yet to take place. Structural–functionalism contains an almost blind faith in the capacity for industrial society to evolve and overcome its material and ideological problem. This, in effect, ties human social interaction to the premise that throughout the world the traditional and irrational will give way to the modern and rational. By contrast, historical materialism posits that capitalism must ultimately give way to socialism and, by implication, promises that future social interactions will be devoid of antagonistic conflict. But there can be no guarantees of the outcome of social change, and the only adequate counter to such falsely deterministic frameworks is to adopt a theory of social change dedicated to the assumption that it is human beings who have produced and who will reproduce society. They are both enabled and constrained by the structural and systemic patterns that they have created, but the outcome of social change can go in a number of directions. To avoid this conclusion is tantamount to allowing the human race to abdicate responsibility for the outcome of its actions.

2

Development and its Denial: Modernization Theory versus Dependency Theory

In this chapter I shall extend discussion of the structural–functionalist and historical materialist perspectives to cover their application in the more specialized field of the sociology of development. It is worth bearing in mind that this involves concepts conceived in the industrialized West as part of a modernization process and then used to address the effects of colonial exploitation which was itself a part of that process. The principles of structural–functionalism as they impinge upon the relationship between developed and developing countries take the form of modernization theory, whilst those of historical materialism emerge as dependency theory (cf. Etzioni-Halevy 1981; Hoogvelt 1982). However, whilst structural–functionalism has a direct connection with modernization theory, the link between historical materialism and dependency theory is more complicated. The principles of historical materialism specify that societies become capitalist before they can go through a further revolutionary transformation to socialism, but dependency theory is based upon the argument that Europe's colonies were brought into the capitalist economic system as dependencies during the colonial period. However, an opposing interpretation posits that the former colonies remain pre-capitalist because they were not industrialized, and on this has hung a crucial question for Marxist analysis as to whether socialism is viable in the Third World. Nevertheless, it is preferable to begin with some consideration of modernization theory.

Modernization theory

Parsons's distinction between traditional and modern societies was expressed in terms of pattern variables at the level of social interaction. In principle, these have formed the basis of a comprehensive prescription for the modernization of traditional societies, known as modernization theory. Stated simply, it involves a fundamental proposition that people in traditional societies should adopt the characteristics of modern societies in order to modernize their social, political and economic institutions. The raison d'etre behind this is that there are certain social characteristics of enterprise, achievement and progress with which the Industrial Revolution has been identified and which subsequently have enabled the USA to provide a model of mass-consumption society. The straightforward implication is that a society which adopts these characteristics will become modernized.

In practical terms, upon the dismantling of the European colonial empires after the Second World War, these principles can be found in the policy for launching the former colonies upon pathways of development. It will be described more fully in chapter 7 how the end of European colonialism became part of the strategic policy of the USA during the Second World War. This relates to the USA's background as a former European colony, to its national ethos as a land of freedom and opportunity, and to a practical desire to exploit globally an enhanced industrial capacity derived from the war effort. All this is significant for an adequate understanding of the post-war notion of modernization and, as the problems faced by former colonies became part of international relations, the development policy of Western nations became synonymous with the principles of modernization theory. It is an example of interplay between historical change and broad social science concepts which in this case produced new global institutions – the United Nations and the Bretton Woods economic arrangements – against a background of the Cold War global military order. In all these developments the USA played a dominant role, and it is difficult to avoid the conclusion that in policy and theory alike there was a fundamental belief that the USA occupied an exceptional place in history as a result of her constitution and ethos (cf. Ross 1991). It is revealing to consider that the European colonies tended to be called 'backward societies' before they gained constitutional independence, 'emergent nations' upon independence and 'developing countries' thereafter (Alavi and Shanin 1982: 2). This reflects the course of Western perceptions of the Third World at the time, but unfortunately the quality of life of its people did not change perceptibly, and in some cases it became worse.

A model for modernization theory

Orthodox modernization theory, perhaps best illustrated by reference to Walt Rostow's *The Stages of Economic Growth* (1960) and its subtitle, *A non-communist manifesto*, is revealing of Western fears about the spread of Soviet communism. In fact, many of the independence movements in the colonies had Marxist as well as nationalist aspirations and these emerged freely after independence. Rostow, an economic historian who became an adviser to the American government, took his model from the British Industrial Revolution and developed it as a blueprint for the implanting of capitalism in all countries as a means to economic growth and modernization and also as a bastion against communism. The principles can be set down from Rostow's work as follows:

Stage 1 (traditional society) in which output is limited without the application of Western science and technology, values are fatalistic and political institutions are undeveloped.

Stage 2 (the pre-conditions for take-off) which include the introduction of ideas for economic progress, involving education, entrepreneurship and the expansion of a commercial infrastructure.

Stage 3 (the take-off) in which traditional barriers are overcome, Western technology is introduced and political institutions developed. Modernization becomes a real possibility when the rate of increase in investment overtakes the rate of increase in population. Both industry and agriculture are mechanized.

Stage 4 (the drive to maturity) when 10 to 20 per cent of the national income is invested, the use of consumer technology becomes widespread and an impression is made on the capitalist world economy.

Stage 5 (high consumption) when the mass production of consumer goods dominates the economy and a large economic surplus is created. Rostow observes that this has been used in the USA mainly for ultra-high consumption, in Europe mainly for the welfare state, and in the USSR mainly for producer and military technology.

The implications of Rostow's theory are clear, and its consistency with the general tenets of structural–functionalism can readily be perceived. Above all, the traditional-modern dichotomy taken from classical sociology and developed by Parsons is paramount. Societies are either traditional or modern as indicated by the pattern of their social institutions, but the modernization process is seen as inexorable given certain conditions, and this is indicative of the evolutionary nature of modernization theory. Variations on this approach can be found in the work of Neil Smelser (1959), B. F. Hoselitz (1960) and S. N. Eisenstadt (1968), who were all influenced by Parsons's work and seek to project the development of Western civilization, in general, and the preconditions of the British Industrial Revolution, in particular, to prospects for the developing countries. The use of the British Industrial Revolution as a case of independent development would seem to signal an inherent flaw in the theory when it is considered that British economic development during the eighteenth century was connected with the rise of London as the centre of a European-based global economy which, in various forms, had been developing since the thirteenth century.

There are two further aspects of modernization theory which should be considered here. The first is 'diffusionism' which, in common with other influences in Parsons's work, comes from early twentieth-century anthropology. This recognizes that societies are not closed systems and that ideas are diffused from one to another. The second is the alternative, but potentially complementary, view that innovation can also take place in parallel but similar social structures. Consequent upon these points is the argument that modernization cannot be a simple linear process, and that in the case of the developing countries attention must be paid to the outside influences which impinged upon them during the colonial period. Ankie Hoogvelt (1978: 65) has taken the broad view that the facts of history tend to contradict the abstract neatness of the modernization model, whilst David Harrison (1988: 44–5) suggests that objections to orthodox modernization theory are exemplified in the work of Reinhard Bendix (1967) who argues that, having occurred in one country, industrialization cannot happen in the same way in others due to diffusionary influences. If modernization theory is accepted in principle, there are implications for the way that Third World countries conceive and apply their development policies. But if it is rejected, the main implication is that we should examine further the circumstances in which Europeans came into contact with the peoples of other countries. The consideration of dependency theory, which constitutes the antithesis of modernization theory, represents the next stage in an examination of the West's relationship with other parts of the world.

Dependencia and the formation of dependency theory

The origins of dependency theory can be traced back to the notion of *dependencia* amongst Latin American economists during the 1930s, to the United Nations Economic Commission for Latin America (ECLA) during the immediate post-war years, and, in particular, to the work of the Argentinian economist Raoul Prebisch. The fundamental principle of dependency theory is that the Third World is not, as modernization theory suggests, an area ripe for development along a pathway taken previously by European countries, but instead is a subsidiary part of the Western capitalist system and has been so since the spread of European colonialism. Part II will discuss how historically this has involved the establishment of an international division of labour, whereby Europe and North America became largely the manufacturers of finished products and the Third World, the supplier of raw materials and cash-crop agricultural products. This carries with it the implication that the Third World is an exporter of relatively low-priced raw materials and an importer of relatively high-priced Western products, a relationship of unequal exchange which Prebisch interpreted as leading to further deterioration in the balance of trade because:

1   Raw material products are subject to substitution by synthetics.
2   Agricultural products are, in economic terms, 'demand inelastic', i.e. during upswings in prosperity increased demand goes disproportionately into consumer goods.
3   Technological progress tends to leave primary producers behind, especially in terms of earning capacity.

There is also the so-called 'Prebisch–Singer thesis' that raw material prices fluctuate in the short term and decline in the long term.

A number of writers contributed to dependency theory as it emerged from the notion of *dependencia* and the deliberations of ECLA. Paul Baran's *The Political Economy of Growth* (1957) is generally accepted as a founding work, but other significant contributors include Andre Gunder Frank (1966) with *The Development of Underdevelopment*, Arghiri Emmanuel with *Unequal Exchange* (1972), Immanuel Wallerstein with *The Modern World System* (1974) and Samir Amin with *Accumulation on a World Scale* (1974). But according to David Harrison's (1988: 81) review of dependency theory, it was mainly through the efforts of Andre Gunder Frank, a Chicago-trained economist, that the concept of dependency came to be popularized in Western academic circles. His work involves the concept of a series of 'metropolis–satellite relationships', developed from Baran's work, which conflate global economic relationships with social class relationships, extended throughout the workings of capitalism. Thus the industrialized West stands in a relationship of exploitation with the Third World, but equally there exist metropolis–satellite relationships within individual countries. In each case, the spatial relationship is related to social class, so the south east of England may be seen as a metropolis to the satellites of British provincial regions, or northern Europe may be seen to contain the metropolitan centres to southern

Europe's satellites. Within Third World countries, the old colonial centres are linked as subsidiary metropolis with Europe and North America whilst other areas are the ultimate satellites of the global economy. Therefore, Frank's whole concept may be seen in the form of a chain which links conceptually the Third World peasant with the New York capitalist. Frank's systematic rejection of modernization theory was first contained in the article referred to above, which sets out his general assertions that modernization theory is empirically invalid, theoretically inadequate and politically ineffective.

An immediate counter-criticism can be mounted against a part of Frank's argument which locates the process of underdevelopment precisely in the relationship between core and satellite and asserts that satellite areas which have had the strongest links with the core are now the most underdeveloped. As Harrison (1988: 82–4) suggests, links of this kind can be taken equally to explain development in Australasia and the lack of it in Latin America. Both areas have been closely associated with Europe but clearly with different outcomes and, although Frank attributes the discrepancy to different class factors, the precise juxtaposition of class and spatial relationship has never satisfactorily been explained. Ian Roxborough (1979: 45), in a work devoted mainly to the appraisal of dependency theory, confirms that Franks' theory of underdevelopment and dependency is meant to conflate the transfer of value through spatial relations, as outlined above, with the Marxist emphasis on the appropriation of surplus value through the class relationship. The exploitative relationship between the capitalists of the core and the peasants of the satellites is seen to exist through a network of spatial relations. But this explanation has certainly never satisfied orthodox Marxists and Frank's work has been termed 'neo-Marxist', due to its emphasis on the metropolis–satellite relationship at the expense of the quintessential class relationship of Marxist theory.

Of equal significance here is the exception taken by Marxist writers such as Ernesto Laclau (1971) and Bill Warren (1980) to any interpretation that the Third World was made capitalist by Western colonialism or to the implication that Europe itself was capitalist at that stage of development. This particular criticism harks back to Paul Sweezy et al.'s *The Transition from Feudalism to Capitalism* (1976), a debate on which the resolution depends upon the degree of adherence to an orthodox Marxist interpretation of history. This work presents an alternative interpretation, drawing from the historical analysis of Fernand Braudel and Immanuel Wallerstein, which regards production for extended market exchange as sufficient definition of capitalist activity. Capitalism, involving economic interdependence in an extending division of labour and global economy, is contrasted with feudalism, involving a high degree of self-sufficiency within the manorial unit, but it seems pointless to regard feudalism as ending at a precise point and capitalism beginning at another, as Sweezy in Sweezy et al. (1976: 46–7) appears to want to do. Capitalism had begun expanding before feudalism declined, and there is evidence that one benefited the other in Europe when the manorial system existed alongside long-distance trade in commodities. This occurred again in Latin America when *hacienda* and *encomienda* agriculture co-existed with capitalist mining (see chapter 6) and in Europe yet again when a 'second serfdom' in Poland supplied grain to the capitalist merchants of the Hanseatic League. In any case, this point remains significant only as long as historical materialism, with its emphasis on a sequence of modes of production, is applied to the analysis of history. But, with the material to be presented in part II, I am supporting the proposition that the feudal system was only one system of production amongst others during the medieval period and that socio-cultural, religious and politico-military developments were just as important as economic ones. This is a point emphasized in the work of successive historians of the French Annales school, and the work of Fernand Braudel (1982: 62) and Jacques Le Goff (1988: 90) will be referred to extensively. When the exchange of goods rises above the system of travelling pedlar–merchants a significant change occurs, as Sweezy (in Sweezy et al. 1976: 42) recognizes, but the resulting economic mechanism is surely capitalistic. In any case, to go back to the original point, the criticism implied by the attachment of a neo-Marxist label to Frank would presumably only matter to him if he were a Marxist but in his academic writings he avoids stating whether he is or not.

Lest the emphasis so far should appear disproportionately focused on Latin America, it is worth including some reference to the work of Samir Amin. He was born in Egypt and educated in France, but much of his inspiration came from Senegal, a former French colony, where he worked as the director of a UN research programme. Senegal may be seen against the broader background of West Africa which has been connected with European trade since the fifteenth century and the early stages of Portuguese colonialism (see part II). Like Frank's, Amin's perspective is a global one, drawing attention especially to 'accumulation on a global scale' and, according to Roxborough (1979: 47), portraying a world proletariat set against a world bourgeoisie. Harrison (1988: 96) also points out that Amin's remedy for this situation is a global socialist society, which goes further than Frank's proposal for the breaking of the dependency chain between metropolis and satellites. Amin argues that the West's maintenance of low wages, combined with the introduction of modern technology and, hence, high productivity in the Third World has increased exploitation and, therefore, dependency. In the language of neo-Marxism, he concludes that the peripheral economies are subject to a logic of accumulation that exists in the metropolis which dominate them. This approach is, like Frank's, criticized by orthodox Marxists because the mechanism by which Amin sees global accumulation taking place is 'the disarticulation of economy'. It clearly has much in common with Frank's conceptualization because the 'disarticulation' in question is of Western-orientated economic activity from the remainder of the economy in a Third World country. This is comparable to the metropolis–satellite split, even if the terminology is different and it emphasizes the integration of only selected parts of Third World economy into the Western economic structure. Amin's claim is that it accounts for the huge differences of wealth and poverty that exist between town and country and between different regions in Third World countries. Thus integration into the global economy is vertical and through selected economic activities associated with specific spatial regions, whilst there remains a chronic lack of horizontal economic integration across and between the economies of Third World countries, which accounts for their lack of development.

These various contributions to dependency theory constitute a comprehensive argument against modernization theory on the grounds that the development to which it refers is palpably a Western phenomenon. Most of the rest of the world has been subjected to it, in various ways, but has in the majority of cases not benefited from it. Western development has been supported by an extended global economy in which the West has been the metropolis, but the consequences for other parts of the world has been the creation of satellite economies disarticulated within themselves and heavily dependent upon the West. The question arises whether the West must remain always the metropolis of this system or whether Third World countries can overcome their dependency. In dependency theory it is set down firmly that they cannot unless the global capitalist system is changed fundamentally. However, the precise focus of the metropolis can be seen to have shifted from Europe to North America during the mid twentieth century and now Japan threatens to eclipse both of these in terms of economic growth and power. Meanwhile, a few other countries in East Asia and one or two in Latin America have been designated by observers as 'newly industrializing countries' (NICs), to signify that they have broken away from their Third World identity and begun to exhibit evidence of independent economic growth alongside the West or Japan. It desirable to expand upon the global aspect of dependency theory through the work of Immanuel Wallerstein.

The concept of the capitalist world-economy

Immanuel Wallerstein brings sociology into contact with history (Wallerstein 1979: vii) and outlines social change in terms of its historical unfolding. The founding fathers of sociology did, of course, use historical comparison, and this is evident, for example, in Weber's extensive studies of world religions or Marx's analysis of ancient civilizations. But, arguably, structural–functionalist social theory failed to realize expectations of it as *the* analytical 'science of society', precisely due to neglect of historical sequences in social change. Wallerstein was influenced by Braudel and their work may be seen as complementary. Braudel has brought history into contact with sociology and provided us with a detailed account of European society from the time when the Middle Ages were giving way to the Renaissance, and Europeans were beginning to extend their culture beyond the physical boundaries of Europe (see part II). This approach is particularly apposite for understanding the origins of modern society, and Wallerstein discerns specific periods through which the development of a single 'capitalist world-economy', centred on Europe, can be traced. Other civilizations contained extended economies but they were confined to relatively limited areas, and trade was always dependent upon the politics of a single imperial hierarchy. For instance, during most of their era, the Romans controlled a singular political and economic domain around the Mediterranean and throughout Western Europe. In a different example, the spread of Islam carried trade with it throughout the Mediterranean and the Indian Ocean but was nevertheless limited to coastal navigation by the principles of a spiritual empire which regarded the exploration of the oceans as impossible (also see part II). By contrast, from the period which Braudel refers to as the 'long sixteenth century', i.e. 1450 to 1640, Europeans began to consolidate what was ultimately to be a true world-economy. Most significant of all, this trade was not controlled by a single political entity as it had been in other civilizations, and it is possible to discern two separate but interdependent systems operating from this time. One is a system of political states, and the other is a world economy through which those states are interdependent.

Wallerstein's framework has much in common with Frank's and this sets them both against orthodox Marxism with its essential principle of the class division. Where Frank talks in terms of 'metropolis' and 'satellites', Wallerstein uses the terms 'core' and 'periphery'. In Wallerstein's scheme of things, between 1450 and 1640 the core of a European world-economy became located in north-western Europe where there was a range of emerging manufacturing industries and relatively advanced forms of agrarian production. The Italian city-states, which had been the foremost centres of trade and a link between Europe and Islam in this respect, lost that central position when Portuguese and Spanish sea-borne trade with the Indian Ocean and the Americas was connected up with Antwerp, a new centre of a European 'world-economy'. With its food supplies threatened, Venice put investment into agriculture on its mainland holdings, the *terra-ferma*, and thus neglected manufacturing to become part of a 'semi-periphery' in Wallerstein's terms. Portugal and Spain, despite their maritime success, never enjoyed core status in this system because they lacked the commercial infrastructure and because the Habsburg kings dissipated the Spanish wealth through the adminis-tration of a sprawling legacy to the Holy Roman Empire in central and southern Europe. Therefore, Portugal and Spain, too, became part of the semi-periphery. Beyond these, the periphery of Wallerstein's framework was made up firstly of Eastern Europe and secondly of the new overseas territories whose exploited wealth was traded throughout Europe. According to Wallerstein, Eastern Europe with its huge agricultural base went into a 'second serfdom' when its landowners failed to diversify their activities and their agricultural produce was traded throughout Europe by merchants of the Hanseatic League, a series of ports along the northwestern European coast.

Subsequent stages for Wallerstein were:

1650–1730 when Amsterdam assumed the centre role in this European world-economy;
1760–1917 when London took that role during the Industrial Revolution; and finally *the period of consolidation from 1917* when the
   USA was in the ascendancy.

The notional core of the system, therefore, remained unequivocally in north-western Europe until the nineteenth century when it began to gravitate westwards towards the USA. More recently with the rise of Japan the definition has become more difficult, but Wallerstein emphasizes in later works (1982, 1984) the growing importance of de facto economic and strategic axes, specifying 'Washington–Beijing–Tokyo' and 'Paris–Bonn–Moscow'. These have become even more intriguing with the wide-ranging changes in Eastern Europe which began to take place in earnest during 1989. Wallerstein's semi-periphery has continued to include the north Mediterranean countries but also now includes the former white-settler colonies of Australasia and South Africa (which Frank, by contrast, sees as fully developed) and, more problematically in conceptual terms, the state socialist countries of the Soviet Union and Eastern Europe. Here arises again the problem of a perspective that is inherently economistic (see chapter 1), for in politico-military terms the Soviet Union was until recently without doubt alongside the USA as one of two superpowers. In mitigation of this Wallerstein (1979: 224) takes pains to stress that his three tiers are not intended to project the detail of reality, but take the form of a pattern to aid us in identifying class struggle at the global level. Harrison (1988: 95) points out that this is reminiscent of Parsons's systems-theory type of abstraction and also (p. 115) that 'world systems theory', as Wallerstein's work has been called, falls generally into the same trap as structural–functionalism with the lack of an adequate social action perspective. The role of the semi-periphery has been interpreted widely as a 'functional' buffer between core and periphery proper, another allusion to the Parsonsian type of analysis. These are undoubtedly weaknesses in Wallerstein's framework.

The crucial factor for Wallerstein is interdependence. From the sixteenth century, early developments in larger-scale manufacturing took place at the core of his world system in north-western Europe, in such areas as textiles, shipbuilding, metalworking and armaments. There were also advances in agriculture with the extensive collapse of feudalism and the spread of the enclosure movement. These developments constitute the creation of free wage labour on an increasing scale, together with the division of labour, and in this respect Wallerstein's framework is consistent with the orthodox Marxist view of the development of capitalism. However, Wallerstein emphasizes that economic activity in the core was increasingly linked with economic activity in the periphery. His notion of the capitalist world-economy is based upon the extension of European colonialism and the participation of a number of politically separate colonial blocs in an increasingly interdependent economic system. As polity and economy became distinctly separated in the absolutist states, largely through the reliance of monarchs for their revenue upon independent merchant capitalist ventures (see chapter 5), so a system of political states emerged to complement the capitalist world-economy.

According to Wallerstein (1984: 40), a true hegemony of this capitalist world-economy has only existed during certain periods. It was first obtained by the city-state of Amsterdam, supported in agriculture and crafts by the Dutch United Provinces, roughly between 1620 and 1672. Then, with an even more aggressive approach to colonial trade and the considerable advantage of the Industrial Revolution, Britain enjoyed hegemony as a fully fledged nation-state, roughly between 1815 and 1873. By the end of this period, Britain had begun to lose the lead in industrial innovation to Germany and the USA. But, during the twentieth century with the defeat of Germany and the destruction of Europe in two world wars, the USA was left clear to assume hegemony, according to Wallerstein, between 1945 and 1967. That position was retained throughout the setting up of a new world order against the background of the Cold War and the dismantling of the European colonial empires, until the economic burden became too much even for the USA. The Bretton Woods global economic arrangements, of which it had been the cornerstone, were finally terminated in 1971 (see chapter 7). Since then the capitalist world-economy has lacked such an anchor role and, with a core made up principally of the USA, Japan and the progressively integrating EC countries, it has been more unstable, with financial and commodity markets often wildly fluctuating.

For all its advantages as an analytical device, Wallerstein's core–periphery framework, like Frank's metropolis–periphery model, is subject to the disadvantage of being grounded in the economic system. By virtue of this, the politico-military aspects of international relations are underplayed. It can hardly be doubted that the Soviet Union has been a 'superpower' in politico-military terms along with the USA, yet in Wallerstein's framework it is part of the semi-periphery because of its economic position. The resources which the super-powers have been able to call upon in their long military confrontation have far outweighed those of other nation-states. For, whilst the proliferation of sophisticated, mass-produced armaments has changed the face of warfare, the nuclear arsenals of the USA and the USSR have formed a separate category of military strength. Of the capitalist world-economy, nation-state system and global military order, none can be reduced to any of the others as part of an adequate analysis. Anthony Giddens (1985: 167–8) encapsulates the weaknesses of Wallerstein's formulation by stating that it involves 'an uncomfortable amalgam of functionalism and economic reductionism'. The existence of the semi-periphery is explained in terms of the needs of the system as a buffer between the economic wealth of the core and the poverty of the periphery. This is its function. States appear merely as territorial sub-divisions in the economic sectors of core, semi-periphery and periphery, rather than as entities capable of wielding military power in the pursuit of political interests which cannot always be explained by reference to the capitalist world-economy.

Reflections

Dependency theory is generally seen as the principle reaction to modernization theory. Yet David Harrison (1988: 70) makes the interesting point that Paul Baran's *The Political Economy of Growth*

(1957), which is widely taken as the founding work of dependency theory, was in fact published three years before Walt Rostow's *The Stages of Economic Growth* (1960) and seven years before the issue of the *American Sociological Review* (1964) which heralded the rise of 'neo-evolutionism'. This confirms the proposition that social theory is a reflection of and a contribution to society. The factors that gave rise to concepts of modernization and dependency were in existence before theories were formulated, but that formulation, in turn, affected the way in which development issues were confronted. The concept of modernization is associated with post-Second World War reconstruction and the end of the European colonial era, as will be described at length in chapter 7, whilst the concept of dependency emerged from recognition of the lack of economic progress in Latin America from the 1930s.

Nevertheless, it is quite clear that most of the subsequent dependency-theory literature and especially the work of Andre Gunder Frank addresses precisely the claims of neo-evolutionary modernization theory. Furthermore, Eva Etzioni-Halevy (1981), Hermann Strasser and Susan C. Randall (1981) and Ankie Hoogvelt (1982) all confirm that the theory of modernization is clearly evolutionary in nature and a part of neo-evolutionary structural–functionalism, whilst the theory of dependency is a variation on the historical–materialist perspective which has been labelled neo-Marxism due to the importance attributed to core and periphery relations at the expense of the class relationship.

The chief weakness with dependency theory is that it is only a kind of mirror image of modernization theory. Modernization theory states that countries will develop if they modernize, i.e. if they change their social institutions from the traditional to the modern, whereas dependency theory states that peripheral countries cannot develop because they have been placed in a position of economic dependency by Western modernization. Frank's own terminology states unequivocally that the West has developed by 'underdeveloping' other parts of the world. By virtue of economic dependency, the Third World is destined to remain a service area for the West. In terms of 'unequal exchange', the Third World supplies raw materials at market prices that remain relatively low, whilst it must obtain most of its requirements in manufactured goods from the West at relatively high prices.

Both modernization theory and dependency theory make absolute statements about the relationship between the developed and the developing countries. Essentially, modernization theory is about the progress of capitalism and the avoidance of socialism, whilst dependency theory is about the need to break up the capitalist system to allow the Third World out of its subservient role. Therefore, just as in broad social theory there is a need to transcend the opposing paradigms of structural–functionalism and the Marxist critique, so in the consideration of global development there is a need to transcend modernization theory and dependency theory.

3

Social Interaction and the Reproduction of Institutions through Time and Space: the Theory of Structuration and the Concept of Inter-Societal Systems

In this chapter I propose the application of principles from Anthony Giddens's 'theory of structuration' as a means by which to transcend structural–functionalism and historical materialism in the analysis of social change and, more particularly, their equivalents in the sociology of development, modernization theory and dependency theory. With structuration theory, Giddens seeks the reworking of social theory, as an underpinning for sociology and the social sciences in general, principally by accommodating more effectively concepts of both social structure and social action. He began this task with *New Rules of Sociological Method: a positive critique of interpretative sociologies* (1976) and its full title reflects the importance of the legacy from the classics and the need to address the widespread swing away from structural to interpretative explanation that was current in sociology during the 1970s. Implicit in this is the need to incorporate the more convincing aspects of each into social theory, and Giddens has continued to develop the core of structuration theory in major works, *Central Problems in Social Theory* (1979) and *The Constitution of Society* (1984), together with a number of subsidiary works. Whilst in a complementary series, *A Contemporary Critique of Historical Materialism* in two volumes so far (1981 and 1985), Giddens proposes the final abandonment of historical materialism, as an inadequate theory of social change, and of functionalist theories, on the grounds that social systems cannot be explained adequately in terms of the functions of their parts. Instead, structuration theory is presented as a non-evolutionary theory in which it is clearly human beings who make a difference in the reproduction of social institutions and therefore create social change.

The safeguarding of human agency in a theory which clearly also involves structure and system is approached through the fundamental concept of the 'duality of structure' (Giddens 1984: 25). This takes up David Lockwood's (1964) distinction between 'social integration' and 'system integration', whereby the former consists of the structural and systemic elements which make day-to-day social interaction possible, and the latter of the longer-term, institutional aspects of society. In terms of the duality of structure, when we enter into day-to-day social interactions we, at the same time, contribute to the reproduction of social institutions. By the same token, we are enabled and constrained by social institutions in our day-to-day social interactions. The structural and systemic elements of society represent 'unacknowledged conditions' for our interactions and, equally, entering into social interactions has 'unintended consequences' in the reproduction of social structure and system. We reproduce routinely the institutions of society as a matter of day-to-day social interaction.

Social institutions represent the 'distanciation' in time and space of social interactions. But in the immediate nexus of action, at any passing moment in time, the distanciation of social institutions in time and space can only be an abstract concept served by human memory traces and the various aids, manual and electronic, devised by human agents to record the symbolic orders and modes of discourse. This basic, underlying concept of structuration theory can be illustrated to some extent in figure 2. It is suggested in the diagram that social interaction is motivated, rationalized and reflexively monitored by participants (the principles of interpretative sociology), yet it has structure and system (the principle of structural sociology). The term structuration means that as human agents we continually reproduce the structure and system of society in social interaction. The precise term social integration is employed to signify that social interaction is meaningful to human agents through the reproduction of structure and system.

Consider the following example. When I go into a lecture theatre to deliver a lecture to students, we come together as a group expecting to fulfil our respective roles in a familiar social situation. I deliver the lecture and the students listen, take notes and perhaps ask questions. But, in the course of undertaking this piece of 'social integration', we reconstruct, routinely, several social institutions which have a duration much longer than the one hour of the lecture. The conventions of higher education in Western culture form 'unacknowledged conditions' of our actions and the 'unintended consequences' of them are that these conventions are furthered in time and space. We do not normally think discursively about our roles as lecturer and students, but we are reproducing a model of higher education which has its

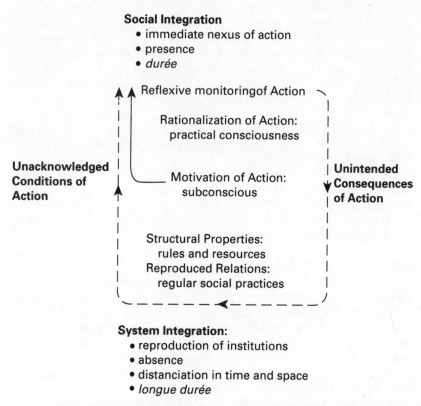

Social Integration
- immediate nexus of action
- presence
- *durée*

Reflexive monitoringof Action

Rationalization of Action:
practical consciousness

**Unacknowledged
Conditions of
Action**

Motivation of Action:
subconscious

**Unintended
Consequences
of Action**

Structural Properties:
rules and resources
Reproduced Relations:
regular social practices

System Integration:
- reproduction of institutions
- absence
- distanciation in time and space
- *longue durée*

Figure 2   The duality of structure (after Giddens 1985)

origins in medieval religious instruction and beyond. Secondly, similar observations may be made in respect of the academic discipline of sociology. I reproduce the teachings of a discipline with its origins in the spread of industrialized society during the nineteenth century. Sociology has not been taught in the same way during all of this time and, hopefully, the content of my lectures is updated usefully in between each annual delivery. This illustrates the power of human beings to 'make a difference' in the reproduction of social institutions. Thirdly, this process also reproduces a bureaucratic organization, the university or polytechnic or college. This exists, physically, merely as a collection of buildings containing various rooms until lecturer and students come together to bring the lecture room 'to life', as it were. It is in ways like these that the structure of social institutions is reproduced systematically in regular social practices, but always with the variations of human agency in the process of structuration. The social integration of the act of tuition, in which there is 'reciprocity between actors in contexts of co-presence', reproduces the system integration of the various, associated institutions whereby there is 'reciprocity between actors or collectivities across extended time-space' (Giddens 1984: 28).

The principle of the duality of structure extends through all institutions of society and of course there are many interlinked levels to its operation, extending from the local to the global. In the broad context of the modern nation-state, the concept is capable of relating the individual as a knowledgeable agent in society to the institutional structure of state administration. The great majority of people in the world today are citizens of nation-states, participating as voters, protesters, tax-payers, claimants, census respondents, fugitives or in a great many other roles, both negative and positive to the ideals of the nation-state. In fact, to be a stateless person in the modern world is to be in an especially problematic position. Furthermore, if we adopt Immanuel Wallerstein's (1974) concepts (see chapter 2), the duality of structure might also link the individual as worker, consumer, investor, etc., with an interdependent capitalist world-economy, especially in terms of the international division of labour. Connections of this kind are at an extreme level of abstraction, yet links between human interaction and larger societal structures are presumably ones we would wish to see not only maintained but also reflected in social theory. Otherwise large institutions tend conceptually to drift out of the control of human beings and we revert to the kind of deterministic theory rejected in the previous two chapters. Equally, differences of power and access in relation to social institutions need continually to be addressed, particularly by reference to historical precedents in the process of structuration.

Modern societies have been influenced by Western culture and take the legal form of nation-states. The model was created out of a process involving the conjunction of 'absolutist states', formed during the Reformation and Counter-Reformation, with merchant capitalism in the form of an extending world economy derived initially from the activities of Renaissance city-states. In the process, the national polity was effectively separated from the international economy in a significant contrast to other societal forms which contained them in one entity as, for instance, in the case of the Roman Empire. The outcome is, Giddens (1984: 183) suggests, that: 'The distinctive structural principle of the class societies of modern capitalism is to be found in the disembedding, yet interconnecting, of state and economic institutions.' In the contemporary period, therefore, the system of multiple nation-states, juxtaposed with that of a single, interdependent capitalist world-economy is a manifestation of this distinctive structural principle. At the same time, nation-states and world-economy are mediated by a global military order, and all three are linked by a system of global communications which has been rendered increasingly effective by technological advances. This terminology is used throughout this book, and, consequently, the next section of this chapter will be devoted to further elaboration of how such terms fit into the time and space dimensions of Giddens's structuration theory.

Inter-societal systems: a non-evolutionary framework for social change

Any framework which is used to compare human societies must of necessity involve arbitrary distinctions. There have been thousands of different cultures during the time that human beings have inhabited the Earth, but an encyclopedia or atlas that included them all could only serve as a catalogue and, in any case, is unlikely to be complete. So a compromise has to be made and the question arises of how it is made. Giddens makes his on the basis of time and space distanciation, that is, according to a society's capacity to extend its culture historically and geographically. His framework is threefold and includes: 'tribal society', 'class-divided society' and 'class (capitalist) society' (see figure 3).

Tribal society

Tribal society is the type that has existed for all of the several hundred thousand years that human beings have inhabited the Earth. It obviously covers a number of variations, including hunter–gatherers, pastoralists and horticulturalists, but the important, distinctive feature for Giddens is that these societies have had very little impact on the world beyond their limited 'locale'. Their modes of transport and communication are rudimentary, and there is a low level of contact and interaction with other societies. Communication is face to face and there is no written language, except where there has been contact with a literate society. Therefore, social integration and system integration are mainly fused together in ritual form involving communal participation, that is, the cultural institutions of the society are expressed face to face, in story-telling and the enactment of ceremonial rituals. To describe such societies as simple is to do them an injustice for there is considerable depth to the culture, but it takes the form of traditional, communal practices so that social organization is vested in kinship backed up by the norms of group sanction.

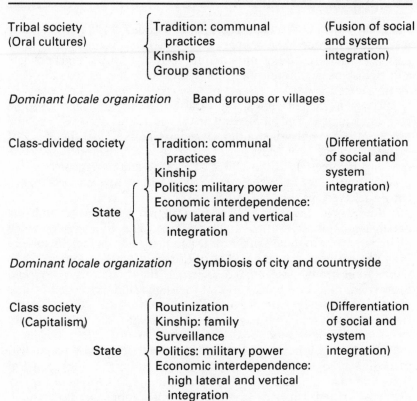

Figure 3   Social integration (Giddens 1985: 181/2)

Class-divided society

By contrast, the class-divided type has existed for the 7,000 years that humans are considered to have existed in 'civilizations'. The distinction between tribal and class-divided society hinges on the emergence of the city against a background of rural hinterland, part of which is controlled by the city and part of which shades off into tribal society or the area of influence of another city. Hence the title, 'class-divided society', because people who live in the city experience a lifestyle and division of labour quite different from that experienced by people in the rural hinterland. There are, therefore, two classes of people, and they are divided spatially between city and countryside. Tradition and kinship remain features of social life for both classes, but in the cities there are 'state' institutions and their controllers hold power as the ruling class of a city-state. According to Giddens (1984: 183), these institutions include, 'The polity, with its officials . . . separated in some part from the procedures of economic activity; formal codes of law and punishment . . . and modes of symbolic co-ordination, based in written texts'.

The city is located amidst the rural hinterland and there is some economic interdependence between the people of the city and the people of the countryside, although it is at nothing like the levels of interdependence that exist in modern societies. Through its state mechanisms, the city is the source of a range of powers which would otherwise not exist and these are broader, in effect, than anything in tribal society. These powers, which are both enabling and constraining for the people involved, include extended government and the organization of agriculture and marketing. The countryside is the major source of food and other basic products, but its social structure is as distinct from the city as that of tribal society. Giddens refers to the relationship in class-divided society as the 'symbiosis of city and countryside' and he emphasizes that the state stands conceptually and physically at the division between the city-based institutions and the rural communities. In most cases the city wall with its politico-military significance is the symbol of this division.

Giddens's main point in the distinction between tribal society and class-divided society, however, is that the latter has a greater impact in time and space. Significantly in this respect, class-divided society includes written language amongst its institutions, a facet which Talcott Parsons also used as a distinction between his categories, 'primitive' and 'intermediate' society. Giddens's emphasis, however, is that the distinction between the two types should not be seen as evolutionary because tribal society continued to exist to form a set of relationships with class-divided society or an 'inter-societal system' in the terminology of structuration theory. The earliest known instance of writing, dated at roughly 3100 BC, was found at Uruk, a Sumerian city-state in what is now southern Iraq. In this case, baked clay tablets bear pictographs of agricultural produce and people and they were obviously developed to help the city-state administer increasing wealth and complexity. Clearly, this is a crucial point in the emergence of the state, because the keeping of written records constitutes a form of surveillance by a recognized authority.

The city, Giddens argues, becomes a 'storage container' in time and space for the society in terms of knowledge and political power, and of physical production through such things as food storage and irrigation systems. Differences of power and access are evident in that literacy as an extension of knowledge was available only to nobility and priesthood, with their joint role in law and sanction, and possibly to merchants, or to the chosen servants of these three groups. Writing as straightforward record-keeping and inventory can easily be understood as significant, for instance, in the polity for purposes of taxation, in the belief-system for tributes, and in the economy for the exchange of goods. These institutions and their written records represent a precise form of the distinction between system integration (relations across extended time and space) from social integration (relations in co-presence). Literacy in communication and the institutions of law, polity and economy enabled a culture to be extended in time and space and the existence of a plurality of cities as concentrations of culture led to forms of exchange between them in art, science, expertise, scarce goods, etc. The rise of Western culture owed much to exchanges between the medieval cities of Europe when these formed a class-divided society in the terms outlined here.

Class (capitalist) society

This third category in Giddens's framework is the form of society recognized by the classical sociologists as modern, but by Marx, particularly, as capitalist, in which the capitalist class relationship becomes virtually universal. However, Giddens distinguishes his categorization by emphasizing that the extension of class is only part of a process which has also involved a number of social and political developments associated with the state and citizenship. Economic institutions are based upon the capitalist exchange mechanism which was extended globally through the transmission of Western culture over five or six hundred years. The school of thought popularized by the work of Immanuel Wallerstein (cf. 1974) and Fernand Braudel (cf. 1981) sees Western merchant capitalism as emerging between the fifteenth and seventeenth centuries.

Giddens uses the term 'class society' because the conflict of interests between capitalist and worker produced by the capitalist economic mechanism is a consistent feature of this type of society. However, during the early stages of Western development, merchant capitalism affected the working lives of only a small proportion of the population, whilst the vast majority were still engaged in traditional agricultural pursuits and locked in a social structure that retained many of the features of feudalism. But with industrialization, the division of labour was extended and the capitalist class relationship came to permeate virtually the whole of society so that, in principle, labour became a commodity to be purchased by the owners of capital, as identified so effectively by Marx. The pervasiveness of the capitalist class division throughout class society contrasts with the spatial nature of the class

division between city and countryside in class-divided society. Yet
the two forms existed together in Europe and its extending colonies
from the time of the Renaissance. There was no process of linear
evolution. Concentrations of merchant capitalism were created and
disappeared amongst the politico-military turmoil of European
development, as in the case of the rise and fall of Portugal or Habsburg
Spain, or of a whole string of powerful city-states, the principal
examples of which were Venice, Antwerp, Genoa and Amsterdam.
Subsequently, Britain emerged as the first fully-fledged nation-state to
dominate Europe and the European colonies. It had destroyed
France's prior claim to this position in colonial struggles over territory
in Canada and India and, ultimately, in the Napoleonic wars. London
became the centre of the capitalist world-economy not as a city-state
but as the capital of a nation-state and the Industrial Revolution took
place in a social structure that was already in many ways developed
and conducive.

When politico-military dimensions are taken into account as well as
economic ones it is clear that the development of modern Europe and
class society was never as simple as suggested by major conceptual
frameworks of social change. Marx's materialist conception of history,
for instance, emphasizes the economic 'substructure' to the detriment
of adequate political analysis, and this has been a weakness of all
Marxist theory, especially in terms of its operationalization in the
Soviet Union (see chapter 8). Structural–functionalism, by contrast,
reduces the role of capitalism, emphasizes a 'logic of industrialism'
and treats political institutions in a similar way to economic institutions. The function of power in the polity is modelled on that of
money in the economy, and so this theory, too, suffers from an
economistic weakness. Even Wallerstein's historical approach is
centred on the development of the capitalist world-economy and so
understates the role of other systems of global proportions, especially
the nation-state system or the global military order.

By the nineteenth century, class (capitalist) society had developed in
the West through a complex series of social, political and economic
developments. These included developments in Britain and such
milestones as the American Declaration of Independence (1776) and
the French Revolution (1789), both of which contributed significantly
to ideas of state and citizenship. A new model of social order had been
produced which embraced not only the ubiquity of the class relationship in society but also notions of citizenship and the transformation
of the state into the nation-state. In Durkheim s view, these changes
involved the stripping away of traditional moral norms and, as Weber
pointed out, tradition became, for the most part, replaced by routine,
especially in the form of rational–legal social organization. Kinship, as

theorists of all types have indicated, became transformed into a supportive institution, with the family as a unit of consumption rather than of production.

Class (capitalist) society, then, is recognizable in the development of Western culture and the concrete form that it takes in social and political terms is the nation-state, a legal–rational, bureaucratic form with well-developed institutions of surveillance and record keeping. A significant aspect of modern class society is the ability of the state to enter into the most detailed aspects of the life of the individual. Yet this must be set against rights of citizenship in law, property holding, representative democracy and social welfare which have been achieved by the general population to an extent evident in no other type of society. Such institutions as policing, taxation, censuses, registration for voting, etc., all represent aspects of class society that may be seen as both enabling and constraining for its citizens.

With extensive urbanization accompanying the industrialization of production, including agricultural production, the environment of class society has become increasingly artificial and, in Durkheim's terms, an 'organic' form of social solidarity and division of labour renders all of its members interdependent. The state has, therefore, ceased to derive its power from the contradiction of city and countryside interests as in class-divided society and, instead, state power in class society may be located conceptually at the point of contradiction inherent in the population's dual role as a socialized labour force and as private citizenry and appropriators of property. The polity may be seen as the arena of society as a social whole, out of which socialized labour is extracted, whilst the economy may be considered as the arena of private ownership, enterprise and appropriation. The separation of polity and economy has been a basic feature of Western development and class society, but the precise location of the division between, in effect, public sector and private sector forms one of the primary issues of party politics in modern times. During the period from the Second World War up to the present day, the extension of the public sector welfare state has been reversed in the privatization of services, as Keynesian economics have been eclipsed by monetarist theories.

At the global level, polity takes the form of the nation-state system, the milieu of international relations between separate state governments; and economy is the capitalist world-economy, the milieu of transnational business enterprise. Here, too, the precise boundary between them is a fluctuating political issue. Additionally, a feature of the mid to late twentieth century was the transformation of some nation-states to the 'state socialist' form. These cases involved the extension of state administration from the polity into the economy with the suppression of private enterprise, but this did not diminish the significance of the capitalist world-economy. However, the creation of state socialist nation-states alongside capitalist nation-states gave rise to two 'superpower' military alliances, NATO and the Warsaw Pact, which until recently constituted a clearly defined global military order.

As with tribal society and class-divided society, Giddens's main point about class (capitalist) society is presented in terms of time and space. Western culture is the first truly global culture and advances in transport and communication have made huge changes in 'time–space convergence'. The world really has become a smaller place. The past one hundred and fifty years have seen progress from travel and communication at the speed of the horse or sailing ship to intercontinental travel measured in hours and global communication, virtually instantaneous. Furthermore, whereas in earlier times travel and communication was only for a few, they have now become commonplace. The electric telegraph, the telephone, sound and televisual broadcasting with the added dimension of Earth satellites have become collectively the media of communication in a global information system to which virtually everyone has some kind of access. As part of the same technological advances, Western culture has been recorded in an extending variety of forms so that there is a wide range of sources available for the projection of its symbolism and discourse. The printing press and nationally and internationally circulated newspapers and journals have been supplemented by sound and picture recording involving records, tapes, film and video, etc. Additionally, electronic, computer technology in the processing of information produces amongst other things the extended surveillance capacity of the modern nation-state, referred to earlier. In class-divided society the city is the storage container of power and resources, but in class society this role is more highly centralized in the administration of the nation-state within broad but clearly defined territorial borders. The concentration of information on this scale gives state institutions the capacity to provide persuasive interpretations of social events. This is system integration on an enormous scale, with individual social interactions at all levels forming an increasingly small part of national and global institutions. As such, it reinforces the argument for the preservation of human agency in theory and practice.

The term, inter-societal systems, therefore, has to be used with caution, especially in view of the tendency apparent in Wallerstein's world-system analysis for historical and geographical distinctions to be oversimplified. At the same time, it should not be forgotten that the purpose of such concepts is to facilitate analysis when the reality of the world situation is continually in flux. Indeed, fundamental changes have taken place in recent decades with the concentration of new and successful industrialization in East Asia, with sweeping political changes in the Soviet Union and Eastern Europe and with the resurgence of Islamic political and military power in the Middle East. It is intended that the terminology used here avoids the traps of economistic bias and exaggerated functional integration, referred to earlier. Giddens (1985: 276) emphasizes that the use of the inter-societal system concept 'does not imply that there is a single dominating dynamic in its development or that the "whole" somehow has primacy over the "parts"'. The contemporary inter-societal system, therefore, may be outlined in terms of four dimensions each of which may in itself be seen as a sub-system:

Symbolic orders/modes of discourse	Global information system
Political institutions	Nation-state system
Economic institutions	Capitalist world-economy
Law/modes of sanction	Global military order

(after Giddens 1985: 277)

The division of labour has become increasingly specialized and any one individual can have no more than a rudimentary grasp of the complexity of interactions which go to make up modern class society in which the individual plays only a small part. This renders the preservation of the principle of human agency all the more crucial in such an overarching conceptualization as the inter-societal system. Any conceptualization of the immediate nexus of action in which human agency and the reproduction of social institutions coincide must take into account the scale of the institutional framework(s). There are many levels of social structure from the local to the global and it is within these levels that the inequalities of power may be discerned.

The rejection of the evolutionary perspective in social change

The final point in this chapter, therefore, is to emphasize the quality of pervasiveness of Western culture in time and space and its manifest capacity to permeate other cultures in the world. The principle of pervasiveness, in fact, replaces the rejected evolutionary principle in this approach to the analysis of social change. The meaning of the contemporary inter-societal system, therefore, is that class (capitalist) society has not simply replaced class-divided and tribal society but has suffused with them in a series of historical conjunctions and, furthermore, has itself been subject to further variation in the form of the state socialist societies. This may be illustrated by reference to figure 4. Hence, an inter-societal system represents a conjunction of societal forms with differential capacities to make an impact in time and space, so that there exist what Giddens (1981: 167) refers to as 'time–space edges'. It is across time–space edges that class society, with its highly developed powers to amass resources (storage capacity), to travel and to communicate, has made an impact on tribal and class-divided society, so engendering a truly global culture. Other societal forms are not discarded along an evolutionary pathway, rather they are subject to the kind of fusions that social scientists and particularly students of social change and development must seek to disentangle.

Figure 4 shows tribal societies as the longest-standing social form but as fragmentary systems with little impact in time and space, subject only to slow migrations and lacking contact with each other except on a localized basis. They are often referred to as 'pre-

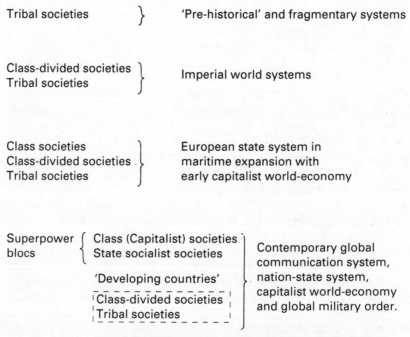

Figure 4   Inter-societal systems (after Giddens 1985: 184)

historical' societies because without literacy their awareness of their place in time and space is not developed or projected to other societies. When class-divided societies were created it was against a background of tribal societies. Cities existed in a rural hinterland and had only tenuous control over the frontiers of their politico-military power. What Wallerstein (1974) refers to as 'imperial world systems' were extensions of the form. The ancient empires, such as China or Rome, were extensive but not of course true world systems even if their emperors liked to think of them that way! According to Wallerstein (1974) and Braudel (1981), however, from the time of the Renaissance, European 'Western' culture began to flourish and to set up a 'world-economy' based on merchant capitalism. More accurately, through complex, social, political and economic processes that were competitive militarily and commercially, class (capitalist) societies were extended throughout Europe and its colonial interests. These societies existed as part of a world otherwise made up of class-divided societies and tribal societies, including several other 'empires' and 'civilizations' such as the Islamic Ottoman Empire, Imperial China or Muscovite Russia.

Figure 4 also shows the contemporary period in which capitalist societies have existed uneasily for much of the twentieth century with state socialist societies which were set up in reaction to capitalism. Side by side, these two forms have constituted the two superpower blocs of the post-Second World War, global military order made up of NATO and the Warsaw Pact. Their status as 'industrialized' or 'developed' has created the familiar distinction between these and the 'developing countries' of the Third World. This leaves the remaining vestiges of class-divided society and tribal society to be found on the margins of class (capitalist) society and especially in the Third World. Consequently, in figure 4, class-divided and tribal society are enclosed in broken lines to indicate how Western culture's impact on them has significantly affected most examples. The principle of time–space edges, relating to the resources and capacities of societies in a global context, may therefore be seen to link up with the question of development and underdevelopment and this conjunction forms the major theme of this book. In the parts which follow, I examine the rise of Western civilization and its impact upon the rest of the world (part II), the culmination of this after the Second World War (part III) and, finally, its legacy in the present day (part IV).

PART II

THE RISE OF WESTERN CIVILIZATION

A study of the formative period of Europe and Western civilization might in itself be taken as a contradiction of evolutionary and economistic theories of social change. Such theories are ethnocentric and specifically about the progress of the West, and yet the development of Western culture was quite clearly never assured and always subject to politico-military outcomes. A wide cross-fertilization of ideas and material developments was associated with the rise of Western civilization and the emergence of Europe as a distinct set of societies. But this all took place against a background of politico-military turmoil, so that it was never certain what kind of social formation would be the outcome. According to the historian John Roberts (1985: 96) in his account, *The Triumph of the West*, even by 1500 the distinct term, Europe, would have been used by few people. The entity to which people living in the area after the fall of Rome would have first felt they belonged was probably 'Christendom', although even the use of this term has not been identified before the eleventh century. However, the importance of Christianity as an integrating force must be emphasized in the social dynamics that produced the European culture. Not that the ideal should be taken as preceding the material facets of the culture, in a Hegelian sense, because ideal and material are quite clearly intertwined.

That a European culture did emerge, amidst continual internal upheaval and the threat of conquest from outside, serves to emphasize two aspects of structuration theory. There were unanticipated consequences in the now distinct European social institutions reproduced between the fifth and ninth centuries, and unacknowledged conditions principal amongst which must have been legacies of the Graeco–Roman past. The term Holy Roman Empire is significant from the eighth century because it refers to an emerging Western European political entity imbued with Christianity as a world religion. This brings us on to the external threats to Europe. The office of pope in Rome, as the spiritual centre of Western Christianity, was subject to an inherently problematic relationship with Byzantine Christian emperors in Constantinople. This was the legacy of the Emperor Diocletian's administrative division of the Roman Empire in the third century, which created two Christianities sharing ideals but with different, and potentially conflicting, social and political forms. From the seventh century, however, there was a much more serious threat to either form of Christianity when Islam burst out of the Arabian peninsula into surrounding areas, to the frontiers of Europe and Byzantium and beyond.

Therefore, three neighbouring cultures were created in and around the area which gave rise to Europe and Western development (see figure 5). The Holy Roman Empire, as a political entity, had an erratic existence in Western Europe and never became a truly European empire except for the period under Charlemagne. The Byzantine Empire prove more consistent, in the area to the north east of the Mediterranean. But from the sixth century Islam swept through the Middle East, North Africa and parts of Asia on a tide of military conquest and religious fervour that threatened Europe and Byzantium alike. As an empire, each was at certain times relatively unified and at others a looser collection of landholdings and cities sharing a combination of culture, religion and military alliance. From the seventh century, each frequently occupied portions of another's territory and, in support of the argument against evolutionary outcomes, it is clear that the physical integrity of Europe and therefore of Western civilization which we now take for granted was at that time never entirely secure. Islamic armies approached Europe from the south west through Spain, which they occupied between AD 711 and 719, and their advance was reversed only at Poitiers in central France in 732 by the Frankish ruler, Charles Martel. To the east, between the the siege of Constantinople in 718 and the second siege of Vienna in 1683, there were many assaults by successive Islamic groupings. In addition to this neighbouring rivalry, there were the long-distance incursions of Mongol raiders from China who were a threat to Europe, Byzantium and Islam, alike. During the thirteenth century they appeared invincible, occupying vast swathes of Asia and the eastern fringes of Europe. They had the military power to continue but, fortunately for European development, the chief interests of their Khan emperors were in central and eastern Asia. This all tends to make a nonsense of European ethnocentric views of societal development as evolutionary or economistic. Such a viewpoint could only be

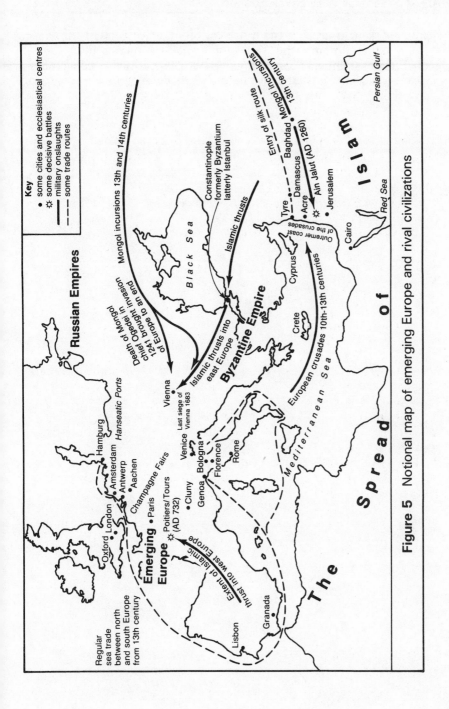

Figure 5 Notional map of emerging Europe and rival civilizations

Key
- • some cities and ecclesiastical centres
- ☆ some decisive battles
- — military onslaughts
- --- some trade routes

Russian Empires

Mongol incursions 13th and 14th centuries

Death of Mongol chief Ogedei in 1241 brought to an end of Europe invasion

Islamic thrusts into east Europe

Black Sea

Constantinople formerly Byzantium latterly Istanbul

Islamic thrusts

Byzantine Empire

Entry of silk route

Baghdad Mongol incursions 13th century

Damascus

Ain Jalut (AD 1260)

Tyre
Acre
Jerusalem

Outremer coast of the crusades

Cyprus

Cairo

Red Sea

Persian Gulf

Islam

The   Spread   of

European crusades 10th–13th centuries

Mediterranean Sea

Crete

Vienna
Last siege of Vienna 1683

Venice
Bologna
Florence
Rome

Genoa

Cluny

Hamburg
Amsterdam
Antwerp *Hanseatic Ports*
Aachen

Champagne Fairs
Paris

Oxford
London

Emerging
Europe • Poitiers/Tours
(AD 732)

Extent of Islamic thrust into west Europe

Lisbon

Granada

Regular sea trade between north and south Europe from 13th century held ex-post facto because the historical process clearly went through a complex and composite series of social, politico-military and economic developments constantly involving for the actors concerned unacknowledged conditions and unintended consequences.

4

The Development of European Institutions as Western Culture

The Europe from which western civilization emerged is nowadays taken for granted as a finite part of the world map but, as outlined already, its emergence between the fall of the Roman Empire and the sixteenth century was always uncertain. The danger was from internal turmoil with the power vacuum resulting from the decline of Rome and from external aggression on the part of military alliances to the east. Yet by the end of this period the identity of Europe and the foundations of Western civilization had been given structure. Two writers who have taken an overview of the medieval period are Jacques Le Goff (1988) of the French Annales school of history and John Roberts (1985), the English historian. In a manner that is consistent with the emphasis in structuration theory on the links between human agency and social institutions, they both observe that there came with European culture a sense of the power of human beings to determine their own destiny and of human actions having direction and 'going somewhere'. Le Goff (1988: 166) tempers this by adding that, given medieval Christianity, the future could be the day of judgement, but Roberts (1985: 75) emphasizes the sense of hope for the future, despite the decline of the Roman Empire, by reference to St Augustine of Hippo's fifth-century work, *Civitas Dei*. He locates the 'birth of the West' between AD 400 and 900 and reflects thus:

> Those centuries – which, patronisingly and ambiguously, we still sometimes call the Dark Ages – produced among other things still with us the primacy of the papacy in the West, the earliest monastic structures, the English monarchy and some of its basic institutions, as well as the fundamental linguistic divisions which still form the basis of

many modern European nations. At the same time there appeared feudal society, the Holy Roman Empire, the first European nobility, the French monarchy, the structure of thought which shaped European culture down to the rediscovery of Aristotle in the eleventh century, and many other things which have now disappeared but which were to have centuries of life in them, as well as enormous influence in the world. (Roberts 1985: 81)

It is further significant that this writer can lay such emphasis on the creation of institutions which give structure to the idea of a Western culture and which in their reproduction have been so crucial to its rise to prominence in the world. This indicates the reproduction of social institutions that, in sum, represents the *longue durée* creation of European culture. It is not acceptable to view this process in terms of the functional evolution of dehumanized social institutions, nor as the result merely of economic relationships.

Christianity and feudalism as Western institutions

The period of European feudalism is characterized by the principle of feuding warlords and land barons determining by their actions the division of territory and the profile of the social structure. More specifically, Le Goff (1988: 90) states, feudalism existed only in embryonic form before AD 1000 when it blossomed mainly in France and Germany, and to a lesser extent in Italy and Spain. Subsequently, the Normans took it offshore to England, Sicily and the Outremer of the crusades but it varied in its precise form from area to area. Fernand Braudel (1982: 464), following Georges Gurvitch and Marc Bloch, points out that there were several facets to the society of the time and that feudalism, an efficient means of agrarian production, was only one of them. Certainly, it seems, the conquest of Roman Europe by 'barbarian' horsemen and the destruction of most of its institutions created a turbulent and floating society which did not become widely settled again until AD 1000. Le Goff (1988: 38–43) describes the Emperor Charlemagne, a Frank of barbarian descent, as instrumental in the Christian reform of barbarianism, albeit by the extreme means of massacre or conversion. It is desirable to consider many reasons for the re-awakening of Europe, but the society that was created was in Anthony Giddens's (1981: 159) terms 'class-divided'. The nobility, the higher priesthood and the wealthy merchants together with their immediate followers lived an urban, literate existence separated from the masses of peasantry who worked the land. Towns grew as a settled and 'civilized' society 're-emerged' and in the terms of structuration theory there was a form of 'symbiosis' or interdependence, as a structural principle, between the two classes. The urban class depended upon the peasant class for the production of food and basic commodities whilst the latter depended upon the former for land tenure through government and military protection in the face of turmoil. Le Goff (1988: 293) describes the separation of two 'worlds' by town walls, whilst Paul Hohenberg and Lynn Hollen Lees (1985: 22), following R. S. Lopez (1963: 27), write of 'a paradox [in which] the city closes itself off from the rural environment in order to enlarge the scope and intensity of communication with the wider world'. It will be emphasized throughout this chapter how the urban network that grew up in Europe, although by no means permanently united in political terms, was important for the circulation of norms, values, beliefs and techniques in a growing culture. Social, political and economic institutions initially reproduced in a limited locale became extended through time and space to be linked up with those from other locales to form the broader European culture. These include ideas and influences derived from Byzantium, Islam and further afield, and they comprise a notion of European culture which is meaningful as the basis for Western civilization.

Throughout this whole period and those that followed it, no state and no individual managed to achieve the domination of the whole continent as the Romans had done. A sociological interpretation by Michael Mann (1986: 376) refers to emergent Europe as 'a multiple acephalous federation'. This is significant because the entity that emerged as Europe was not an empire like the Roman Empire. Instead it consisted of a variety of separate states, continually in military competition over territory and influence, but collectively making space for a rather inconsistent but, nevertheless, increasingly recognizable system of political and economic relations. The establishment of a number of relatively secure politico-military states made possible the more stable exchange of commodities and even reasonably secure mechanisms for investment in such activities. This system became merchant capitalism on an extending scale and it was the forerunner of modern industrial capitalism. But again it needs to be emphasized that history cannot be explained in terms of an evolutionary pathway from merchant capitalism to industrial capitalism because there were concomitant changes in social and political institutions on which the transformation depended.

In medieval Europe, there had been attempts to unite the area as a single political unit. Clovis, at the turn of the fifth century a predecessor of Charles Martel and of Charlemagne himself as King of the Franks, converted to Christianity quite clearly as a political expedient which he used to further his military ambitions throughout the former Roman province of Gaul (Le Goff 1988: 21; James 1988: 70). Then Pope Gregory the Great, as head of the Roman Church, achieved a degree of unity between AD 590 and 604. But above all it was Charlemagne, actually referred to as Emperor and sometimes as *Europae Pater*, for whom real success can be claimed at the turn of the ninth century. His leadership brought a fixity to European society after the wanderings of the barbarian period (Le Goff 1988: 134–5), using the military power of cavalry as the barbarians had done against Roman foot soldiers in the first place. Charlemagne had well-developed technical skills at his disposal, such as metal working for weaponry and geographical knowledge for campaigning, both of which are significant features in the longer-term European development (metal working for cannon was later to be crucial in European maritime expansion, as was geographical knowledge for navigation). Charlemagne established a series of courts and encouraged scholarship and the arts, setting the model for a social form that was also significant for the future. The court at Aachen enjoyed precedence over the others, according to Le Goff (1988: 39), and some of the infrastructure survived in the region, so that in a later period it contributed to developments which enabled the city-state of Antwerp to become an important European cultural and commercial centre. Charlemagne's Holy Roman Empire and its culture were small when compared with those of his contemporaries, the Byzantine emperors or the Islamic Abbasid caliphs. It lacked an enduring existence, and Europe was subsequently broken up into its characteristic form of independent political units. It should be remembered, however, that Charlemagne was crowned by a pope and that Christianity remained a consistent and unifying force for European culture.

That Western Christianity was called the Roman Church is broadly significant because it carried forward some of the institutions on which Roman society had been structured. Foremost amongst these, in terms of the rationalizing effects of literacy and the universalizing potentialities of a common language, was Latin as a mode of discourse. Latin became not only the language of the church but also of its centres of learning and the medieval universities of Bologna, Paris and Oxford became models of their kind (Duroselle 1990: 210–11). As late as the eighteenth century the Swedish botanist, Carl von Linne (Carolus Linnaeus) published his classification of plant species in Latin so that it could be read throughout Europe. The principles of Roman Law were also carried through the Middle Ages and, as Max Weber (1978: 852–5) observed, these were of great importance for later periods, since they contained 'general formal qualities' which fitted in well with the growth of 'the practice of law as a profession'.

A rival civilization to the East: Islamic Empire

During the seventh century a rival world religion, Islam, grew out of the teachings of the prophet Muhammad and served to unite the nomadic Beduin tribes of the Arabian peninsula. The faith spread enormously through conversion by means of the *jihad* or holy war which, according to Mann (1986: 302), was a striking contrast with the ideological propagation of Christianity. Despite this aggressive approach and the Arabs' initial reluctance to share their religion on equal terms with outsiders, Islam had popular appeal with the masses, as Malise Ruthven (1984: 144–5) points out. By the early eighth century the first extensive Islamic empire had been created under the leadership of the Umayyad caliphate, the latter word a term signifying the succession to Muhammad. Its centre was Damascus, but it stretched from Spain in the west, through North Africa and the Middle East, to the River Indus in the east. With their nomadic Beduin origins, the Arabs as horse soldiers were used to living off the land, and they moved quickly and effectively to their military successes. Other travellers carried the influence of the religion and elements of the culture even further, into China and South-East Asia. After initial expansion, however, the lines of communication became enormously stretched and Islam varied at different times from being a large unified empire under a single caliph to a loose collection of emirates and sultanates (lesser rulers) connected by a religious hierarchy. Mann (1986) has drawn attention to such examples of dynasties in extended military empires which last only a generation or two, before the pressures involved in the pacification of territory cause the power structure to fail and the empire to break up. In Islam the political centre was moved from Damascus to Baghdad under the Abbasid caliphate from AD 750, and then to Cairo in the tenth century with a series of different caliphates, including the Seljuks who with their military strategist, Saladin, successfully ejected the European crusaders from the Middle East. Ultimately, from the fourteenth century the Ottoman Turks began to affirm their power in Islam and they established their capital at the former Byzantine city of Constantinople which they renamed Istanbul. The Ottoman Empire survived for six centuries until the First World War from whence its demise will be described in chapter 12.

Islam provided a widespread and effective network for scholarship and trade, as well as religion, and quickly outpaced Christian European development. The Arabs were an oral culture until the coming of the religion but Arabic script became the language of Islamic scholarship which, like the early Christian church, did not distinguish between lay and ecclesiastical study. Scholarship within Islam created a unity through popular cultural assimilation and, between the eighth and the thirteenth centuries, its culture was unrivalled anywhere for institutions of government and quality of learning and science. The Al Azhar University in Cairo was founded in the tenth century and survives today as a revered centre of Islamic scholarship and reputedly the world's oldest surviving university. Christian Europe and the Islamic Empire met as rivals both in religion and in culture. Both societies were of the class-divided type in the terms of structuration theory, that is they consisted of cities, which were the carriers of the culture, and the countryside, where most of the population lived and worked in agriculture. Cultural exchange took place between cities and between cultures, for instance through Spain during its occupation by the Umayyad emirs of *al-Andalus*, the Arabic word for Spain from which the present-day Spanish province of Andalucia takes its name.

The other great medium of exchange was the crusades. Jerusalem is of great significance to each religion and, having been restored initially by the eastern Roman Emperor, Constantine in the fourth century as part of the foundation of Byzantine Christianity, it fell to Islam in AD 638 as part of the push north into Byzantium and Persia. It was not until the eleventh century, however, that Christian kings and princes in Europe, with the encouragement of the Byzantines, pursued their own holy wars or crusades to free the Holy Land from Islamic control. Despite many abuses, the crusades are significant for their association with ideas of piety and chivalry. Such ideas are crucial for the definition of an ideal character, especially amongst the nobility in the developing European culture and have long-term implications for Western notions of culture and civilization. At the same time, the establishment of feudal estates throughout Europe represents an overall improvement in agriculture, and this gave the nobility wealth and power to support such projects as the crusades and eventually the exploration of the oceans as a means to circumvent the Islamic land blockade of routes to the spice and silk trades of the east.

Piety and chivalry, together with associated ideals such as courtly love, became characteristics which set a minority nobility apart from the rest of the population, whilst the higher clergy, although nominally restricted to piety, in practice shared a much wider range of these contemporary ideals. Monasteries, such as the archetypal example of Cluny in Burgundy (cf. Whitton 1988: 136–8), became centres of politico-economic power alongside those of the lay nobility. In fact, the Cluny model became an instrument of administrative reform emulated by nobles and bishops alike and, in this way, the courts of 'those who fight' and 'those who pray' extended the spread of

European culture. The lands which the crusaders settled at the eastern end of the Mediterranean were known as Outremer and they contained a concentration of urban literate culture. Its occupants combined their own ways with those of Islam which were mostly more sophisticated and such cross-fertilization is an important feature of European cultural development. Peter Denley (1988: 285) and Malcolm Vale (1988: 346–51) emphasize the significance of the broad characteristics of medieval culture for the subsequent and far-reaching changes of the Renaissance period and beyond. However, as a pointer to the exploitative effects of the rise of the West and subsequent comparisons between the two cultures, Mansfield (1985: 83) observes that 'The first crusaders found much to admire and envy in the living conditions of their Saracen enemies [but] eighteenth century European travellers to the area were unanimous in their descriptions of the human misery that they found.' Moreover, the crusades changed the relationship between the two religions; before there had been tolerance and even acceptance, afterwards there was hatred and mistrust.

Whilst the Islamic peoples continued to be a threat to the independence of Europe, the spirit of the crusade in its various forms was a focus for European culture, and it became an institutionalized part of the structure of society. Ironically, the fourth crusade was diverted to achieve something that Islamic armies had long failed to achieve, the fall of Constantinople and the Byzantine Empire in 1204. This invasion received strong encouragement from the Venetians who were by then building up their trading empire in the eastern Mediterranean and consequently had an interest in seeing Byzantium subdued. The Venetian trade network extended into Islam and served as a commercial bridge to bring oriental produce into Europe, which made it effectively the first centre of a co-ordinated European 'world-economy', in Braudel's or Wallerstein's terms. The associated rise of Venice along with other Italian city-states consitutes a different manifestation of European cultural advancement, the Italian Renaissance.

The Renaissance: the affirmation of Western civilization

Further developments in European identity and the cultural self-confidence of European people can be found in the Renaissance. This period has a primary connotation looking back to the perceived glories of classical times, and is associated primarily with art, architecture and scientific advancement. Aristotle's writings had been rediscovered as early as the eleventh century and, despite the general Christian suppression of pagan antiquity, there were often Greek figures on churches to represent the seven liberal arts, as in a celebrated example over the doorway of Chartres cathedral in France. In this connection, too, the contact with Islam is significant because it was the Arabs who had maintained many Greek texts, especially from Alexandria during the Ptolemaic period, and with translation into Latin these became available to European scholars. In more pragmatic terms, the elite of the Italian city states added to the model of medieval court circles by providing such services as administration, law, medicine and commerce. This required an expansion of secular education and brought about an exchange of skills throughout Europe. The 'notary' was a role formerly associated with Roman Law but probably derived through the Roman Empire from the Middle Eastern civilzations (Weber 1978: 682–3). This 'professional' drew up contracts and was the intellectual of business life when merchants were often less educated (Denley 1988: 287; Le Goff 1988: 219). By the fourteenth century, the itinerant merchant of medieval times had become rare as merchandise came to travel unaccompanied, subject to written correspondence and bills of exchange (Braudel 1981: 419). The Italian city-states traded widely, and Genoa as well as Venice, created a trading empire in the eastern Mediterranean to provide points of contact with Byzantium and Islam. These are good examples of the power and influence of cities with guilds, confraternities and corporations wielding power independently and alongside the landowners in the class-divided society of Renaissance Europe. Hohenberg and Lees (1985: 45) further describe the competition between merchants and guildsmen in their study, *The Making of Urban Europe 1000–1950*.

All such examples are indicators of a growth in exchange of goods and ideas. As early as the thirteenth century, the Hanseatic League consisting of merchants in northern Europe, had established regular exchanges by direct sea route with Venice and Genoa, replacing the tortuous land routes which hitherto had come together in the Champagne fairs of north-eastern France (Le Goff 1988: 79). Thus trade across Europe was extended, indirectly, far beyond the Mediterranean, through Islam to India and China. Direct routes were yet to be developed, but it is probably no coincidence that the point of departure for this was to be a haven on the route from northern Europe to the Mediterranean, the port of Lisbon. This would have served as a receptacle for maritime innovation from northern Europe, the Mediterranean and beyond and, under the patronage of Prince Henry 'the Navigator', it was subsequently to blossom as a home base for the 'navigators' and notably Vasco da Gama who pioneered the direct ocean route from Europe to India. It was as though Christian Europe was feeding from sources that it despised, such as Islam, in terms of both ideas and luxury goods (Le Goff 1988: 152). The wider implications of this are the enrichment of the European elite and the furtherance of European culture.

The arts, skills and the discoveries that emerged during the Middle Ages and the Renaissance were circulated between the increasingly numerous cities and towns of Europe: through the courts of royalty and nobility; the abbeys, cathedrals and universities of the Christian religion; and the markets, fairs and merchant houses of the evolving European economy. All of these developments were facilitated by the copying, mainly by monks, of documents that were exchanged widely in time and space. As a single example, a bible in Michelangelo's chapel at Florence proved to have been produced in Bede's *scriptorium* in Northumberland. Laborious copying was gradually superseded by the introduction of printing and moveable type at various centres, an innovation widely attributed to Gutenberg of Mainz, although there are other contenders and this may have been another practice brought from China. The printing press certainly liberated ideas throughout Europe, which contrasts with its prior, but restricted, use in Chinese civilization (Dawson 1964: 245). By means such as these, the urban class in a European class-divided society developed, within the cities, concentrations of power and wealth, legitimized by religion, protected by military force, and supported by the administrative facility of literacy. These urban centres may, therefore, be seen in Giddens's (1981: 144) terms as having 'storage capacity' both materially, as centres for the development of agriculture and trade, and ideologically, as collection points for information of all kinds. This makes possible the 'time–space distanciation' of culture through institutionalized methods of reproduction and transmission. The storage capacity of the city is instrumental in the generation of power, through both the production of goods, or 'allocative resources', and the reproduction of knowledge or 'authoritative resources' (Giddens 1981: 94). Renaissance Europe *was* a class-divided society but it included also 'long-term divergencies' which set it apart from the other civilizations and these were significant in the rise of the West. Giddens describes it as follows:

> Class-divided society is marked ... by some disentangling of ... four institutional spheres. ... The polity, with its officials, is separated in some part from the procedures of economic activity; formal codes of law and punishment exist; and modes of symbolic co-ordination, based in written texts, make their appearance.
>
> Modern capitalism is not [however] one type of 'civilization' among others, and it does not mark an evolutionary development 'out of' class-divided societies. The first genuinely global type of societal organization in history, it has its origins in a double discontinuity in the

development of the West. There are long-term divergencies in the formation of the West, as compared with that of the other major 'civilizations', over a period of some two millennia; Europe remained a 'state system', and no dominant imperial centre was re-established in its midst after the disintegration of the Roman Empire. Within this broad divergence, however, a range of massive discontinuities from other types of society was introduced by the intertwining of political and industrial revolutions from the eighteenth century onwards. The distinctive structural principle of the class societies of modern capitalism is to be found in the disembedding, yet interconnecting, of state and economic institutions. (1984: 183)

Social, political and economic institutions from limited locales were joined up with those from others to form a broad European culture which also drew freely from the cultures of other civilizations. The European culture was, however, developing characteristics now recognizable which were to set it apart from the others in terms of self-conscious progress, politico-military and economic power.

The Reformation and the opening for rational explanation

The Protestant Reformation has to be seen as essentially a breaking up of the religious unity that had been a kind of adhesive for medieval society and the Renaissance. The routine reproduction of social institutions by human actors admits of change but authoritative resources are necessary for the reform of a major social institution. The ideas of the Reformation were relatively long in developing, and Martin Luther was not so much their originator as the first to get them listened to successfully. Roberts (1985: 106) suggests that Luther's teachings suited European politics at the time, and that he was supported by some sectors of the nobility, whilst others were distracted by yet another wave of Islamic expansionism in eastern Europe. Luther, he maintains, would have been appalled by the outcome of the Reformation because he was a man of the Middle Ages, whilst the unintended consequences of the reforms that he set in motion constitute an important dimension in the transition from medievalism to modernism. The enabling factor in these changes was release from the restrictiveness of the Roman Catholic church which contributed significantly to the further advancement of European culture and to the whole panoply of discoveries and invention that followed. The constraining factor was that, through the institutions that they created, Western people tended towards an overweaning belief in their own ideological and technical superiority in the world which led to some excesses, and was not significantly checked until the twentieth century.

Max Weber's thesis, *The Protestant Ethic and the Spirit of Capitalism*, has been over-interpreted in terms of a link between these two elements, but it is unlikely that the development of science and technology would have taken place in the way that it did without changes to the dominant belief system of European culture. Joseph Needham (1956), in a much-quoted paper, suggests that the application of mathematics to science, after the work of Galileo Galilei in the sixteenth and seventeenth centuries, is the single most significant factor in the advancement of Western science and technology. The claim is based upon the conspicuous lack of such a combination in Chinese science, which was otherwise ahead of its Western counterpart before this time. Needham also refers to the concomitant social changes in Europe which opened the way for gentlemen of the nobility to associate with technicians, an illustration of the interlinking of changes in ideas and social mores. Weber set great store by his perceptions of the development of rational thought as part of these advances. In terms of his 'ideal types', he distinguished between the *zweckrational* and the *wertrational* in social action and feared that the former, involving an emphasis on goal-orientation, had increasingly displaced the latter at the expense of values in the developing society. Thus Western society was becoming more of a calculating and 'means-to-ends' culture, in which the classical economists had observed changes in the allocation of resources. The capitalist economic system was capable of reducing almost everything to the status of a commodity with a market price. Money had become the universal medium of exchange, and rational bookkeeping and accounting procedures could be developed in order that the precise financial position of any enterprise could be calculated at any particular time.

Merchant capitalism and the beginnings of the capitalist world-economy

Braudel (1984: 57) does not entirely share Wallerstein's (1974) emphasis on the sixteenth century but agrees with Marx that European capitalism began in Italy in the thirteenth century, although, as he points out, Marx went back on this. The Hanseatic–Mediterranean trade with its indirect links to India and China, as mentioned earlier, provided for Europeans the experience of international trade involving the setting up of an infrastructure of merchant houses, financial arrangements and paper transactions. Some of these techniques were not new, Braudel (1981: 472) suggests that the bill of exchange was re-discovered by the West in the thirteenth century and that its use in some form or other is as old as trade between cities. Elsewhere (1982: 556) he refers to the Islamic *sutfaya* in use before the European equivalent. Such comparisons are important for an adequate perspective on these developments, but as with many other things, Europeans went further in the institutionalization of the innovation than their precursors.

Venice, with a string of trading posts along the Levant coast and the Hanseatic link, emerged at the end of the fourteenth century as the centre of what Braudel (1984: 124) calls the first European 'world-economy'. Peter Burke (1986: 223) affirms that it did so by seizing the position of a link between Europe and the eastern trade. But the commercial methods used in Venice were emerging in cities throughout Italy and the rest of Europe. The systems of economic exchange became relatively secure, with the creation of stable political institutions, and the latter were buttressed by the production of economic wealth resulting from the former. Professional specializations were created in these societies to accommodate the growth of social, political and economic activity. In manufacturing, craftsmen organized themselves into guilds and were often in conflict with merchants, although in the case of Venice they rarely made an impression on its mercantile-dominated politics. Venetian manufacturing, in fact, went beyond the guild system with the establishment of the Arsenal, a state-run manufactory where the Venetian fleet and its armies of *condottieri* mercenaries were equipped and where advice on naval engineering was taken from Galileo. The Venetians put cannon into their galleys in the fifteenth century, although the Spanish and English had in fact used naval artillery about a century earlier. Such armaments were needed to protect Venetian interests from the Ottoman Turks who had developed or obtained cannon, too, and were taking advantage of the demise of Byzantium to become a greater military force in the north-eastern Mediterranean. It is estimated that by the sixteenth century Venice's Arsenal employed three thousand workers, and may, therefore, be seen as a forerunner of those ordnance manufactories which subsequently were a feature of the military strengthening of many European states. It is also indicative of the employment of considerable wage labour by the Venetian city-state although much the work would have been contracted out to guildsmen.

Sophisticated commercial techniques were widespread by this time. At the height of Venice's commercial success, the ownership of trading galleys was divided into transferable shares or *partes*, as practised in other European maritime cities at about the same time. By the fourteenth century regular commercial exchange had been institutionalized under the porticos of the Rialto in Venice where merchants, bankers and others could meet to carry out their transactions, but equivalent arrangements had existed even earlier in Lisbon (Braudel 1982: 98). In the fifteenth century, Luca Pacioli of Florence published a treatise on mathematics which was widely used as a textbook and which included an explanation of *partita doppia* or double-entry bookkeeping (Denley 1988: 287). The technique thus formalized was passed on to other Italian cities and thence to the rest of Europe to become the foundation for modern accountancy. There was clearly cross-fertilization of techniques and specializations across Europe and some of the great bankers of the time were based in Florence, a city that was also important throughout Europe in the manufacture of wool-cloth. Of the bankers, the Bardi and the Peruzzi bankrupted themselves through loans to royalty that were not repaid, notably including those made to Edward III of England to finance his wars with France (Burke 1986: 224). That royalty could renege on their debts in this way is a confirmation of the relative power of the kings and the bankers or merchants of the period, but equally, it is an indication of the growing dependence of state rulers on mercantile finance, and therefore of the separation of political and economic institutions in the developing European societies. The infamous Medici family were bankers, too, as were the Welsers and the Hochstetters of Germany, and the highly successful Fugger family of Augsburg, whose financial ascendancy coincided with the commercial success of the Flemish city of Antwerp when it eclipsed Venice as the centre of the European 'world-economy'.

All of this confirms early developments in merchant capitalism, but they apply only to the more successful activities. To keep a perspective on scale, Roberts (1985: 266) points out that a modern merchant ship could carry a year's tonnage landed on the quays of medieval Venice. On the other hand, the profits were relatively much greater, and made it possible to retire on the proceeds of a single successful voyage. Taking Europe as a whole, however, the greater part of its aggregate social and economic activity was still traditional, and, in terms of changes of lifestyle, merchant capitalism affected only a small proportion of the population and almost exclusively those living in the towns. The medium of merchant-capitalist activity was family firms which tended to operate for only a few decades, their lack of permanence due as often to a switch to *nouveau riche* rural life as to actual commercial failure. The most dominant centres of trade superseded each other in succession (Braudel 1984) and after Venice, as mentioned already, Antwerp became the centre of the European 'world-economy' in a rather fluctuating episode between 1501 and 1568. Then there was Genoa (1557 to 1627), followed by Amsterdam, as the Counter-Reformation and the Thirty Years War (1618–48) opened a religious division between northern and southern Europe. With this the focus of commercial operations was moved permanently northwards, which Wallerstein (1974) has interpreted as the establishment of a core to the 'world-economy' in north-western Europe. Meanwhile, the declining Mediterranean area, including Spain, Portugal and the Italian city-states, became in his terms a semi-periphery, whilst a 'second feudalism' in grain production in eastern Europe reduced that area to a periphery roughly equivalent to the new European colonies overseas.

In this broad process of Western social development, political concentration and economic consolidation, the land blockade posed by Islam to the east became the prime factor in Europe's emergence as a set of maritime powers. There had for centuries been piecemeal and indirect trade routes extending from Europe to India and China. There was even a branch of the Nile known as 'Nechao's canal' which flowed into the Red Sea for a period of several centuries, long before the Suez canal was built (Braudel 1981: 402). But none of the eastern routes were under the control of Europeans who in land battles could do no more than hold their own ground against Islamic forces or Mongol raiders alike. It was by sea that the Europeans made progress and the voyages of the 'navigators' were initially an extension of the Christian crusades against Islam. But, with royalty as their patrons and merchants or bankers often acting directly as their financial backers, the navigators also discovered direct routes to the long-coveted riches of the 'Indies'. These ventures and the later trading empires of the Dutch and English will be described at length in chapter 6.

Both Wallerstein (1979: 37) and Braudel (1984: 22) distinguish between a world-economy, which could apply to the 'world-empires' of ancient times, and *the* world-economy, which can apply only to the subsequent maritime expansionism of the European states and constitutes the first truly global culture. This European expansion was capitalist in the social sense that it involved the creation or extension of wage labour both in manufacturing and in agriculture, albeit at first for only a minority of the total workforce; in the political sense that economic institutions were allowed to be separated out from the polity; and in the economic sense that it involved the exchange of commodities through the medium of money, banking and investment. The transformation of European society into class (capitalist) society was already progressing when, through maritime expansion, it created an inter-societal system involving class-divided and tribal societies in other parts of the world (see chapter 3). The appropriate social, political and economic institutions are discernible in the development of the European states amidst politico-military conflict and religious divide, from the Hanseatic–Italian exchanges of the thirteenth century to modern times. Giddens (1981, 1985) describes the expansion of the state as one of the crucial features of the transformation from class-divided society to class (capitalist) society. In class-divided society, the state is embryonic and created out of the conflict of interests between city-based institutions and rural communities. The urban elite is as far removed from the countryside, existentially, as it is from tribal society. The city walls enclose the state power and resources and the separate lifestyle of its inhabitants despite the fact that city and countryside are to an extent economically interdependent. In class (capitalist) society, by contrast, a more developed state embraces city and countryside through the pacification and surveillance of extended, but clearly defined territory. When London took control of the European world-economy during the eighteenth century, it was not as a city-state like its predecessors but as the capital city of an emerging nation-state known as Britain after the Act of Union in 1707. The state in class (capitalist) society enforces its borders so that the activities which take place within them are in various ways subject to centralized monitoring and surveillance. As a day-to-day illustration of the effects of this, Braudel (1984: 289) describes foreign visitors to Britain during the eighteenth century who expressed surprise and irritation at the thorough customs check which they received at the port of entry. But this was tempered with relief that there were no further checks at tolls within Britain's borders, as would have been normal throughout Europe at the time. The collection of excise duties had clearly been taken over by a centralized state administration.

A consistent feature of state development is the increasing separation of polity (the public sector) and economy (the private sector) and state intervention may be conceptualized as follows:

1   In class-divided society, the state may be seen to intervene at the point of contradiction between city interests and rural interests. This is characterized by the city-state's maintenance of city walls.
2   In class (capitalist) society, the state may be seen to intervene at the point of contradiction between socialized production and private appropriation. This is less easy to define precisely amongst the industrialized and urbanized population living in a 'created environment' within the much broader borders of the nation-state. As such, its location, seen as the division between the public and the private sector, has remained predominant on the political agenda of the modern liberal democracies.

In both class-divided society and class society, therefore, the state exists at a point of contradiction of interests and therefore of potential conflict. For Giddens, this transformation of the state is a better index of social change than the machinations of class struggle as emphasized by Marx. We shall return to this issue in chapter 5, when the development of the state is addressed in more detail. Let us now consider the broad development of Western culture during the Enlightenment.

The Enlightenment as the threshold to industrial society, liberal democracy and the nation-state

The term Enlightenment extends that sense of the power of humans over their environment and of a direction to history which has already been linked with the development of Western culture. It is impossible in the space available to do justice to the whole panoply of advances that go to make up the Enlightenment, but there are a few threads of particular relevance which can be drawn out. European society arose out of medieval Christianity and religious institutions remained a powerful force in the sixteenth and seventeenth centuries. This remained so despite the dividing of the Christian church during the Reformation and the resulting secular advances especially in northern Europe. As Robert Zaller (1984: 88) observes, it is well known that Galileo (1564–1642) was persecuted by the Catholic church and driven from the Catholic University of Padua, but less so that his contemporary, Johannes Kepler (1571–1630), was expelled from the Protestant University of Tubingen. What scientists needed was the establishment of a specific institutional focus for scientific advancement, recognized by the state, and this was achieved with the chartering of the Royal Society in London by Charles II in 1662, four years after Oliver Cromwell's death. This was followed by the Academy of Sciences in Paris in 1666 and then equivalents in other northern European cities.

It was against this changing background that Isaac Newton (1642–1727) provided an integrated framework for science that took Europe by storm and, as Roberts (1985: 244) points out in terms of the mores of the time, by 1737 his work was acceptable reading 'even for ladies'. Given this chapter's emphasis on the combination of diffusion and independent innovation in the development of European institutions, it is perhaps also significant that the German, Gottfried von Leibniz, who was not always in agreement with Newton, nevertheless independently discovered calculus at approximately the same time (Zaller 1984: 90). Newton's *Principia Mathematica* of 1687 was central to the development of the physical sciences, as Charles Darwin's *The Origin of Species* of 1859 was to the natural sciences. The extent of the application of mathematics to science may be regarded as fundamental to the scientific, technical and commercial advancement of European culture as compared to that of China or even Islam.

In the field of social and political ideas, Thomas Hobbes (1588–1679) and Jean-Jacques Rousseau (1712–78) reflected during this period on the origins of society and its government, particularly in terms of the relationship between the individual and the collective. These are issues clearly addressing the enabling and constraining characteristics of social institutions as discussed earlier. In a similar vein the French Philosophes and in particular Francois Marie Arouet, known as Voltaire (1694–1778), advocated religious tolerance and the notion of secular progress. This all represents a thread of development which leads to the upheavals of the American Revolution and Declaration of Independence in 1776 and of the French Revolution beginning in 1789. Such events produced pragmatic new models of citizenship, government and the state, interwoven with economic changes which were taking place at the same time as a result of the development of capitalism from the mercantile to the industrial form. The American Declaration of Independence was a reaction against European colonial government by settlers who were Europeans themselves in origin, whilst the French Revolution was a reaction against the constrictions of the absolutist state and the ancien regime. Each proclaimed the 'rights of man' (and of the citizen), a principle which had been set in print in 1791 by Thomas Paine who was an Englishman associated with both revolutions. The resulting changes in the way that Europeans would run their societies can hardly be exaggerated. The American Constitution was the first comprehensive legal codification of government and as such it must be seen as central to an age in which Europeans sought to codify and draw up laws directed at all the phenomena of the universe: physical, natural and social.

Yet such documents as the American Constitution are of the order of ideals and their limitations in practical day-to-day terms should not be neglected. As Kenneth Karst (1989) points out, the 'rights of man' in the American Declaration of Independence excluded, in practice, at the time not only women, slaves and Indians but also Germans, 'Scotch-Irish', Catholics and Jews. Thomas Jefferson, the author of the Declaration, denounced slavery but continued to keep slaves himself with the rationalization that it was not safe to release them into a society dominated by white men (Roberts 1985: 259). It has often been argued that in England whilst things were not set down in a written constitution, the effects of such milestones as the early Magna Carta (1215), the later Civil War or English Revolution (1642–58) and the Glorious Revolution (1688), along with the succession of nineteenth-century reform movements, all represent a more effective pathway to freedom and justice. In fact, in all these revolutions and reforms, their unacknowledged conditions and unintended consequences, there was and continues to be, interplay between day-to-day social practices and social institutions viewed in the longer term, as suggested in the principles of structuration theory. These historical events serve to illustrate the varying routes taken by Western cultural development, through the individual histories of separate states, yet producing principles of citizenship, liberal democracy and capitalism which they hold in common.

During the Enlightenment, progress continued in the economy also and, if we pick up the threads left earlier, Amsterdam was taking over from Genoa as the centre of the European 'world-economy' at the beginning of the seventeenth century. Braudel (1984: 175) points out Amsterdam's role as an intermediate stage between the 'age of the city' and that of the 'modern territorial state', because when London subsequently took over it was as the centre of the British nation-state. It is, in fact, debatable whether a nation-state was constituted by the government of the United Provinces, Amsterdam's surrounding agricultural base, but in any case there was little evidence of state intervention in Amsterdam's leadership. European maritime tradition was maintained at the Saardam shipyards just outside of Amsterdam, where the extensive use of mechanical hoists and saws was pioneered and fifty ships of the *fluyt* or *vlieboot* design were launched per year. This design was capable of carrying huge cargoes and yet it required only a small crew, which has prompted Nick Rowling (1987: 38) in his history of commodity trading to describe them as the bulk-carriers of their day. Not only were these ships cheaper to build and operate through superior technology, but there was also a second-hand market for them, with the participation of yet another commercial specialization, ship-brokers. Amsterdam's hold on trade was established first in European waters and then further afield, and on the strength of this the Amsterdam Bourse (stock exchange) was operating by the sixteenth century. It predates the Royal Exchange of London (1695) and the Paris Bourse (1724), but it should properly be regarded as a successor to the less formal exchanges of the Italian city-states, such as at the Rialto in Venice. The Amsterdam Bourse dealt mainly in government stocks including those of the empire-building Vereenigde Oost-Indische Compagnie (VOC) which was established in 1602, two years after the English East India Company, which it nevertheless overshadowed until the eighteenth century.

The East India companies were instruments of colonialism common to several European states and it was in the wake of the Portuguese but before the English that the Dutch established a substantial Indian Ocean and Far Eastern trading empire. Keeping out of the Thirty Years War, from the early seventeenth century they patiently built up a chain of trading posts and forts, initially in Indonesia, then moving for a time into India. At first they proceeded peacefully and then more aggressively, in some cases displacing the Portuguese, Spanish, French, English and myriad Asian peoples who were trading in the area, until by the middle of the century the Dutch dominated the entire eastern trade (cf. Boxer 1973). As a result, Amsterdam enjoyed a golden age during the second half of the seventeenth century but in the end it was a victim of its own success. The policy of non-intervention pursued by the Amsterdam city-state is an illustration of the unintended consequences of thoroughgoing laissez-faire capitalist institutions. Its merchants would pursue trade by whatever means appeared necessary and with a ruthless expectation of early returns. This cost them a strong position in the Americas when different groups of Dutch venturers pursued different economic goals. Some invested in the production of slave-grown sugar, but others took up the short-term expedient of plundering the Portuguese, to whom yet others were prepared to sell arms. This type of conflict of interests also denied them outright victory in a series of wars against the French when, in 1697, vigorously independent Dutch merchants using flags of convenience relieved a grain famine that was about to bring France to its knees (Rowling 1987: 43).

The rise of Britain at the centre of an industrializing world-economy

Towards the end of the eighteenth century the British were in the process of taking over from the Dutch as the centre of the world-economy at a time when the Industrial Revolution was already under way. As already noted, London's role in this was as the capital city of the British nation-state and not as a city-state. Without the full range of changes to be wrought by the industrial revolution, Britain was not yet a fully fledged nation-state in the modern sense. But it was well advanced in the process and was already through what Charles Wilson has called *England's Apprenticeship* (1965). In politico-military terms Britain turned against the Dutch during the 1780s and was victorious in a series of Anglo-Dutch wars. With the Italian city-states already declined and the wealth of Spain, Portugal and their colonies largely dissipated by the pan-European imperial designs of the Habsburg monarchs, only France might have offered an alternative to Britain. Braudel (1984: 315) argues that France *was* the first modern state, 'receiving her final shape from the cosmic midwifery of the 1789 revolution', and in this respect the earlier administrative reforms instituted by Colbert and his *intendants* will be discussed in the next chapter. But France was also a victim of its size and the metropolitan rivalry between Paris and Lyons, so that by 1783 its bid for economic primacy against Britain may be seen to have failed. Britain on the other hand continued to expand its empire, confirming its hold of India after the battle of Plassey in 1757, and Canada after the conquest of 1762–3, both at the expense of France. Until the Indian Mutiny in 1857 when the British government assumed direct responsibility for colonial administration through the Indian Office, it was the officials of the East India Company who were instrumental in the setting up and maintenance of the institutions of the Raj in India, the centrepiece of the British Empire. There, and in trading enclaves on the coast of China and throughout South East Asia, British people imposed their customs, but also absorbed elements of the local culture. As with the crusaders in the Levant much earlier, this illustrates the extension and evolution of Western culture through interaction with other peoples.

In Britain the economic infrastructure was further entrenched. The Bank of England was established in 1694, the Royal Exchange with its informal coffee-house network became the Stock Exchange in 1773 and around these the 'City' financial institutions were created. At this point we should take note of a particular disjuncture between merchant capitalism and industrial capitalism. The City was for a long time far from supportive of the industrial developments in the Midlands and North of England and the celebrated entrepreneurs of the Industrial Revolution were nearly always dependent upon their own resources. This was especially so for pioneering production processes which had not been successfully set up and organized before. As J. D. Gould (1972: 63) points out, there was a 'dramatic contrast between the desperate activity to which Matthew Boulton was reduced in an effort to raise the four thousand pounds needed to keep the engine-making partnership of Boulton and Watt solvent, and the ease with which eighty years earlier a two million pound loan to the new East India Company had been over-subscribed in three days'. It is also worth bearing in mind that the innovators tended to be practical engineers touched in only the most general terms by the scientific advances of the Enlightenment which nevertheless formed the broader intellectual environment. Formalized engineering training on any significant scale came later and contributed to incremental improvements rather than to the original breakthroughs. This was most particularly true in Britain which in engineering training tended to lag behind its European competitors (cf. Weiner 1981: 132–3). In fact, the

Industrial Revolution tended to be a process of innovation fighting inertia and for each of the successful entrepreneurs there were others who failed and are now forgotten. Technical failure was not the only problem, there was also the need to organize the operation of new processes at a time when convenient precedents did not exist. For instance, factory owners at first resorted to the employment of whole families as self-regulating units, and the railway companies initially looked to models of military organization for their sprawling national operations.

The progress of the Industrial Revolution is replete with cross-cutting connections and unintended consequences. Despite the problems described in the last paragraph, it forced huge changes in markets especially through its archetypal industry, cotton. The 'machinofacture' of cotton garments dramatically cut their cost and made regular changes of clothing, which represented a significant advance in hygiene, a possibility for the general population. But the industry was developed, argues K. N. Chaudhuri (1978: 273), as much in response to cheap competition from India, imported by the East India Company, as to the growth of internal demand. A burgeoning Lancashire cotton industry certainly increased the call for raw cotton so that Liverpool was expanded to handle imports from the slave plantations of the USA. The connections between colonialism and raw materials for the Industrial Revolution are immediately apparent, but there was also increased demand for home-produced coal and, in fact, this created more revenue than the cotton industry. Coal, in turn, is connected with the replacement of increasingly rare and expensive wood-charcoal by coke in the iron-smelting process. Stimulated by the steeply rising demand, iron was produced more cheaply and efficiently after Abraham Darby's innovations of 1709, and these were adopted widely during the middle of the century. A hundred years later, similar reductions in the price of steel were made possible by Henry Bessemer's 'converter' of 1856 and the Siemens-Martin open-hearth furnace of 1866, the latter reflecting the contribution of German technological training which was rapidly advancing at the time (Mathias 1969: 410–11).

The application of steam power was made possible by improvements in the production of metals, in combination with techniques of cylinder casting and boring derived originally from artillery manufacture. Stronger and more reliable metals also made possible the introduction of railways and steamships which changed the pattern of transport and communication. Sailing ships, for all the improvements in their effectiveness over the years, remained subject to weather conditions and could spend half their time or more in harbour. The wooden-walled merchantmen and even the faster 'clipper-ships' could not compete with iron-built steamships, but the transition was not as straightforward as sometimes thought. Until coal stations could be set up at various points around the world, Isambard Kingdom Brunel had to design his steamships with the capacity to carry all the coal they needed for long-distance voyages (Rolt 1970: 308–9). From the 1840s, railways not only improved the penetration of the continents with cheap but efficient travel and transport, but also permitted the prompt distribution of daily national newspapers when before they had been restricted to local distribution. In this case, developments in metals and energy joined with printing to provide mass communication on an unprecedented scale. The harnessing of electrical energy made possible the electrical telegraph which, of huge significance, separated for the first time the transmission of information from the transporting of people and goods. These revolutions in transport and communication effected enormous adjustments to the time–space dimensions of Western culture. The implications of this are of course enormous for the propagation and reproduction on a global scale of the symbolism and institutions of Western culture.

Industrial capitalism and class society

During the period of industrialization, the precise relationship between the individual and time and space was, for an increasing number of people, changed fundamentally, primarily in terms of time discipline arising from the routinization of employment but also in terms of travel and communication associated with new lifestyles. The European societies became class (capitalist) societies through a process which also involved the creation of an inter-societal system bringing them into contact with class-divided and tribal societies in other parts of the world (see also chapter 3). Ultimately, these changes applied to the majority of people in Europe and North America and to an increasing proportion of others within the ambit of Western activities elsewhere in the world. A first confirmation was when the British census of 1851 showed that more than half of the population was living in towns or cities. The implication is clear: that large proportions of the populations of industrial, class societies would be urban dwellers and that institutions originating in the urban areas would dominate and be extended to transform the countryside too. Agriculture was as much transformed as manufacturing, and its activities were developed, mechanized and industrialized to support the growing urban masses. In fact, a 'created environment' was formed within the borders of the modern nation-state, determining that there would be a diminishing difference between town and countryside in terms of social institutions.

Within this 'created environment', the application of the capitalist economic dynamic to productive activities involves the rendering of human labour itself to the status of a commodity, along with other commodities. The price of labour became calculable in relation to time and the overall exchange value of what is produced. Marx's *Labour Theory of Value*, derived from the classical economics of Adam Smith and David Ricardo, hinges on the fact that the capitalist owners of the means of production are able to calculate the price of a finished product by aggregating the costs of raw materials, plant, machinery and labour in order to anticipate profitability. But the crucial principle seized upon by Marx is that, of all these commodities, it is labour that is active in the conversion of raw material to finished product and, therefore, in the addition of value. Thus, he argued, in extracting a profit, the capitalist entrepreneur or investor appropriates part of the true value of labour, its transformative capacity in relation to the product. For Marx, it was irrational that the production by human beings of their needs should be subject to exchange values determined by market mechanisms, especially through a process in which part of the value of human labour is appropriated by a small elite simply on the basis of their ownership title to machinery and plant, the means of production.

Although Weber was pessimistic about the general drift to rationality in modern society, he nevertheless recognized the extreme rationality of the capitalist labour process. The rendering of all elements of production, including labour, to commodity status enabled more sophisticated calculation and record keeping to take place. For Weber, this was the essential component of the capitalist economic mechanism, for it enabled entrepreneurs to calculate the viability of their activities and it rendered production to a much more predictable format (Weber 1978: 86). There is a history to commercial calculation dating back to the Renaissance and beyond, but up to the nineteenth century economic activity remained, in general, subject to slow and uncertain communications and a high risk of failure. It may be seen that mathematics applied to science and to economics or business calculation, combined to ameliorate these difficulties. Modern business is not without risk but more precise calculation has made possible a huge growth in scale, as exemplified by the transnational corporations with portfolios of counterbalanced profit centres and the facility to extrapolate profit making into the future even against the fluctuations of markets. Equally, however, this process appeared to Weber to be leading to empty social structures geared to goal attainment and efficiency, but increasingly devoid of human values, in his terms, the *zweckrational* at the expense of the *vertrational*.

Further advances in technology and the rise of Germany and the USA

By the final quarter of the nineteenth century, Britain was tending to concentrate on exporting aspects of its original industrial revolution to its huge colonial empire and other parts of the world, such as the independent Latin American countries, and in the process extending its interests in commercial and financial dealings ('invisible exports'). As a consequence, it had begun to lose its industrial lead and contemporary accounts (cf. Barnett 1972; Weiner 1981) relate that British entrepreneurs lacked the determination to reproduce their role in succeeding generations. Instead, it is suggested, they preferred to raise new generations of landed gentry, sheltered from industrial activities with the result that the key specialization, engineering, continued to lack prestige and even respectability in British society. The links between social norms and government policy in this case appear to be clear. In Germany and other parts of northern Europe, state-sponsored *technische hochschule* with university status were established before the end of the nineteenth century, whereas in Britain, for the most part, there were only low-status 'mechanics institutes' founded by middle-class reformers. Certainly towards the turn of the century it was primarily in Germany and the United States that strategic new industries to produce synthetic chemicals, electrical technology and the components of the internal combustion engine became securely established, even though in several cases the technological breakthroughs had taken place in Britain and elsewhere.

The connections between technological advance and social organization may be further illustrated by reference to two significant examples from early twentieth-century America. Firstly, there was the introduction of 'scientific management' pioneered, against considerable opposition, by Frederick Winslow Taylor against a background of breakthroughs in metal-cutting technology in the US steel industry. Secondly, there was Henry Ford's mass production techniques, which at first entailed simply dragging the frames of Model 'T' Fords through the production shed on ropes whilst the workers attached components stacked in sequence on the sidelines (Herndon 1970). In each case, the principles were simple but the implications were enormous. With 'scientific management', the routine study of human actions in the production process made possible the elimination of wasteful effort through the redesigning of tasks in the division of labour and the precise calculation of labour costs against time. 'Time and motion study' and work study in general also drew a rigid line of separation between the planning and the execution of work, the provinces respectively of management and workers. For the critic, this represents the embodiment of Marx's more philosophical reflections on the alienation of labour, interpreted more recently as the 'de-skilling of labour' by Harry Braverman (1974). In the case of Ford's mass production, the principle may be put crudely as follows. Small quantities of hand-built products can be produced at a profit, but huge quantities of standardized versions at a price that almost anyone can afford will not only generate much larger profits but also will improve the quality of life for more people. In the production of the Model 'T' the die was cast for mass-production or 'Fordism', the form of manufacturing that has dominated industry throughout the twentieth century, at least until the Japanese developed more flexible 'post-Fordist' techniques (see chapter 11). Fordism became a symbol for the United States as the archetypal mass society of the twentieth century. Mass-participation was a cornerstone of the USA's political foundations and it was extended into the economic sphere with mass production, mass communication and mass consumption.

In overview, this might be seen as the culmination of the 'rise of the West', involving Western culture extended through the global institutions of an inter-societal system to the rest of the world, and at first it appeared to offer limitless possibilities for the future. But this has proved to be a false hope in the twentieth century when world wars and all that they have encompassed have starkly demonstrated the destructive side to technological advancement and destroyed faith in the infallibility of human progress. More than anything else, this should add weight to the argument that human society does not develop through a process of evolution guaranteeing certain things at the outcome. In chapter 1, structural–functionalist social theory was associated with the 'logic of industrialism' in human advancement, whilst historical materialism was associated with the notion of a 'scientific' pathway to socialism. Neither of these perspective are tenable because it is human beings who produce and reproduce social institutions, not through any overriding logic but through their actions and interactions. The concept of distanciation is employed here to refer to the way in which social institutions may be projected through time and space by means of the storage capacity developed by human beings. This storage capacity exists in human memory traces, but has been extended by the many techniques, manual and electronic, developed for recording symbolic orders and modes of discourse in relation to social institutions. But these can have no finite existence beyond their reproduction in the interactions of human beings at any passing moment in time. There can be no formulae to the outcome of human society and it is the realization of this on the part of human actors, including, particularly, specialized observers like sociologists, that is the best safeguard for the future outcome of society.

The industrialization of warfare

Perhaps the most shattering blow to the confidence of twentieth-century Western society was the First World War and it has often been described how so many hopes for the future 'sank into the Flanders mud'. The important feature of this war for any consideration of social change is that it demonstrated on the battlefield the economic and technological power released by the various advances of previous centuries. The American Civil War had already offered an indication of what industrialization could provide in the development and supply of weapons and their effects on flesh and blood human beings. But the First World War was so named because of its widespread impact upon Western society, although as many observers have pointed out it was really only a European civil war. In an oversimplified way, this war may be interpreted as a contest in the production of explosive shells to be rained down upon the enemy's defences, because on either side a huge proportion of industrial production was given over to these and associated munitions. Improved steel cutting, synthetic chemicals, electrical power and the internal combustion engine were available to the combatants for the production of rifles, machine-guns and modern artillery. There were warships constructed of steel, including electrically powered submarines; military vehicles, including tanks and aircraft, powered by petrol engines; and horrific new chemical weapons, including poison gas.

The recruitment and organization of armies had also been subject to advances and reforms with the professionalization of the officer class, the reform of organizational practices and, during the war itself, the routinized conscription of the male population. All these things reflected advances to social, political and economic institutions during the nineteenth and early twentieth centuries, and they served to intensify the conflict to an unprecedented extent. Tragically, the pattern of military strategy itself had not advanced very much from Napoleonic times. Setpieces on the battlefield and even cavalry charges were tried at first, but in the face of the devastating new weaponry the tactics deteriorated to trench warfare on fixed lines. Human beings were continually and persistently ranged against the mechanized weaponry with little immediate concern for the huge number of casualties. This, and the political machinations that lay behind the military strategy, were reminders of old human frailties now displayed in an age of technology and mechanization. As Roberts

(1985: 368) has pointed out, it is no accident that when Oswald Spengler's book, *The Decline of the West*, was published in 1918, it 'captured a mood and an audience much wider than his obscure, difficult text made likely'.

Reflections

Social change cannot be explained by reference to any single factor. It is only by appreciating the breadth of European culture, including those features derived from other cultures, that one can understand how and why Western culture was extended and the range of consequences. The model of class (capitalist) society employed here portrays people organized socially and politically into nation-states made interdependent by the global institutions of an inter-societal system. This has clear time and space implications, in that other types of society have had to come to terms with Western institutions during the process of development of Western class society. This is the meaning of the term inter-societal system. There has not been an evolution of modern society but rather a 'triumph of the West' in its contact with other cultures, and even within that an alternative form of industrialized society derived from the Marxist critique of Western capitalism. The state socialist societies have in recent times stood alongside the capitalist societies. Now it is desirable to examine in greater depth two crucial features of the modern inter-societal system, namely the formation of politically separate nation-states together with their interdependence in the capitalist world-economy. Chapter 5 covers the development of the Western model of the state and chapter 6, the development of European colonialism with an international division of labour operated through the capitalist world-economy.

5

Western Societies as a State System: the Development of the Nation-State

The historical material in chapter 4 illustrates the series of episodes and transformations through which European society was developed from a class-divided form to a class (capitalist) form, using the terminology of structuration theory. The emphasis now will be turned to more specific aspects of the change process and in this chapter the development of the state in Western society will be examined. In the formation of European culture states have been organized in a variety of forms at any one time and over periods of time, but amongst the plethora of historical examples certain principles can be discerned which have been identified in European culture as beneficial for statehood. Therefore, we can speak of a Western model of the state, accepting that it is derived from a variety of sources, including those classical Greek and Roman antecedents to which Western civilization has tended to look back. Examples of more recent formative influences are provided by the English Glorious Revolution of 1688–9 with its notions of republicanism and libertarianism (Hill 1972); by the eighteenth-century administrative reforms of Frederick the Great in Prussia; by the American Declaration of Independence (nationhood) of 1776, or by the French declaration of 'the rights of man and of the citizen' after 1789. These examples vary considerably in their content but combined they provide the essentials of the ideal modern state administration, subservient to a democratically elected representative body or parliament. The notion of a Western orthodoxy is reinforced by some twentieth-century examples which have been regarded as 'deviant', such as Marxism–Leninism in the soviet Union (see chapter 8) or National Socialism (Nazism) in Germany during the 1930s and 1940s. Each of these resulted in conflict with the 'orthodox' Western states. Clearly, the outcome of state formation is not guaranteed through an evolutionary process any more than the other institutions of society. The interactions of human beings bring about changes in social institutions and we should, therefore, try to identify the institutions that have been significant in the creation of the Western model of the state.

In chapter 3, emphasis was placed on the significance of storage capacity to state administration and more particularly the storage of authoritative (political) resources. The state possesses the means by which the surveillance of society can be carried out, using devices that have varied through history from the clay-tablet inventories of ancient Mesopotamian cities to modern electronic data storage. Surveillance entails the reflexive use of knowledge about society in the reproduction of society and it is a process that is both enabling and constraining. In modern society people generally submit information willingly in the belief that, in a broad sense, it will benefit them, and less commonly, they withhold it when they consider that it will not. Consequently, state officials have available to them huge amounts of privileged, centralized knowledge through the storage capacity that has been developed in birth, marriage and death registers, censuses, tax records, police records, etc. This obviously renders their position powerful in terms of authoritative resources for the government of society. The process of state administration binds time and space together through the routine gathering of information, making possible historical analysis, spatial comparison and future projections which carry authority over a large territorial area. The process may be extended internationally, too, through international agencies of the nation-state system.

There is a relationship between the form of surveillance and the type of society, as outlined earlier in figure 3. In tribal society knowledge about the social system is in the form of familiarity with the tradition of communal practices, kinship and group sanctions. Formal institutions consist of the ritualized enactment of phenomena or events that are significant for the society. As a random example from Basil Davidson's studies of Africa, the Dogon of Mali in West Africa have ceremonies involving elaborate and colourful costumes in which those plants and animals in their environment which are important for the tribe are portrayed symbolically. Through the ceremonial the society binds time and space together in a limited way by reinforcing images of the traditional past and the expected future against the background of the spatial environment (Davidson 1984: 57–8). But in this type of society day-to-day social interaction and the ceremonial reproduction of the society take virtually the same form: each is a matter of communal practices and tradition enacted face to face in conditions of co-presence. In the terms of structuration theory, the long-term system integration of the society can be projected, or distanciated, in time and space with virtually only the same means as are used for day-to-day social integration. There is no substantial container for knowledge about the society other than human memory traces and a few artifacts. In other words, in tribal society there is no state.

In class-divided society, the city within its walls is the storage container for authoritative resources because it is the location of whatever political, military and religious institutions serve to constitute the state. In a different sense, it is also the storage container for allocative resources as the central point for the control and development of agriculture in the surrounding countryside and the market or point of exchange for produce. A state-controlled irrigation scheme linked with a market system, for instance, is a good example of the extension and conservation of production resources. The city contains institutions with which to exercise surveillance over the population both within the city and within relatively loose and often fluctuating frontiers outside. An important factor in the maintenance of this surveillance is the existence of writing and literacy for the storage of knowledge.

The form of class-divided society can be identified in the kingdoms and city-states of medieval and post-medieval Europe, as described in the last chapter. According to the example chosen, the elite consists of combinations of nobility and priesthood with merchants and others forming a bourgeoisie. Each group is capable of ascendancy, diversification and decline through interactions in the reproduction of institutions over time. The use of literacy is a factor in the control of both authoritative (political) and allocative (economic) resources and is mainly restricted to the elite. Institutions are diversified and some aspects of system integration, such as symbols of kingship or of religion, are stored in the city and effectively separated from the day-to-day life of the great mass of the population which is mostly located in the rural hinterland. The state, therefore, is integral to the class-division between city and countryside and may be seen as standing at a line of potential conflict (Giddens 1981: 237). Throughout European history such conflict erupted from time to time in the form of peasant revolts.

In class (capitalist) society the state is the nation-state and its administrative apparatus is the storage container. The process by which nation-states came into existence involved the centralization of administration with the enclosing of broad territories within fixed borders, instead of merely cities within walls. The state, however, remains integral to the division of classes and may still be conceptually located at the point of potential conflict. In class society this is equivalent to the structural contradiction between socialized labour (the public sector) and private appropriation (the private sector) in the capitalist labour process (Giddens 1981: 238). The physical enclosure of broad territories and their populations was achieved with more efficient centralized state administration, backed by military force that was better equipped and organized. The people within these borders were encouraged and sometimes coerced into regarding themselves, if they did not already, as the nationals of these states. In the much quoted example of France under Louis XIV, people who had hitherto regarded themselves as Normands, Bretons, Languedociens, Gascons, Basques, etc., were enjoined to regard themselves as French. Thus, larger more powerful 'nations' came into existence capable of supporting the scale of administration and military activity already referred to. This occurred in Europe coincidentally with the expansion of merchant capitalism during the sixteenth, seventeenth and eighteenth centuries. Typically, the state through the person of the monarch granted charters to mercantile monopolies which generated resources for the state as well as for the mercantile bourgeoisie and there was a growing distinction between political (state) institutions and economic (private enterprise) institutions. The modern nation-state did not come into being until the nineteenth century after significant upheavals, particularly in the societies and governments of England, the United States of America and France, at a time when capitalist development was being transformed by industrialization. The conjunction of capitalism and industrialization completed the transformation of Western society into class society with the extension of the capitalist labour process to virtually the whole of the population.

This brings us to the question of the transition from the state in class-divided society to the modern nation-state. Consistent with the arguments already put forward in favour of structuration theory, this should not be seen as an evolutionary transition but the results of human agency through a complex series of institutional transformations not necessarily always in the same direction of progress. For example, since the development of the state was intertwined with the development of capitalism, there were struggles between the traditional landed aristocracy and the mercantile bourgeoisie for influence in the state. Furthermore, with the extension of the domestic system into the countryside as part of the embryonic textile industry in various parts of Europe, it was not in the interests of either of these two parties to support the urban-based guilds. However, the significant intervening entity was the absolutist state, created out of absolutist monarchy with state power centralized in the person of the king to the detriment of other parties in the state arena and it is this to which we shall now turn.

The absolutist state

The process of absolutist development was, in crude terms, one whereby larger territories were appropriated and subdued more effectively by monarchs using a combination of armed force and centralized administration. Borders were delineated more clearly and fixedly (although not necessarily permanently) at a time when trade and the control of domestic production were also becoming increasingly centralized and when individual city defences were losing much of their effectiveness through the development of artillery. 'The king,' as Michael Mann (1986: 453) puts it, 'could batter down the castles of the feudal nobility.' The political map of Europe at the end of the fifteenth century was beginning to consist of strong territorial states, or else of areas not yet transformed in this way, such as the residual 'Holy Roman Empire', smaller principalities and ecclesiastical landholdings or the vigorous mercantile city-states of Venice, Antwerp, etc. (see figure 6). The rulers who began the absolutist trend were, according to Perry Anderson (1979: 229), the 'new monarchs' of the late fifteenth century such as Louis XI of France, Ferdinand and Isabella, who were joint rulers of Spain, Henry VII of England and Maximilian of Austria. But it is generally accepted that the archetypal examples came later in Louis XIV of France, the 'Sun King', and Elizabeth I of England. England, France and Spain in particular were shaped out of centuries of bitter warfare and the process of state building involved a reduction in the number of states. Charles Tilly (1975: 12) counts 500 states of various kinds in the Europe of 1500, reduced by 1900 to only 25. The absolutist states were not only the survivors of wars and conquests but the continuing patrons of those improvements in weaponry and military organization which were being diffused throughout Europe at the time. Those kings who could manage their affairs best, or else find people to do it reliably for them, could afford the biggest standing armies equipped with the highest levels of new weaponry. These were the ones who established strong states and successful dynasties and, as Mann (1986: 455) suggests, with the rising cost of warfare the very poor states were in trouble.

The profile of power in the absolutist state was steeply hierarchical, contrasting with the flatter profile of feudal society. The absolutist monarchs were richer and more powerful than their feudal predecessors and yet this did not touch the majority of their subjects. Anderson (1979: 17) asserts that the culture of serfdom did not disappear with feudalism, and the introduction of the wage bargain did not at first change the social structure of the countryside or the expectations of its participants. A most significant aspect of the absolutist state was its

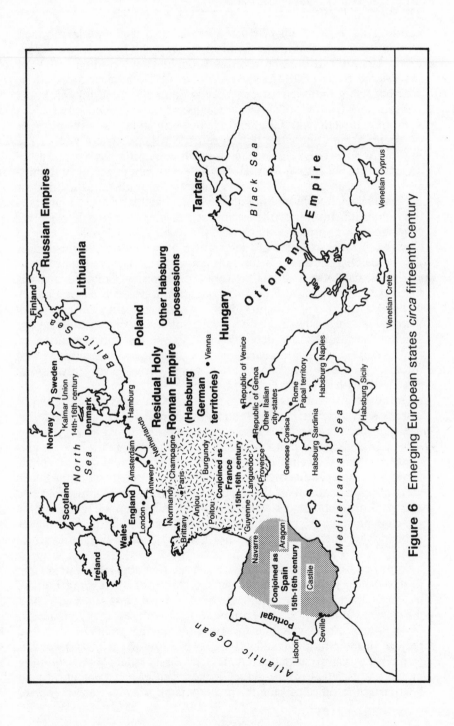

Figure 6 Emerging European states *circa* fifteenth century

administrative mechanism which operated at first alongside and then in place of the clerical hierarchy hitherto provided by the church. This can be seen clearly in the changes brought about by Louis XIV of France and Henry VIII of England (Elizabeth I's father) who both put the position of monarch firmly before the church establishment. Louis refused the counsel of priests because he considered himself to commune directly with God, and Henry went so far as to dissolve the link with Rome upon the pope's refusal to bend to his will in the matter of divorce. Yet, despite this self-conscious concentration of separate and absolute power, Henry VIII was recognized as maintaining a 'European court' and he was determined to make it the finest in Europe through cosmopolitan arts and scholarship. This is a particularly good illustration of the notion of European culture in a fiercely separated state system.

An archetypal example of the creation of absolutist administration is provided by Louis XIV's appointment of Jean-Baptiste Colbert, one of the secular 'new men', as his foremost minister. Colbert set about his task, which was nothing less than the modernization of France, through a provincial structure of *intendants* replacing the governors who had been the heads of the local feudal structures (Zaller 1984: 38–9). The job of these new officials was the institutionalization of routine surveillance and collection of knowledge for the state. Their interactions with the population created new social institutions connected with the state. Colbert had more power than his equivalents in earlier reigns, such as Cardinal Richlieu, but he exercised it as the instrument of the king rather than as a separate power in the state. In fact, the focus of administrative power was centralized literally in the person of the king so that Louis XIV could have said quite accurately, 'l'etat, c'est moi', even if the often attributed statement is apocryphal. Gianfranco Poggi adds that in the absolutist administration, the court was no longer made up of the upper section of the royal household but consisted of public offices. The king himself was a public figure and in the case of Louis XIV conducted all his personal and private life in public. 'The ruler, then, ruled from his court rather than through it' (Poggi 1978: 68–70).

Anthony Giddens (1985: 103) observes that the most bureaucratized absolutist state was in the eighteenth-century Prussia of Frederick the Great, where there was 'one civil servant for every 450 inhabitants' but, at the same time, compares this with 'Germany in 1925 [where] there was one for every 46 of the population' in the pattern of most modern states. Poggi (1978: 74–81) contrasts Prussia with France asserting that Frederick the Great ruled *from within* his more comprehensive bureaucracy rather than *over* it, thus effectively separating the office of king from the person. Max Weber, of course, regarded the replacement of personal roles with impersonal offices as of crucial importance in the development of 'rational–legal' authority in modern society. The key feature in the Prussian model was (Weber 1978: 641–4) 'public law' as opposed to royal commands, serving to separate the state from civil society. This is significant for the development of the Western state model because it represents an antecedent to the laissez faire type of policy whereby the demands of the private sector in economic affairs can be accommodated, whilst the rule of civil society remains in the public sector. Mann (1986: 476) sees the principal components of the absolutist state as law and permanent bureaucracy, whilst Anderson (1979: 25) and Poggi (1978: 73) both see Roman law specifically, with its civil code and its properly formulated property rights, as a strong element against medieval privilege and traditional rights in the process of modernization of state administration. The principles of Roman law were never lost in the emergent European culture through the Middle Ages and the Renaissance, but in the absolutist state they find a fuller flowering. With the recourse to law and the use of professional lawyers there is a reflection, too, of the earlier introduction of professional notaries into the Italian city-states of the Renaissance. Giddens (1985: 185) adds that the principles of republicanism inherent in Roman law also sustained one of the countervailing forces against absolutism, the use of assemblies against the ruler as in the case of the French *parlements* which Louis XIV felt he had to suppress. Another countervailing force, mentioned earlier, was peasant revolts which occurred quite frequently throughout Europe (cf. Tilly 1975: 22–3). However, these could be put down more easily with better trained armies and the use of foreign mercenaries not at all sympathetic to the peasantry. The embracing of Roman law with in its enabling and constraining features was undoubtedly significant in the development of European culture and a pointer forward in time to the modern liberal–democratic nation-state.

However, it should not be assumed that these centralized administrations, for all their undoubted effectiveness, were comparable with a modern, legal–rational bureaucracy. The purchase of office remained an accepted practice especially in fiscal matters, where it was expected that official encumbents would, in the process of tax gathering, make personal gains sometimes in the order of 300 to 400 per cent. Anderson (1979: 34) describes this as persisting in France, Italy, Spain, England and Holland during the sixteenth and seventeenth centuries and, according to Weber's definitions, the practice is dated as pre-modern. The administrative and military infrastructure of the absolutist state was, therefore, extremely expensive to maintain at a time when monarchs were already often in debt to bankers. According to Fernand Braudel (1984: 151), the Habsburg Charles V who still used the title Holy Roman Emperor and had at his disposal all the wealth of Spain and its colonies as well as that of Milan, Naples and Sicily and the Habsburg territories in central Europe, still 'could not do without the services of the Antwerp money market'. His state could never be described as absolutist or centralized and it was centralization that was the key to raising money without debts to bankers. A favourite means was 'mercantilism' or the banning of imports and encouragement of exports in certain goods for which chartered merchant companies enjoyed monopoly conditions. All duties were then paid into the central exchequer as goods crossed borders that were more clearly defined and guarded as a matter of routine. The complicated networks of provincial excise duties were abolished in favour of centralized collection.

Military organization and the balance of power

There are a variety of ways in which innovations in military organization can be related to developments in state organization but, in particular, to the capacity for the state to have a monopoly of the means of violence. Advances in weaponry represent good indications of the assertion of state power over larger areas of territory, and when associated with general advances in manufacturing ability form a part of the transitions in social, political and economic institutions which are inherent to the absolutist state and its subject population. There has consistently been exchange between general technological progress and the technology of armaments, as in the case of gunpowder for mining and for cannon; cast iron for cheaper, stronger metal products including cannon; and gun barrel boring techniques for steam-engine cylinders. The Chinese had gunpowder by the ninth century and firearms by the eleventh, before Europeans, yet by the end of the fourteenth century European cannon were superior and in their seaborne form struck terror in the Far East during the sixteenth century. The Ottoman Turks had built or acquired cannon for their successful bid to the leadership of Islam, but the naval battle of Lepanto in 1571 ended their control of the Mediterranean and subsequently Islamic sea power presented no difficulties to the Portuguese caravels which spearheaded the European entry into the Indian Ocean (Braudel 1984: 468). Europeans had very effective mobile artillery by the fifteenth century and cheaper cast-iron cannon through the use of blast furnaces by the sixteenth (pp. 387–8). Arms production tended to become concentrated in state arms manufactories or arsenals, as in the prototypical case of the Venetian Arsenal.

There were also military academies which included artillery schools to ensure that European gunnery remained superior to that of the Ottoman Empire, India, China or Japan (pp. 393–6).

In terms of military organization, France had Europe's first regular units, the *compagnies d'ordonnance* of the mid fifteenth century, financed, according to Anderson (1979: 32), by a special tax known as the *taille royale*. This writer also attributes the introduction of infantry drill and line to the Dutch Prince Maurice of Orange and Nassau, the cavalry salvo and platoon system to King Gustavus Adolphus of Sweden and the unitary vertical command to Count Albrecht von Wallenstein of Czechoslovakia. The latter acted as a kind of military contractor in the growing professionalism (p. 29) and trained mercenary groups or 'free companies'. These were often hired by absolutist monarchs for their military campanigns or, since they were free of local ethnic or kin connections, for putting down peasant revolts. According to Zaller (1984: 2), this lasted until the Thirty Years War, which heightened divisions between Europe's Protestant north and Catholic south, but was the last one to be fought with this kind of mercenary army. The armies of absolutist monarchs were larger and more efficiently recruited whereas those of their predecessors had been put together ad hoc. They were better trained and equipped, too, in both small arms and artillery. The widespread adoption of artillery meant that defensive structures had to be redesigned and, star-shaped, *trace Italienne*, low fortifications were characteristic of northern Europe during the eighteenth century, such as in the Dutch United Provinces' successful defence of its small but wealthy territory. Navies were also improved and became organized on a regular basis with the final disappearance of the privateer. For example, the regular navies created during Anglo-Dutch conflict in the seventeenth and eighteenth centuries contrast sharply with the sixteenth-century Spanish Armada, only a small percentage of which actually belonged to Philip II, with the rest made up of converted merchant ships, chartered Venetian galleys, etc.

The absolutist states reflect substantial changes not only in the model of the European state but also in the pan-European state system, such that the dealings between absolutist states represent the foundations of modern diplomacy. However, Anderson (1979: 39) and Poggi (1978: 68) note the proviso that the legitimacy of absolutism lay in the dynasty of the monarch and not specifically in the state or its people, which contrasts with the modern nation-state. The supreme diplomatic device of absolutist diplomacy and alliance was marriage, although it did not always go to plan if the several 'wars of succession' during the period are an indication. Nevertheless, the principle of diplomacy did develop during the sixteenth century, notably as a result of the initiatives of Louis XIV and his ministers. Congresses and treaties began to appear from the seventeenth century onwards, as in the example of the Congress of Westphalia which brought to an end the Thirty Years War. These contrast with the international meetings of earlier centuries which were normally organized through the offices of the prevailing Roman Catholic church. The institutionalization of congresses and treaties, however, did not prevent war but merely put it on another footing, involving formal recognition of the existence of states, and a notion of the balance of power in Europe. Equally, the disruption of this balance of power or the breakdown of diplomacy provided new reasons for war. These were surely pointers for the future, as were the vague stirrings of an idea of European politico-military unity, at that time to repulse the Ottoman Turks during the Siege of Vienna in 1683 when the territorial existence of Europe was last threatened by outsiders.

Capitalist industrialization and the nation-state

Although it is tempting to conceive of a neat transition from the absolutist states to the modern nation-states, it would be a mistake. There were many concomitant changes in European social institutions during the seventeenth and eighteenth centuries which affected a broadening spectrum of society at a faster rate of change. As the scale and extent of capitalist institutions increased in the emergent indus-trialized nations of nineteenth-century Europe, they did so 'into an already constituted state system' (Giddens 1981: 189). When London took over from Amsterdam as the centre of the European 'world-economy' it did so as the capital city of the British nation-state within an emerging nation-state system and this marked the end of the era of the mercantile city-states. France, too, was developed as a nation-state, probably more developed in this way than Britain, but it lacked a comparable level of trade. The European states in general had been going through a process of consolidation and reduction in number. Thus, on the 'eve' of the Industrial Revolution there existed an embryonic nation-state system with a capitalist 'world-economy' centred on London, representing in terms of structuration theory global institutions in an inter-societal system. No one had consciously devised these systems, they were the unanticipated consequences of the whole panoply of developments described in these chapters. They grew out of myriad transformations of existing social, political and economic institutions by human agents in the manner illustrated in the historical material of the last chapter. As Poggi (1978: 88) put it with reference to the state system, 'the states do not presuppose the system they generate it'. Equally, the history of the European 'world-economy' demonstrates how even in its early, piecemeal and fluctuating development the innovations of capitalism were institutionalized and spread from merchant city to merchant city. The gradual extension of these techniques into an international infrastructure through colonialism accounts for the growing speed with which the industrial and commercial opportunities of the Industrial Revolution could subsequently be taken up.

As industrialization spread, urbanization and the mechanization of agriculture spread, too. In fact, a virtual 'created environment' came to cover north-western Europe, thus destroying finally the medieval distinctions between city and countryside and the structure of class-divided society. As the structure of societies became dominated by industrial capitalist production the wage bargain became not only an economic relationship but also a social relationship with the resulting class division inherent throughout society. The removal of the city–countryside distinction took the coercive compulsion out of labour relations, to be replaced by what Karl Marx referred to as 'dull economic compulsion'. Two distinct social movements may be identified in the emergence of this class (capitalist) society. The first involves pressure on the state from the capitalist bourgeoisie for conditions conducive to industrial capitalism and the second, pressure from reformers and mass movements for a range of citizenship rights. As suggested earlier, the occurrence of the English Civil War (1642–58) and Glorious Revolution (1688), the American Declaration of Independence (1776) and the French Revolution (1789), together with comparable but less celebrated developments in other countries, are of signal importance.

The role of states and the state system has largely been the provision of centralized administrative infrastructure from which rulers and governments have been able to pursue their particular politico-military objectives. This also provided stable national and international conditions for a burgeoning economic system which became increasingly useful in the provision of state finance. However, merchant capitalism, although dynamic and significant for change, was periphral to most of society whereas industrial capitalism came to involve virtually the whole of it. Therefore, whilst the Western state has throughout its development been brought increasingly to terms with capitalism, the distinction between public sector and private sector has nevertheless been made more clear. Institutions established during the period of merchant capitalism, such as fiduciary currencies and workable channels of international exchange, were expanded and refined in order to accommodate the greater potential of industrial capitalism. The period of industrialization was also a time of intensified colonialism and so commercial facilities were extended across the world through the global institutions of an inter-societal system. It will be discussed at length in the next chapter how European colonial frontiers penetrated the continents making available increased supplies of many commodities and creating price mechanisms in international commodity markets. These have been interpreted elsewhere as primarily developments in the capitalist world-economy but it can readily be seen that they were interdependent with systems of global communication maintained through the politico-military activities of European states.

The exchange mechanisms of earlier centuries were supplemented by a plethora of specialized markets not only in existing commodities but also in future options on their purchase, 'the futures markets'. The proud boast in these markets has been that they are self-regulating and self-policing and therefore do not require state intervention. In fact, the auditing of financial mechanisms together with its general regulation became the province of professional, chartered organizations. The auditing of financial documents in business firms by separate firms of accountants is a good example of the regulation of capitalist institutions outside of the state structure, maintained separately from the taxing of the system itself which is a centralized state prerogative. But in either case the principles of accountancy, developed from fifteenth-century Florentine *partita doppia*, have become the universal and sophisticated form of present-day financial regulation. It enables business companies' taxes to be externally negotiated with the state at the same time as their 'profitplans' are internally extrapolated into the future. It affords, therefore, an avenue between public- and private-sector finance through which standardized techniques have been established.

Financial and other calculations became quicker and more precise as the technology of the Industrial Revolution speeded up transport and communication. Before the steamship, sailing vessels took months over their voyages, spending overall more time in port than at sea due to the uncertainty of wind and weather. Travel by land was even more difficult before railways or surfaced trunk roads. Braudel (1981: 428) cites an extreme example of early settlers on the east coast of North America importing coal from Britain because it was cheaper than wood transported overland from the interior when transatlantic shipping, even by sail, had been made comparatively regular. But the railways transformed overland travel and made possible timetables that even the best stage coach and turnpike road combinations could not match. More significant still, for the first time in history the electric telegraph enabled information to be routinely transmitted separately and much more quickly than the transport of passengers and goods. Schedules of all kinds could be

monitored at a distance, including the railway timetables which are a
time–space ordering device similar to the application of 'scientific
management' principles in manufacturing. In fact, the time-space
distanciation of Western culture was extended to such an extent that
by 1884 it was necessary to standardize time and at the International
Meridian Conference in Washington: despite French dissent, Green-
wich near London was chosen as the baseline for global space–time
measurement.

The separation of polity and economy

In the absolutist states the separation of political and economic
institutions had begun to take shape. The affairs of the king and the
affairs of the merchants were interdependent but the institutions of
trade developed separately from those of state and diplomacy. As
capitalism progressed, the separation was maintained and modern
nation-states emerged with this division as a fundamental part of their
institutional structure. The state in class-divided society may be
conceptualized as operating simply at the class division between city
and countryside, but in modern class society the equivalent location is
at the line of potential conflict between private economic appropriation and socialized production. Economic relations are ideally
depoliticized as the private sector, whilst the affairs of the state are the
public sector. The nineteenth century ideal of laissez faire was
indicative of this structural principle, but in fact there has never been
a total lack of state intervention in the economy. Party politics in the
Western societies have ever since been largely concerned with the
extent of government intervention in economic and social affairs.
Parties of the 'left' have generally preferred to 'de-commodify' certain
goods and services and bring them into the state or public sector,
whilst parties of the 'right' have opted to 'commodify' or privatize
them. Poggi (1978: 138) refers to this as a process by which state and
civil society displace each other.

Despite the insulation between these two sectors, the nation-state
remains dependent on the private sector for economic stability and
competitiveness in terms of the capitalist world-economy. Whenever
left-wing governments have attempted to implement radical socialist
policies on behalf of socialized labour they have mostly found
themselves deprived of economic support from the private sector and
consequently disadvantaged in the international economy in comparison with right-wing governments. As Poggi (1978: 94) puts it, capital
provides a means of economic domination in civil socity that is quite

independent of state political domination. The problems faced by socialist parties in government have provided the rationale for the state ownership of industry or 'nationalization' which is the ultimate form of state intervention in the economy. Such ventures have tended to be restricted to national undertakings in the form of public utilities like railways and energy supply which are regarded as public services, or private-sector enterprises facing problems and maintained through subsidies by the state in the interests of the employees. Meanwhile, the transnational corporations have been at the spearhead of economic development, especially since the Second World War. These operate across nation-state borders and they have become the archetypal private-sector organizations of the capitalist world-economy. Their greatest advantage is the flexibility to organize themselves in the optimum way across the fiscal and labour policies of the various nation-states in which they operate. They have the capacity to purchase raw materials and labour, to locate manufacturing plant and to market finished products wherever it is most advantageous to them. Thus, in the contemporary period, nation-state governments have relied to an increasing extent for economic buoyancy upon a private sector increasingly dominated by the relatively fluid and mobile operations of transnational corporations. Only in the USA, where the majority of these companies have their headquarters, has there been a measure of protection against this trend. But even American transnational business has in recent decades had to compete with that generated by the resurgent economies of Germany and Japan. More recently still, the Japanese model of manufacturing efficiency has been extended into other East Asian economies to great effect. Now, attention will be turned from the nation-state system/capitalist world-economy relationship to the role of the individual in the nation-state.

Citizenship and the nation-state

We may begin by looking at something discussed already in connection with class-divided society and the absolutist state, that is, the concept of surveillance of the subject population. With the application of computers and electronic data processing the modern nation-state administration has a much extended range of information storage techniques at its disposal and it collects a far wider range of data than the absolutist state's relatively simple fiscal records. The transition from one to the other was brought about by the application of what Weber (1978: 217–23) referred to as 'legal authority with a bureaucratic administrative staff', a form of organization applied to state administration which he associated with the development of rationality in the West. This has not only extended the state's power to influence the day to day lives of the citizenry but also has conferred upon it the legitimacy of 'rational–legal' authority. The nation-state, therefore, has routinely probed into the lives and private affairs of its citizens to a much greater extent than any previous form of state administration and yet has equally provided them with an unprecedented measure of security in terms of citizenship rights. This is a prime example of the enabling and constraining qualities of social institutions. The citizens of the modern nation-state must open their personal affairs to it in a variety of ways in return for their rights of citizenship. However, as with the question of the boundary between public and private sector in relation to political and economic affairs, the extent to which the state should be allowed access to the privacy of the citizen as an individual has been consistently on the political agenda in the nation-states of the West.

The modern nation-state is an institution of social organization derived from the broad spectrum of Western development, and the model has become virtually universal in principle. In terms of the orthodox model, citizenship rights of freedom and equality before the law are secured by a liberal–democratic political system, supported by a rational–legal bureaucracy and backed up by the state's formal monopoly of the means of violence. However, for the most part, citizenship rights have not been awarded automatically through a process of enlightenment or social evolution, but have been actively achieved by people in the course of specific struggles or in the more mundane reproduction of social institutions over time. The liberal-democratic state is intended to be a reflection of the people who make it up – rich and poor, weak and powerful – but as part of class (capitalist) society it must continually attempt to reach a compromise over the potential conflict between socialized labour and private appropriation. Liberal democracy implies not only the democratic citizenship rights of all but also the right of the individual to hold property even against the interests of others. This apparent contradiction may be conceptualized as the location of the state in class society.

T. H. Marshall's (1950) summary of citizens' rights is idealistic but nevertheless useful as a basic framework with three categories. Firstly, civil rights are sustained through the law, if necessary by recourse to the courts. Secondly, political rights are sustained through democratic elections to representative bodies with the participation of political parties and pressure groups. Thirdly, social rights are sustained, according to Marshall, through such things as the extension of public education which constitutes society's awareness of the citizen's need for self-improvement. In all three areas the question must arise of differential access, given such issues as, for instance, the high cost of professional legal representation, the differential resources available to alternative political parties and the potential advantages of a privileged private against a public education. Additionally, since labour is socialized, the full extension of social citizenship rights would presumably include participation in the control of work for the individual-worker-as-citizen. Yet for most people work takes place in the private sector and therefore outside of the public-sector domain of the state and citizenship rights. Even public-sector work organizations have tended to follow the pattern of those in the private sector, and their workers have no overall rights of control. Only in a few societies, notably Germany, the Netherlands and the Scandinavian countries, have workers been granted some limited participation in management as a result of state legislation. Only in Yugoslavia, a state socialist society outside of the Soviet bloc, and in the Mondragon area of northern Spain have workers co-operatives been made into a substantial basis for industrial organization. But in the first of these cases, the Yugoslav state has always been able to override the co-operatives in the interests of centralized planning. In the second case, the success of the Mondragon co-operatives is to a great extent attributable to Basque nationalism and the determination to overcome previous neglect by the Spanish state under the dictatorship of General Franco (cf. Campbell et al. 1978).

The struggle for citizenship has clearly been a cornerstone of the establishment of the liberal–democratic model of the state which in some form or other now provides for the socio-political constitution of Western and other societies throughout the world. Yet in a number of ways the nature of the citizenship role is defined by consensual patterns institutionalized over time and operating at various levels of the society that may conflict with detached ideals of freedom or liberality. At the centre of this issue is the concept of normalcy and its reverse, deviancy. Some aspects are undisputed and are subsumed under a relatively straightforward definition of crime as characterized, for instance, by murder or theft. These are confirmed in common law and reinforced by religious teaching. The changes that have come with liberal democracy mainly involve the raising of murder to the top of the crime scale and its separation from killing in war (Giddens 1985: 187), together with the adoption of more humane forms of punishment (Poggi 1978: 109). But other categories which have been perceived as abnormal, such as insanity, or deviant, such as homosexuality, are clearly much more controversial and yet have resulted in loss of liberty. This impinges on the question of individual freedom and the conduct of the individual as does the issue of state security.

Even when liberality and democracy are at a high level, the area of state security can be shrouded in secrecy and in draconian provisions. The work of Michel Foucault (1977) has drawn attention to the origins of incarceration during the period of the absolutist states, but his work seems to conflate all forms of administrative power in contrast to Erving Goffman (1961) who regards 'total institutions', such as prisons and asylums, as a separate category. The question of which people should be deprived of freedom and citizenship in a liberal–democratic society is one that has yet to be satisfactorily resolved. It is taken as a sign of healthy liberal democracy that such an issue should remain open to debate.

Whilst it is possible to identify the principles of Marshall's model in real-life examples, there are none that conform entirely and each nation-state has unique characteristics. For instance, at the most fundamental level, the USA has a written constitution which guarantees a range of citizens' rights, whereas in Britain these have been enacted by parliament in a piecemeal fashion or even are simply implied by precedent. There is also the question of abuses of citizenship rights for political purposes by a goverment in power, as in the persecution of individuals designated as 'dissidents' or 'subversives'. All governments in all states are surely guilty at some time of these abuses and, unfortunately, there are many instances of countries which have formally emulated the Western model of the liberal–democratic state but in which the most appalling violations of human rights have been perpetrated. It would be surprising if such differences did not exist, given the nature of the nation-state system comprising separate and independent socio-political units and the fact that the societies which they enclose are made up of human agents engaged in historical networks of social, political and economic relationships. As Giddens (1985: 205) suggests, it is better to think of Marshall's three areas of citizenships rights in the Western socieities as three areas of continuing contestation and conflict, normally close to the centre of the political agenda.

Not far removed from the rights of freedom and incarceration is the prerogative of the nation-state to demand conscripted military service from the individual citizen. The enabling characteristic involved in this social institution is that standing armies were the chief means by which the centralized state was able to take a monopoly of the means of violence and thereby provide security against the potential threat of private armies pursuing sectional interests. But the constraining characteristic is that this freedom does require a proportion of citizens to render military service to the state. Conscription has its origins in the French *levée en masse* of the post-revolutionary, late eighteenth-century period and it goes hand in hand with the establishment of a professional officer corps. By the early twentieth century, a discarding of ritual and colour amongst Western armies had taken place as warfare had become transformed by the adoption of industrially produced weapons, transport and communication. Greater numbers of recruits than ever before were required for the kind of wide-ranging conflict that came with the First and Second World Wars. Volunteers had often been sufficient to supply required numbers when standards of living were low but with the increased expectations of the twentieth century the need arose for high levels to be assured by other means. This has called into question the selection of citizens to be put at risk in armed conflict and the exception of such groups as 'conscientious objectors' who might be spared this on grounds of belief. It is an issue allied to citizenship and conceptions of patriotism, which are a part of nationalism and nationality, and it has been complicated by the industrialization of arms production, the proliferation of weapons supply, and the extension of warfare from the setpiece battlefield to society in general. This takes up to the question of nation-states in the global military order.

Reflections: nation-states in the global military order

We speak unproblematically of two world wars in the twentieth century but each was in the first place a war between European states which brought about a breakdown and reformation of the European state system. Arguably, the First World War remained at its core a European war, but the Second World War became truly a global conflict and fundamentally changed the global balance of power. Another distinction is that the Second World War was the first major conflagration in which the number of civilian casualties exceeded those of the military. The First World War caused appalling numbers of deaths and casualties but they were mainly in the trenches as industrialized warfare clashed with traditional ideas of 'glorious death' (Poggi 1978: 100). It was aerial bombing of course which brought mass slaughter to civilian populations in the Second World War, and this is another aspect of the development of weapons technology and the industrialization of armaments production. As the First World War might be crudely reduced to a contest of shell production, so might the Second be seen as one of aircraft and bomb production. In either case, the industrial infrastructure became geared to the production of weapons and munitions, but with aerial bombing the productive infrastructure and therefore the general population actually became targets too. In the history of Western civilization, military and industrial developments are consistently linked and the technology which has advanced the one has advanced the other, but the process has intensified since the nineteenth century. Examples were cited earlier of links between industrial and weapons technology but, during the approach to the Second World War, there was the notable case of Nazi Germany concealing as industrial advancement much of the military preparation forbidden by the terms of the First World War armistice. More recently, it is impossible to make a distinction between the development of rocket-propulsion technology for space exploration or missile development, and between satellite systems for global communication or military surveillance and weapons guidance.

The existence of an independent nation-state with defined borders is accepted universally as justification for the maintenance of armed forces, and the global military order therefore overlaps the nation-state system and the capitalist world-economy. Armed forces require credibility in terms of equipment consistent with technological advancement and so the world-economy and international division of labour are partially devoted to armaments production. Thus, nation-states engage in the purchase of weapons from a network of suppliers dispersed throughout the world-economy. The only clear distinction in this arrangement has been the conflict between NATO and the Warsaw Pact, each of which nation-state alliance has devoted considerable effort to the protection and secrecy of its weapons technology. But even this has not been a complete distinction because, in a growing number of cases where legitimated nation-state forces have confronted non-legitimated 'terrorist' forces, the potential has been created for weapons to be supplied from one side or other of the global military confrontation. In fact, the industrialization of arms production and the proliferation of the supply of sophisticated weapons constitutes a new challenge to the nation-state's monopoly of the means of violence. Within the world-economy there are clandestine and semi-clandestine routes for the trade in arms, and advances in weapons have enhanced the military capacity of smaller states and officially proscribed terrorist organizations. In the light of such events we may more precisely define the phrase, proliferation of armaments, in the contemporary world. The invasion of one state by another is as old as civilization itself, but alongside nuclear diplomacy operates the diplomacy of terrorism with more sophisticated weapons and, similarly alongside battlefield warfare, the execution of violence against civil society. The development of the nation-state has produced the nation-state system and the global military order interconnected through global communications with the capitalist world-economy.

6

Colonial Episodes: the Implanting of Western Institutions around the World

I shall now concentrate on that side of European development which involved the colonization of territory in other parts of the world. Europe became an 'exploring civilization' whereas China, India, Islam or Japan did not, despite the fact that the first three of these developed the means of long-distance navigation earlier. John Roberts (1985: 175–6) suggests that it was largely due to the 'world-view' of Europeans which differed from the Islamic belief that the oceans could not be explored and from the Chinese emperors' lack of interest in such enterprise. To this we can add that a European world-view was developed collectively (as a set of social institutions) through the activities of various individuals (human agents) across a number of European nations and states in competition with each other for politico-military and economic success (as against the singular and hierarchical nature of the other civilizations). Europeans exploited naval and armaments technology in an age of sailing ships and cannon and, as a result, gained 'global knowledge'. This short phrase speaks volumes because, in organized human activity, knowledge and the ability to record it have proved crucial in the generation of power. In the previous chapter the development of the state was described in terms of its 'storage capacity' for society and a crucial feature of this is the containment of knowledge (Giddens 1981: 94–5). Whilst Europe never became a unitary empire again after the Romans, the European states acquired colonies and administered them as separate empires. In this process, the institutionalization of knowledge about the world, its continents and oceans was a means to global power.

However, the circumstances in which European global power was realized are not always properly understood. An early depiction of the world is Ptolemy's *Geographia*, from second-century Graeco-Egypt, which later reappeared first in Islamic, then in European, scholarship. It shows the Indian ocean as a huge lake even though it has been claimed that Phoenicians had sailed around Africa at the bidding of an earlier Pharoah. On the other hand, Fernand Braudel (1981: 402) suggests that the Suez isthmus was never a barrier to East–West trade whatever the status of the Cape route. At certain times a branch of the Nile flowed into the Red Sea and was kept open to navigation. At other times goods were transported overland and there is evidence that the Ottoman Turks transported a whole fleet in this way during the sixteenth century. North Africa and the Middle East were under the control of Islam and therefore of no direct benefit to the Europeans as an independent route to India and China.

Ironically, the *Geographia* was unknown to Christopher Columbus when in 1492 he sailed westwards into the Atlantic intending to find a new route to India and the spice trade. Equally, the discovery of a passage around the Cape of Good Hope into the Indian Ocean was a tentative affair. Portuguese expeditions approached this project by sea and land in stages between 1418 and 1498, as much to link up with the mythical Christian prince, Prester John in Abyssinia, and launch further crusades against Islam, as to establish trade routes. However, they progressed further and further down the west coast of Africa until in 1487 Bartholomew Diaz's expedition found itself around the Cape almost by accident and his crew refused to go any further (Beazley 1968: 317–18). The route to India was completed by Vasco da Gama in 1497–8. Each of these epic voyages was laying the foundations not just for European trade with the East, which after all existed already via Islam, but for comprehensive global knowledge and politico-military power in new European-dominated routes. The cosmopolitan nature of these enterprises was evident from the start, as was Europe's debt to other cultures. When the Portuguese reached Calicut on the Indian coast, it was with the help of Ibn Majib, a Muslim pilot originally from Gujerat in India (Braudel 1984: 430). Vasco da Gama had been advised by separate land expeditions of the usefulness of East African Swahili seafarers to the final stages of his expedition and took him on board at the trading city of Malindi in what is now Kenya (Beazley 1968: 319). Less than a century before, the Chinese had reached this coastline as part of a series of long-distance voyages under the command of the admiral Cheng Huo, a eunuch in the service of the emperor. He was also a Muslim convert, probably taking the opportunity to make a pilgrimage to Mecca. But the Chinese long-distance voyages of the fourteenth century were not repeated as the Ming emperors faced renewed threats from the north and the shipyards which had built huge ocean-going junks were allowed to fall into disuse.

This thumbnail sketch from the history of ocean exploration indicates some of the links between cultures and civilizations. Columbus was Genoese but, having been turned down by the Portuguese crown, sailed under the flag of Castilian Spain and with the financial backing of Genoese merchants in Seville. Vasco da Gama's expedition was heir to a whole series of voyages which had sailed from Portugal under the patronage of Prince Henry 'the Navigator', a former crusader who set up a centre for the study of navigation within his court at Sagres (later Cape St Vincent). Both used triangular 'lateen' sails to sail across the wind, which Europeans had copied indirectly from India via the Arab dhow and the eastern Mediterranean galley. India and Islam had for some time traded on routes stretching from east Africa to the China Sea. Early navigational equipment was used too, including: the compass which was derived via Islam from China; the complex astrolabe, also via Islam but attributed to Hypatia of Alexandria; and the simpler 'Jacob's staff' for taking sightings from the sun and attributed to Jewish origins. To improve ship-handling, in place of an oar over the side, there was the stern-post rudder which came from northern European, but originally probably from elsewhere. Knowledge of discoveries had percolated through existing trade routes between the civilizations, and the Europeans used this to circumvent the land blockade to the east posed by Islam and the Russian Muscovite Empire further north. Europeans went on to dominate the world through the imposition of their Western institutions (see figure 7) and as part of the process world trade was extended through the capitalist world-economy and an increasing international division of labour. In the course of European contact with the rest of the world an inter-societal system was created in the terms of structuration theory as outlined in chapter 3. As European society developed it embarked upon the pathway to the class (capitalist) model but a part of that process was its interactions with class-divided societies and tribal societies elsewhere. This involves the concept of the 'time–space edge' whereby the capacity of Western institutions for 'distanciation' in time and space clashed with the lesser capacities of other societies to form inequalities which have in the long term produced the 'development issues' of today. To illustrate this it will be helpful now to look at the historical development of colonialism.

Portuguese trading posts

In the course of their voyages, the Portuguese established fortified trading posts and settlements on the Atlantic islands and on the west

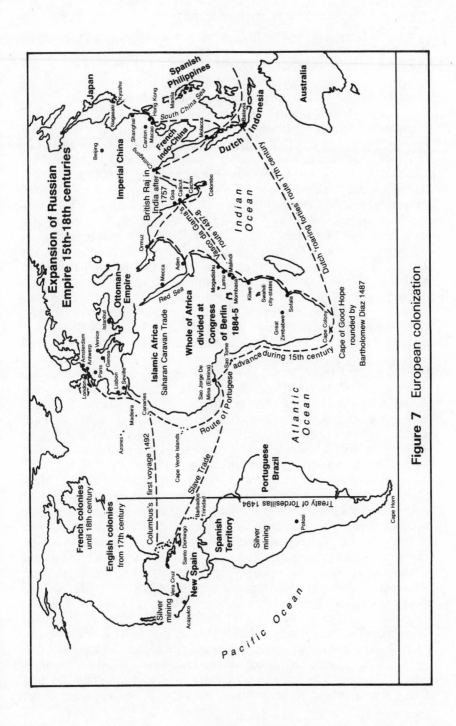

Figure 7 European colonization

coast of Africa. Between 1420 and 1471 the islands of Madeira, the Azores, Cape Verde, Fernando Po and Sao Tome had been reached or even settled, despite Spanish opposition. Sugar was introduced there to supply an existing market in the Mediterranean and by 1460 it had replaced wheat as the main crop of Madeira. Reflecting the embryonic European 'world-economy' there was Florentine, Genoese and even Flemish investment in these ventures, with much of the produce for onward transmission via the mercantile city-states, and in 1481 the building of a fort at Sao Jorge da Mina on the Guinea coast established military backing for the Portuguese monopoly of the African trade. These voyages, despatched by Henry 'the Navigator', were still nominally crusader expeditions ostensibly to join forces against Islam with the legendary christian prince, Prester John. But it was equally clear that with every trip to the Guinea coast there was a handsome profit to be made from ivory, gold and African slaves sold as servants or as labour for the sugar plantations. According to Basil Davidson (1984: 85), a specialist on African culture, the Guinea coast had for centuries been a source of gold distributed via the Saharan caravan routes and this had provided a form of coinage standardized throughout North Africa, the Berber dinar. Some of this gold had already reached Europe via North Africa and had similarly provided the basis for European currencies of the Renaissance.

Beyond the Cape of Good Hope the Portuguese set up forts on the east coast of Africa too. Here, their naval strength was used to subdue a chain of coastal city-states of the Swahili, Africans who were Islamic converts trading with Arabia and India. Roland Oliver and J. D. Fage (1988: 81–4) describe a flourishing scene from approximately 1350 to 1500 with Kilwa trading gold from inland Great Zimbabwe and Katanga; Malindi and Mombasa exporting iron ore to India; and Mogadishu shipping cotton and camel-hair cloth to Egypt. This formed a significant branch of the Islamic trade network and the gold and precious stones obtained by the Swahili from the interior were later to be the goal of waves of Europeans who went into southern Africa. For the Portuguese and the other Europeans who followed them, these ports became stepping stones on the way to India and China. After they had opened the way to India, the Portuguese attempted to block the Red Sea route of the old pepper trade but they never managed to do it permanently. However, pepper landed at Lisbon by the Cape route was a fifth of the Venetian price for supplies obtained via Islam, and Braudel (1984: 142–3) describes Italian, German and Dutch merchants visiting Lisbon soon after da Gama's return. Most significant of all, when the Venetian galleys went to Alexandria in 1504 there was no pepper to be had at all. By the time that Ferdinand Magellan completed the first circumnavigation of the globe in 1522, the Portuguese were established across the Indian Ocean at Goa on the west coast of India (1510), Ormuz in the Persian (now Arabian) Gulf (1515) and Malacca at the entrance to the South China Sea (1519). Evidence of the spread of European economy was subsequently confirmed by German bankers operating through Antwerp, the Fuggers and the Welsers (see chapter 4), who is 1587 established a representative at Cochin and then Goa, both on the west coast of India (Braudel 1982: 186). By 1557 the Portuguese were further established at Macao on the south coast of China, having been repulsed from Canton; by 1571 they had a foothold at Nagasaki; and by the end of the century over forty such bases around the world (Roberts 1985: 187–8).

The Spanish Empire in America

As the Portuguese became dominant around the coast of Africa and in the East, the Spanish concentrated on America where Columbus had pioneered the way to the off-shore islands. By the Treaty of Tordesillas in 1494, however, these two nations divided up the world between them with reference to no one else by means of a line 1,500 miles to the west of Cape Verde. This illustrates the confidence, or perhaps arrogance, of the Europeans with their knowledge and power to which only the pope had to give his blessing. Under these terms Brazil became Portuguese whilst the Spanish who followed in Columbus's wake established themselves over the remainder of the southern part of the continent. In 1496, only four years after Columbus's breakthrough and a year before John Cabot sailed from Bristol to Labrador, the first European city in the Americas was established at Santo Domingo on Columbus's island of Hispaniola (Roberts 1985: 207). This is today divided as the separate states of Haiti and the Dominican Republic but the cornerstone of Santo Domingo's cathedral was laid in 1523 and fifteen years later the New World's first university was founded, a century before Harvard. This demonstrates the Europeans' determination to reproduce European society and its institutions across the Atlantic and provides a very concrete example of the distanciation of European culture in time and space as it was transformed into the first truly global culture.

In 1501 Alvarez Cabral made a Portuguese reconnaissance of the Brazilian coast whilst, for Spain, in 1513 Vasco Nunez de Balboa crossed the isthmus of Panama to see the Pacific Ocean and in 1519 Herman Cortez set out from Cuba to land at Vera Cruz (Bethell 1987: 21). Cortez had with him only a few hundred men but significantly these included 16 horsemen which the Indians interpreted as terrifying composite creatures, never having seen horses before. The first action upon landing was to burn the boats so that there was no turning back and thus began the conquest of Mexico. These were the first of the *conquistadores* and they were followed by Pedro de Alvarado in Guatemala, Francisco Pizarro in Peru, and Diego de Almagro and Gonzalo Pizarro in the upper Amazon basin, to name only the more notable ones (cf. Bethell 1987: 2). With a combination of personal ambition and religious fervour they destroyed two civilizations, the Aztec and the Inca, and by 1600 had claimed for Spain what is now the south-western United States, almost all of Mexico, Central America, islands in the Caribbean, Venezuela, Colombia, Ecuador, Peru, Chile, and the coasts of Argentina and Uruguay. The soldiers were followed by priests of the Franciscan, Dominican, Augustinian and Jesuit orders, and it was mainly amongst these that benign or kindly attitudes towards the native inhabitants could be found (Roberts 1985: 217). Christian missions set up schools and hospitals as well as churches and, centuries later, the independence movements against colonialism were to succeed largely through the efforts of individuals educated in these missions. This is a further illustration of the constraining and enabling aspects of social institutions. Europeans required the colonized people to participate in institutions which became eventually the instruments and means to their independence, but this is jumping ahead several centuries.

Silver was the most immediate and significant commodity in the furthering of Spanish wealth and the sailings of galleons back and forth across the Atlantic were soon established in regular patterns. The regular Acapulco–Manila galleon went far beyond the Americas across the Pacific to the islands renamed the Philippines after the Spanish king, where Peruvian silver could be exchanged for Chinese silks. This route truly was innovatory, independent of any other and virtually free from interference by rivals. What were at first voyages of discovery became, within a few decades, regular trade routes. The silver came from mines which were set up early on in the colonization process and which provide another illustration of the transplantation of social institutions. They were 'European' mining towns, operating within the merchant capitalist system, and in the nature of such towns they produced high earnings, bonuses and heavy spending. Potosi was the largest of these during the sixteenth century and although perched high in the Peruvian Andes it is said to have attracted 160,000 inhabitants by 1610 (Bethell 1987: 183). Although these Spanish and Portuguese colonies were linked into the developing European 'world-economy', neither Spain nor Portugal was at the centre of the system. Spain's silver in fact served to provide Antwerp with its second phase of mercantile and financial dominance between 1535 and 1557 (see chapter 4). German bankers, especially the Fuggers and the Welsers, dominated the Antwerp markets and the Habsburg Holy Roman Emperor Charles V, who was also king of Spain, 'could not do without the services of the Antwerp money market' (Braudel 1984: 150–1). In addition to financial investment, Spain and Portugal were in no position to supply many of the materials required by the American colonies and so goods had to be imported from all parts of Europe. By 1537 the large influx of Spanish silver was being disbursed about the Habsburg Empire, which included parts of the Netherlands, Germany and Italy, and in turn loans made to Charles in anticipation of silver imports served to reverse the economic recession entered by Antwerp just prior to this. Later, during the second half of the sixteenth century, the same source of wealth benefited Genoa for a while after its eclipse of Antwerp and before the rise of Amsterdam in the European 'world-economy'.

The slave trade

Not all the wealth of the Americas was in the form of precious metals. Plantations were established for new crops, such as sugar, or for maize which became the staple cereal of the colonies. The *hacienda* system which put Indians and poor settlers into peonage was a form of feudalism, but there was also the *encomienda* system which entailed no rights to land but merely to Indian labour (Bethell 1987: 17). Each of these instruments of colonialism indicates the instituting of a form of social process and structure with norms, authority and symbolism. In the mining settlements, there was a handful of people who were very rich, either on their own account or as the representatives of large-scale investors in Europe. There were prospectors of varying origin and fortune and there were the Indians who provided *mita* or forced labour. On the land there were landowners or title-holders, small tenant-farmers, poor settlers and Indian *peones* (a word meaning literally pawns) treated mostly as beasts of burden. Shortages of labour on the plantations subsequently drew large numbers of African slaves shipped initially to the Caribbean and Brazil early in the sixteenth century (Bethell 1987: 20) and later to North America. The development of plantation agriculture in the American colonies can be divided up into periods according to the type of labour used. In the first place, the plantations were worked by Indian forced labour but the demands went beyond their physical and psychological capabilities. Consequently, for various reasons, including the diseases introduced by the Europeans, the Indian population was dramatically reduced during the early stages of colonization. The next stage, up to the 1670s, involved indentured labourers or *engagés* who went out from Europe on fixed-term contracts upon the termination of which they often became smallholders (Braudel 1984: 396). This accounts for some of the poorer but otherwise free European immigrants and their descendants in South America. In the third stage, African slaves were transported in increasing numbers after other supplies of labour diminished or dried up altogether. Thus a new landed aristocracy of slave owners was created throughout the Americas, one legacy of which may be seen in the distinction between autocratic conservative planters and pragmatic northern industrialists in the USA of the nineteenth century.

Subsequently, most of the European states maintained trading enclaves on the west coast of Africa and these were mainly for purposes of the slave trade. It is often referred to as the 'Atlantic trade' or alternatively the 'triangle trade' because it comprised three stages in a trading venture. The first leg of the triangle involved the carrying of relatively cheap goods to West Africa and, although the Portuguese had striven to prevent the spread of arms in Africa, they came to be included in the cargoes so that one African tribe could be set against another in the procurement of slaves. The second leg was the shipping of slaves to the Americas and overall figures of ten million landed are, according the Basil Davidson (1984: 216), probably underestimates. The aggregate loss to the African continent is likely to have been as high as several tens of millions, most of whom were skilled in tropical cultivation. In the Americas the survivors of the packed slave ships were sold as plantation workers at a handsome profit but this in turn was used to finance the third leg, the shipping of scarce and highly priced commodities to Europe. Thus there were profits to be made at all three stages of the voyage and investment in a slave ship during these centuries was one of the most successful examples of merchant capitalism.

The capitalist world-economy

It is based on these ventures – the slave trade, the plantations, the *haciendas* and the mines – that Andre Gunder Frank (1967), Immanuel Wallerstein (1974) and others have extended their concept of a capitalist world-economy with a metropolis, or core, in Europe and satellites, or a periphery, in the colonies (see chapter 2). I have used the term, 'European world-economy', consistently in the sense in which Braudel uses it to describe the interdependent commodity dealings between European states. But as the colonial empires were extended to form an inter-societal system in which Western institutions increasingly came to dominate those of other types of society, Wallerstein's term '*the* capitalist world-economy' becomes particularly appropriate to describe a single European-led global economy operating on the basis of the capitalist economic mechanism. As international trade increased, it provided extra wealth not only for the strengthening of the European absolutist monarchs and the further development of European society as a state system, but also for the enriching of the merchants and bankers who increasingly served to finance these monarchs, and in doing so, laid the foundations for class (capitalist) society. The dealings of the latter were connected up through the European 'world-economy', as described earlier, and their growing power in the absolutist states was central to the separation of the economy (private sector) from the polity (public sector). As part of the process, an international division of labour was created in which core areas became increasingly concerned with the manufacturing of ships, munitions and equipment and the peripheries with the provision of foodstuffs, precious metals and raw materials. During the seventeenth century, Wallerstein sees first the Italian city-states and then Spain and Portugal relegated to a semi-periphery, when the core of the capitalist world-economy was moved irrevocably from southern to north-western Europe. This takes us on to the period of Dutch ascendancy.

The Dutch Empire

In chapter 4, the rise of Amsterdam was described as forming a new centre of the European 'world-economy' in the middle of the seventeenth century. Charles Boxer (1973: 24) sees the Dutch as 'rapidly expanding their trade in the Mediterranean, the Levant, and the South Atlantic during the early 1590s, [and so] it is hardly surprising that they tried to extend it to the Indian Ocean region about the same time'. After some uncoordinated forays into the Far East and some unsuccessful attacks on Portuguese forts, the Vereenigde Oost-Indische Compagnie was formed in 1602 precisely with the aim of bringing discipline and policy to these activities, in order to challenge the Portuguese for control of the Indian Ocean trade. From 1568, Amsterdam and the protestant Dutch United Provinces which surrounded it were at war with the Catholic Habsburg monarchy in Spain, a conflict which lasted until 1648, but which played a crucial part in the establishment of Protestant northern Europe. This did not stop the Dutch following in the footsteps of the Portuguese and building small trading enclaves around the coast of Africa and on the shores of the Indian ocean. Boxer explains that these 'Dutch *factorijen* and the English "factories", whether fortified or not, were directly descended from the Portuguese trading agencies, or *feitorias* [which] in their turn, stemmed from and had much in common with the medieval *fondachi*, the residential quarters of Genoese, Venetian and other Italian merchants in the Muslim sea-ports of North Africa and in Ottoman harbours' (Boxer 1973: 209). It is enlightening to consider that these familiar institutions of European colonialism, which were such a feature of the Far East during the seventeenth to nineteenth centuries, had a direct antecedent in the Venetian Levant trade. But at the same time, Boxer points out, the original Indian and Islamic participants in trade which extended from the Persian Gulf to the South China Sea maintained comparable bases in each other's territory. It is the mark of the long-distance trader's insecurity in an alien environment.

Above all, the Dutch needed a central base in the East Indies to get a grip on the spice trade, having failed to take Malacca from the Portuguese, and so in 1619 Jan Pieterzoon Coen, a conscious empire builder, took possession of Jakarta. He did so against the wishes not only of the local sultan but also of the Vereenigde Oost-Indische Compagnie directors in Amsterdam who preferred peaceful negotiation. This type of independent action was typical of Dutch mercantile enterprise with its vigorous laissez-faire ethos. Jakarta was destroyed and out of its ashes the Dutch colonists built Batavia which became the centre of their colony in Java and of their operations in the whole region (Boxer 73: 211). However, they could not maintain their presence in the East Indies without gaining a foothold in India from where existing trade, before the Europeans, had been controlled and so between 1605 and 1665 there came to be of a chain of *factorijen* in India and by 1638 in Ceylon (Braudel 1984: 215). There was also trade with Canton, by-passing Portuguese Macao, and contact with the Japanese at Kyushu, a move which in 1638 led to the expulsion of the Portuguese in favour of the Dutch. Transport and communication was sustained by the innovative 'roaring forties' route from the Cape direct to the East Indies, passing south of Madagascar.

In West Africa, Prince Maurice of Orange and Nassau took several possessions from the Portuguese in 1637, including the central slave fort of Sao Jorge da Mina. This was not to last for long but it marked the Dutch entry into the slave trade. Whilst, in Cape Colony the Dutch flag was planted in 1652 and the settlement of *boers*, or farmers, began in the 1680s with significant consequences for later developments in southern Africa. But most of the Dutch bids for a share of the Americas failed through their conflicting strategies in jealous defence of their mercantile freedom of action. Nevertheless, by about 1660 Amsterdam was the centre not only of the capitalist world-economy but also of the richest colonial empire, a position surpassed only by the British almost a century later.

The British Empire

The Cabots, father and son of Venetian descent, crossed the Atlantic from Bristol to Newfoundland in 1497, only five years after Columbus. Sir Francis Drake circumnavigated the globe in 1578. Yet Britain was late in becoming as aggressively imperialistic as the Spanish, Portuguese or Dutch. During Elizabethan times plunder was preferred and it was relatively easy to pick off heavily laden Spanish galleons or Portuguese carracks on their way home. However, the structures of colonialism were in the process of formation. Sebastian Cabot was an early governor of the Company of Merchant Venturers which was set up to coordinate the exporting of English wool and wool-cloth to Europe. Later some of the crown's proceeds from Drake's privateering were invested in the separate Levant Company to market the lightweight 'new draperies' of the wool trade in the eastern Mediterranean. Profits from this subsequently went into the setting up of the East India Company which became the significant instrument of English colonialism in India and the Far East, as will be described later.

Apart from this, there was the movement of settlers across the Atlantic to the New World. In 1607 Jamestown was established and became the capital of Virginia which together with the catholic colony of Maryland came to specialize in tobacco growing. Originally, the cultivation was by white smallholders but between 1663 and 1699 there was expansion which culminated in the slave plantations (Braudel 1984: 397). The American colonies were often refuges for religious groups and for a while also received people sentenced to transportation. Cromwell transported large numbers of Scots and Irish and, between 1717 and 1759, 50,000 are estimated to have been exiled, including the original inhabitants of Georgia which was founded as a debtor colony by John Oglethorpe in 1732. By 1757 there were 13 British colonies on the Atlantic seaboard, containing some two million people and including British, Irish, Dutch, German and French immigrants plus African slaves. However, the 13 were not integrated because they were scattered and suffered slow communication which meant that they developed separately in terms of social, political and economic institutions (Roberts 1985: 222). People who lived there faced huge distances of travel so that isolation, insecurity and the notion of the frontier was normal. Robert Zaller (1984: 61) suggests that British colonies in the Americas can be divided into three economic categories. Firstly, there were the southern plantation colonies from Virginia to the Caribbeans islands which were modelled in economic terms upon Portuguese Brazil. Secondly, there were the middle colonies which produced grain and timber mainly for the burgeoning trade within the Americas. Thirdly, there were the New England colonies whose shipping often competed with the home fleet as part of increasing economic activity which eventually lead to the struggle for independence.

It was the first group with their slave plantations that was initially of the most economic value to Britain, especially the islands of Barbados and Jamaica which were acquired in 1627 and 1655, respectively. Braudel (1984: 411–2) maintains that at this time the Caribbean islands were more valuable than mainland possessions to either Britain or France, which helps to explain French acquiescence in British occupation of French Canada in 1762–3. Zaller (1984: 64) estimates that during the eighteenth century the British controlled half of the African slave market and the French a quarter. Until 1762 the French held a huge swathe of sparsely populated land stretching from south-eastern Canada to the Gulf of Mexico, as well as caribbean islands, but nowhere were their colonies as valuable as those of the British.

On the other side of the world the British East India Company failed to get a toe-hold in the East Indies spice trade, and so was compelled to resort to the Indian coast, a move that served it well in the end. Zaller (pp. 65–6) notes it might have been the French who took possession of India but for the fact that they lost their nerve when the Nabob of Bengal attempted to resist European incursions with the storming of the fort and the subsequent 'black hole of Calcutta' in 1756. This gave the British the excuse that they needed for the crucial Battle of Plassey in 1757 and after General Clive's victory British India became the 'biggest single agglomeration of peoples ever ruled by a European state' (Roberts 1985: 348), with the Raj eventually stretching from the frontier with Afghanistan to that of Siam. The French and all others were squeezed out except for tiny enclaves and it was British institutions that were implanted into an existing Indian Empire and trade network. Notable amongst the spoils were the land revenues of the Mogul emperors, built up since 1526 but in decline at the takeover, and access to the Indian opium crop. Hitherto, European traders had been forced to pay for Chinese goods in silver because there were few European goods that the Chinese needed or wanted, but by introducing opium into China from 1780 the East India Company changed the balance of trade in Britain's favour. The practice was not approved by the Chinese imperial administration, and it is a remarkable insight into the morality of colonialism that the trade was imposed upon the Chinese in a series of opium wars during the nineteenth century. By then the European colonial nations plus an independent United States of America were able to coerce the Chinese into trade, with concessions granted at Macao, Canton, Hong Kong and Shanghai.

Roberts (1985: 303–4) points out that after Waterloo in 1815 Britain had the pick of former Dutch and French colonies and, with the most powerful navy in the world, assembled the richest empire, despite the loss of the American colonies. The Spanish colonies grew under absolutist monarchy and the Dutch from a vigorous mercantile city-state; but the British Empire came into ascendancy with the infrastructure of an industrializing nation-state and a hegemonic position in the capitalist world-economy. Wallerstein (1979: 29) defines Britain's period as 'workshop of the world' from 1815 to 1873 and asserts: 'Even to those semiperiphral countries that had some manufacture (France, Germany, Belgium, the US), Britain in this period supplied about half their needs in manufactured goods.' In Australia the first settlement of convicts was established in 1789 and during the nineteenth century the British began displacing the Dutch in southern Africa, especially through the efforts of Cecil Rhodes and his fellow adventurers in the British South Africa Company. The final major division of colonial territory, however, was enacted not with military force nor even on the spot but at the Congress of Berlin (1884–5) when the 'scramble for Africa' was resolved around the conference table. All the old colonial powers were there with the exception of the Dutch and to these were added the newly constituted nation-states of Germany, Belgium and Italy. Lines were drawn on a map setting boundaries that had not been surveyed on the ground and in this arbitrary way were determined what, after the colonial period, came to be the borders of the emergent African nation-states.

European colonies and the imposition of a culture

The success of the European states in setting up their colonial empires gave Europeans a tremendous sense of their own superiority. This coincided with the Age of Enlightenment and the Industrial Revolution so that there appeared no limits to the frontiers, abstract or physical, that Europeans could push back. The fusion of a culture of rationality with political and economic power created the positivistic world-view. Europe was seen to have eclipsed the Ottoman Empire and India and other powerful empires like Russia, China and Japan were at least prised open for trade. The persistent application of diplomatic pressure for the freedom of trade was always backed up with the presence of military force. From the sixteenth century onwards, the continuous expansion of colonial frontiers had significantly added to the wealth created within Europe through the development of a form of merchant capitalism to surpass the introverted and protectionist 'mercantilism' to which the absolutist states were at first inclined. Some of the colonies, especially the settler colonies, actually drew wealth out of Europe, but there was always a net return overall and, most important of all, circulation of wealth within the capitalist world-economy. The result was a huge increase in taxable wealth available for the European states to expand their social, political and economic institutions and further propagate trade and colonialism.

The extension of colonialism implies the creation of an inter-societal system in which the developing European society came into contact with other types of society. Western institutions were in a process of development as global institutions, the time–space capacities of which clashed unequally with those of class-divided society or tribal society in other parts of the world. Colonial administration involved the imposition of European institutions but only partial integration into European culture and there were variations in the way that this was applied. In the British case the colonies were administered at arms's length through a colonial civil service, whereas the official French policy was assimilation of subject populations as citizens of France, although in practice this was never taken very far. European states applied their legal and fiscal systems, and European languages, education systems and other cultural institutions were adopted in the colonies.

In settler colonies, to which Europeans emigrated in large numbers, the practical situation was often straightforward because the Europeans replaced or at least overshadowed indigenous peoples, but in others a form of 'dualism' was created. European institutions were paramount, but local ones existed too, and it became routine for colonized people to have two cultures manifested in all kinds of ways. Education was scarce despite the efforts of the mission schools but it produced an educated underclass that was useful to colonial administration. These colonial servants typically led a dual existence, working within a European institutional setting, with its links to global culture, but going home to their families in a different role within the limited locale of a native social structure. In the British West African colony of Nigeria the entire northern territory was of little interest to the British, but was at all cost to be denied the French. The result was 'indirect rule' whereby it continued to be ruled by the emirs of the Islamic Hausa city-states under the routine surveillance of British

district commissioners and tax officials. These are prime examples of
an inter-societal system in which colonial institutions of global
proportions derived from Western class (capitalist) society impinge on
the institutions of a tribal society (the indigenous connections of most
colonial subjects) or of a class-divided society (the Hausa city-states).
In terms of the differential time–space capability of colonial (global)
and indigenous (local) institutions, this has been termed in structuration theory as a 'time–space edge' (see chapter 3).

Colonies were established basically for commercial gain but also to
deny territory to other European states, with the possibility of future
gain in mind. As Europe developed an international division of labour
the colonies assumed the role of suppliers of raw materials and
plantation farming served to supply cash crops which could command
commodity prices on world markets. Europe therefore developed an
interdependence with its colonies not unlike the symbiosis between
city and countryside in class-divided societies. Certainly the final
'scramble for Africa' during the last decades of the nineteenth century
contained an acute awareness of the strategic nature of mineral
deposits and possibilities of plantation agriculture for an already
industrialized Europe.

The coming of constitutional independence

The increasing intensity of colonialist exploitation in the industrial
age required the creation of ever more sophisticated forms of
administration and social infrastructure. In the colonies more and
more trained officials were required from the indigenous population
and it is amongst these educated people that, ironically, the seeds of
the independence movements were sown. Nationalist movements in
the colonies were first set up mainly in the period between the two
world wars and, as Anthony D. Smith (1983) has pointed out, these
should be seen as quite different from earlier manifestations of
resistance to colonialism. Colonized peoples now used the European
institutions of education, law and politics against the colonialists.
The two world wars played a crucial part in these developments
because many colonized people were drafted into the European
armed forces and transferred to the various war zones which gave
them a new perspective on the world and an awareness of the
fallibility of white people. But the instruments of the independence
campaigns were Western institutions like those, for instance, used by
Mahatma Gandhi, the catalyst for Indian independence. He had a
long apprenticeship in British law, especially during a period in
South Africa, before going on to become India's spiritual leader.

Independence for India had been postponed because of the Second World War and it could not be denied for long afterwards, being achieved in 1947.

It was the United States which emerged, post-1945, as the most powerful nation on earth and, being an ex-colony itself, was opposed to the resumption of European colonialism. This was not only a question of ideals of freedom and opportunity, however. With the destruction of European industry, the war had made the USA the world's foremost manufacturer and its government wanted to exploit this position in a world free of colonial trading blocs. In 1941 President Franklin D. Roosevelt and Prime Minister Winston Churchill had signed the Atlantic Charter to guarantee all peoples self-determination. It was aimed primarily at those countries occupied by the Nazis, but it could equally be applied to the European colonies. Therefore, in the longer term, one of the prices for the USA's aid in the rebuilding of Europe was the end of colonialism (see chapter 7).

With its economy actually enhanced by the war, the United States could afford to take the lead in the establishment of the United Nations and the Bretton Woods economic institutions. In 1945 there were 51 nation-states as members of the UN, whereas in the 1990s there are more than 150, and this increase is mainly due to the granting of independence to Europe's colonies. Indonesia gained its independence from the Netherlands in 1949. Ten years later Ghana became the first of Africa's 'emergent nations' in a series of British and French withdrawals from that continent. The 1960s became the 'decade of independence' as, with the exception of Portugal, the European colonial powers went through a process of divesting themselves of their colonial possessions. Portugal was ruled by a right-wing dictatorship which held on in the colonies until futile guerilla wars not only ended colonialism but also brought down the regime itself. In southern Rhodesia, the white settler minority declared independence unilaterally (UDI) to the embarrassment of Britain which was about to grant the colony independence, but again a guerilla war eventually reversed the situation. In each of these resistant cases the result has been a Marxist government, usually demanding support from a Soviet Union that was always reluctant to get involved in Africa.

Reflections

The constitutionally independent nations created by the end of European colonialism have been referred to in a variety of terms, which are themselves revealing. Before independence they tended to be called 'backward countries' and upon the granting of independence, 'emergent nations' (Alavi and Shanin 1982: xi). Afterwards they became known as 'developing countries' in order to fit into the West's notion of universal development or, alternatively, as 'underdeveloped countries' in the terminology of the dependency critique (see chapter 2). French observers recognized their impotence in relation to the NATO/Warsaw Pact military conflict and dubbed them *troisième force* and *tiers monde* or Third World (Worsley 1984: 307). This was a term widely used until the Brandt Commission encouraged the use of the simplified notion of rich industrialized North and poor deprived South at the end of the 1970s.

In a more specialized context, some political scientists have referred to post-colonial countries as 'state-nations' because the building of a state out of the colonial administration actually preceded the building of a nation typically consisting of several ethnic or tribal groups. Normally, the independent state administration was formed from the same native-born intelligentsia that had made up the anti-colonial independence movement. Immediately prior to independence, the Western system of representative democracy was formally adopted and elections were held to decide which of a range of political parties, formed out of the broad independence movement and its critics, should take over government from the colonial administration. Revealingly, in some notable cases such as those of Kwame Nkrumah in Ghana, and Jomo Kenyatta in Kenya, the independence leader went directly from a colonial jail to the presidential palace. Such leaders, however, had invariably been educated in colonial schools and colleges and so were socialized in Western institutions which therefore continued to make up the infrastructure of the independent state. In fact, in a serpentine process, Western institutions had been used against Western colonialism in the struggle for independence only to become the structure of such independence when it was achieved. These events are examples of long-term institutions being reproduced through a series of historical events, despite the constitutional transition from colonialism to independence. More fundamentally, such countries have retained the boundaries laid down arbritrarily by the colonists. This has frequently caused some indigenous ethnic groups to object to the persistence of colonial divisions on what have been traditionally their tribal lands.

In the terms of structuration theory, the inter-societal system of the post-colonial era had involved the marginalization of class-divided and tribal societies in the face of a world order centred upon the confrontation between Western capitalism and Soviet state socialism. In the emergent nation-states of the Third World, governments seek to fit their societies into the time–space dimensions of Western global institutions but some of their citizens see things differently, for instance in terms of the localized dimensions of tribal society. New governments based upon European institutions have had to face the job not only of maintaining uncomfortable amalgams or divisions of tribal groups but also of creating new national identities based upon Western notions of nationalism. This has lead to civil wars and insurrections where, typically, civilian governments have been replaced by military dictatorships and one-party systems. Some examples have oscillated continuously between civil and military government. In Vietnam, tragically, the throwing off of French colonialism through guerilla war was followed by an American-led anti-communist crusade, and even then the outcome was Marxist government. The alignment or non-alignment of Third World countries to the USA or the USSR in terms of the post-war global military order is an issue that will be taken up in part III. This will raise questions of economic dependency, aid programmes and the concept of 'neo-colonialism', together with the attendant issue of the transnational corporations, all of which arise from the colonial episodes described in this chapter.

Part III

THE DEFINITION OF THREE 'WORLDS' AFTER THE SECOND WORLD WAR

The Second World War represents a watershed in the history of Western civilization because it was the first truly global conflict and it resulted in radical revisions to the world order. These took place, however, through global institutions which already existed in an inter-societal system created through the expansion of the West as described in Part II. There were considerable changes to the system of nation-states particularly in Europe but also in other parts of the world especially when the dismantling of the European colonial empires is taken into account. The United Nations Organization was established by the victorious allies as a global forum for nation-states, with the failures of the League of Nations after the First World War clearly in mind. This may be interpreted as official recognition of the global existence of nation-states representing a culmination to the long development of the Western state model. There was clearly determination to maintain the capitalist world-economy and avoid especially the alternative of Soviet state socialism, but only the USA emerged from the war with sufficient resources to provide the scale of public-sector intervention which was needed to initiate private-sector economic recovery. The USA therefore became the main sponsor of new global economic organizations established as agencies of the United Nations. The International Bank for Reconstruction and Development, better known as the World Bank, and the International Monetary Fund (IMF) became known as the Bretton Woods arrangements after the place where they were founded and they may be taken to represent a formal recognition of the global significance of the capitalist world-economy in relation to the nation-state system.

Casting a shadow over all of these arrangements, however, was the post-war global military order. The US leadership at first intended to withdraw back into isolation after the war but was then persuaded to recognize the military threat posed by a consolidated Soviet Union with new allies in Eastern Europe. Thus was created the 'superpower' confrontation between NATO and the Warsaw Pact which gave rise to renewed competition for military supremacy and resulted in a balance of power secured, in theory, through the deterrent effect of nuclear weapons. The continued emphasis on advanced technological development has also transformed the global information system through the enhancement of a range of communication devices to which increasing numbers of people have access. Time and space have become further compressed and bound together and aspects of Western culture have been more widely broadcast through the expansion of fast long-distance air travel and virtually instant electronic communication. All of these changes have become institutionalized since the Second World War as part of an overall inter-societal system in which Western class (capitalist) society is extended as the model throughout the world and other types of society become increasingly marginalized.

The inequalities inherent to the inter-societal system in all of its cultural, political, military and economic dimensions gave rise to the term, Third World. It describes the poorer, mostly post-colonial countries in which most aspects of Western culture are reproduced without the scale of resources available in the First World. Also located there are most of the remaining alternatives to Western society, that is, the surviving examples of class-divided and tribal societies which have become marginalized in the contemporary world. This part of the book, therefore, is divided into three chapters. Chapter 7 will describe the First World's post-war reconstruction programmes under the leadership of the USA. Chapter 8 will trace the consolidation of the Second World, backtracking to the Russian Revolution in order to understand the effects of circumstances upon the formation of Soviet institutions. Chapter 9 will address the dilemma of the Third World in the light of the legacy of European colonialism and of Western-dominated global institutions.

7

Post-War Reconstruction and New Global Organizations: the Confirmation of an Inter-Societal System

In this chapter, I shall regard the foundation of the United Nations Organization with its agencies as formal confirmation of the existence of an inter-societal system of global communications, nation-states, world economy and military order. The United Nations coincides more or less with the nation-state system, whilst the World Bank and the IMF were set up as agencies of the UN to facilitate the recovery of the capitalist world-economy. In their official policies it is possible to discern the principles of modernization theory, since development aid has always been intended as primarily a pump-priming exercise to facilitate private investment. Development programmes in the Third World have been designed to transform the infrastructure of a society from traditional to modern forms in order to enable and encourage private enterprise. From this point it is not difficult to see the conceptual links with structural–functionalist social theory and its emphasis on the dichotomy between the traditional and the modern, derived from the work of classical sociologists. Out of this have emerged notions of modernization, progress and the achievement-oriented society which have been at the heart of official development policy. This kind of interplay between events, policy and theory is a feature of all social science concepts.

Structural-functionalism and modernization theory

In chapter 1, I set out some reasons for rejecting structural-functionalism as a theory of social change but there is still need to consider the effects of Talcott Parsons's work in terms of the interplay that always exists between social theory and its subject matter. This includes various aspects of policy making in the nation-state and, in the case of the USA especially, the global systems with which it connects. Louis Coser (1979: 318) notes that Talcott Parsons's theoretical orientation was tremendously dominant in American sociology from the late 1930s until the mid 1960s and, whilst much of the original material is rarely referred to now, the orthodoxy which grew out of its principles is still relevant for any consideration of modernization theory (cf. Hoogvelt 1978, 1982; Etzioni-Halevy 1981; Strasser and Randall 1981). As a school of social theory structural–functionalism not only maintained the importance of the distinction between traditional and modern society established in classical sociology, but also provided a conceptual basis for the practical transformation of traditional social institutions. This kind of thinking became particularly apparent in visions of 'modernization' which emerged upon the formal dismantling of the European colonial empires after the Second World War, with the USA in a newly consolidated position of power and influence in the world. It is perhaps odd that such an abstract set of ideas as Parsons's should have a practical import, but Guy Rocher, in an overview of his work, explained it thus:

> It is something of a paradox that out of the prevailing empiricism of American sociology should have sprung the most abstract theorist in contemporary social science. Parsons is by no means typical of American sociology. With his formidably theoretical approach, the high level of generality at which he works, and the difficult language he uses, Parsons swam against the stream of almost all American sociology, which he has continually nettled and offended. His work has met with widespread opposition, vigorous criticism and persistent resistance in American sociological circles.
>
> But, at the same time, Parson's sociology is closely bound up with America and American sociology. American society has given Parsons much food for thought and served as his principle research laboratory – to the extent that some critics of Parsonian sociology have seen it as no more than a pseudo-expert formulation of American ideology. Moreover, Parsons has influenced several generations of American sociologists; more than anyone else he founded a school of thought, and amongst those he has influenced can be counted many of the leading figures of contemporary American sociology, such as Robert K. Merton, Robin Williams, Neil Smelser, Edward Shils, Robert Bellah and many others. (Rocher 1974: 1)

This quotation encapsulates many of the points about Parson's work that I wish to amplify in this chapter. First of all I shall take up the criticism that his concepts represents 'a pseudo-expert formulation of American ideology'. The inference here is that Parsons's social theory, based as it is on consensus, and formulated initially during the 1930s, owes its success to the political climate of the USA at that time. President Franklin D. Roosevelt's socio-economic New Deal was introduced during the 1930s depression after the considerable blow to the national psyche caused by the Wall Street Crash of 1929. This took place against a background which included the so-called 'Bolshevik spectre' of continuing socialist revolution spreading from the Soviet Union. Alvin Gouldner (1971) in his appraisal of structural–functionalism suggests that the historical background explains Parsons's embracing of consensus and equilibrium rather than conflict and revolution. Parsons may also have derived from this the respect that his reputation commanded outside of the academic world over a period of time which included the McCarthyite anti-communist 'witch hunts' of the 1950s. In the above extract, Rocher points to the close binding between Parsons's sociology and American society, which no doubt influenced the structural–functionalist school of social theory in terms of the emphasis upon social order rather than social change. Elsewhere Dorothy Ross (1991) argues that American social science in general was modelled on natural science and liberal politics, and nurtured by the idea that the USA occupied an exceptional place in history. Parsons sought a universal model for society but in adopting a biological metaphor attributing explanation to function and form to structure, he succeeded only in providing a blueprint for an idealized and uncontested version of Western society.

In chapter 2, modernization theory was presented as a theory of potential change for all societies. What it represents is the articulation of ideas about development and modernization which became an orthodoxy during the period when the European colonies were gaining constitutional independence. A new range of organizations was introduced to deal with global politics and economics against a background of international relations created by the outcome of the Second World War, including independence campaigns in the European colonies which the the war had interrupted. The connections between academic social science and policy-making are important in understanding the place of structural–functionalist principles in the emergence of modernization theory, particularly in the USA which exerted the most influence in the formation of the UN and the Bretton Woods arrangements. Alvin Gouldner (1971: 141–2) observes in general terms that in the USA during the Second World War sociologists began to be employed in the federal bureaucracy and gained experience of the state apparatus. But Walt Rostow's *The Stages of Economic Growth*, which might be taken as a paradigm for modernization theory, was published in 1960 and represents essentially the amalgamation of an economic historian's ideas about the

British Industrial Revolution with the kind of principles which were enshrined in the Bretton Woods arrangements. The result is the fundamental notion that sufficient application of modernization to the social institutions of a society must result in its 'take off' and 'drive to maturity', to use Rostow's own terminology. That is, the adoption of patterns of social change equivalent to those that first modernized Britain at the time of the Industrial Revolution will result in a process of economic growth. Capital growth will exceed population growth, culminating in the high production and consumption patterns of economic maturity or, in other words, something akin to a twentieth-century United States' world-view. Bretton Woods policy, therefore, has been to support projects which seek to improve the infrastructure of 'modernizing' nations sufficiently to encourage independent capitalist–industrial development. The aim is not to intervene as such in the capitalist world-economy but merely to facilitate. Additionally, the definition of infrastructure typically involves such things as transport and communication which are of course as fundamental to the governance of a society as to its economic prospects. In this example of the extension of Western institutions, therefore, we may perceive the encouragement of projects consistent with a modernized society, but ones that are also able to maintain stability against potential alternative models, with the global military order and the spread of Soviet influence particularly in mind.

Post-war reconstruction, the United Nations and the global military order

Before 1945 the major allied powers were making plans for what amounts to nothing less than the reorganization of the world after the conclusion of the war. The wartime governments of the USA, Britain and the USSR actually engaged in a process of bargaining over the probable international relationships after the war and it was clear that of these the USA alone would come out of the war with its infrastructure intact to take up the most powerful position. According to E. A. Brett's *The World Economy Since the War* (1985: 63), 'the USA [in 1945] controlled some seventy per cent of the world's gold and foreign exchange reserves and more than forty per cent of its industrial output'. By contrast, Paul Kennedy's *The Rise and Fall of the Great Powers* (1988) suggests that, even with the support of its empire, Britain had in fighting the war severely run down its gold and dollar reserves, worn out its industry and become more dependent upon imports. Nevertheless, American policy was firmly against the resumption of European colonialism. This was partly because of its own past and the feeling that colonized peoples are treated badly, but mainly because of the expansion of its manufacturing capacity during the war and the resultant desire for global markets without restriction from the privileged currency and trading areas of the various European colonial blocs. In 1941 the agreement between Britain and the USA, prior to the latter's entry into the war, involved the Atlantic Charter of which Clause 3 affirmed that both countries 'respect the right of all peoples to choose the form of government under which they will live; and [. . .] wish to see sovereign rights and self-government restored to those who have been forcibly deprived of them'. This was aimed primarily at Nazi-occupied Europe but it had equal relevance to Europe's colonies, a point not lost on their future independence leaders, and it was followed in 1942 by a preliminary United Nations declaration which underlined the broader interpretation.

During the war there was a series of 'big three' conferences which involved Prime Minister Winston Churchill of Britain, President Franklin D. Roosevelt of the USA and Josef Stalin, head of state of the Soviet Union. These included the meeting at Yalta in February 1945 from which an image of the three leaders, Churchill on Roosevelt's right and Stalin on his left, has tended to become an icon for the power politics of the time. Despite his distaste for communism, Roosevelt respected the Russians' role in the war effort, and recognized that they would play a major part in the post-war world. His intentions were that the American forces would return home after the war and the USA resume its separate existence in a free world. Churchill was suspicious of the Russians, both as communists, and, historically, as a potential threat to Europe. Stalin, having led the USSR ruthlessly through a period of political purges and intensive industrialization programmes, wanted to gain some buffer territory, especially in Eastern Europe. As a Marxist–Leninist, state socialist society, the USSR was isolated in the world, and consequently Stalin felt keenly the need for its position to be consolidated. Dimbleby and Reynolds (1988: 152–8) describe how at Yalta in February 1945, as at Tehran before, Roosevelt kept his distance from Churchill to ensure that the meetings really did involve three-cornered negotiations. After D–Day, 4 June 1944, the USA had more troops in the war than Britain whilst the Russians were advancing on Germany in large numbers. Therefore Churchill saw that there was nothing he could do to prevent the realization of Stalin's ambitions in Eastern Europe. Apart from anything else the Russians could be seen to have paid in blood for their gains with a reckoning of twenty milllion dead, whereas Britain and the USA together had lost less than a million. As Adam Westoby (1981: 7) points out (following Turnbull Higgins 1957), 'from early 1941 until the Normandy landings, the British and Commonwealth armies engaged between two and eight German divisions, whereas for most of the same period the Soviet armies faced an average of 180 German divisions'. In fact, the victory over Nazi Germany on the eastern front, in what was propagandized as 'The Great Patriotic War', made Marxism a piece of the Soviet national heritage. Meanwhile, Europe lay shattered from the war and the days of its colonial empires were numbered.

Against this background the United Nations Organization was set up as a global forum for international relations, composed of six 'principal organs' with which to achieve its objectives. According to Sydney D. Bailey (1989: 3–4) in his political guide to the UN these are:

1   The General Assembly of all UN members.
2   The Security Council, with limited membership.
3   The Economic and Social Council, with limited membership and the responsibility for creating the World Bank and the International Monetary Fund.
4   The International Trusteeship Council for the temporary administration of stateless nations.
5   The International Secretariat, with the office of the Secretary General to be recruited on as wide a geographic basis as possible, i.e. not from the big powers.
6   The International Court of Justice, with a panel of 15 independent judges.

Outside of this basic structure there are numerous 'autonomous inter-governmental agencies' covering a wide range of concerns extending, for instance, from international mail services (the Universal Postal Union), through labour relations (the International Labour Organization [ILO] inherited from the old League of Nations), to child welfare (the International Children's Emergency Fund [UNICEF]). The agencies have created a reputation for working very independently. Each has its own budget and administration, but in some cases, such as that of UNESCO (the United Nations Educational, Scientific and Cultural Organization) during the 1980s, the consequence of independence has been the withdrawal of funding by the USA and the UK.

William Ashworth (1975: 272) observes that at the time of the UN's foundation the seriousness of the political split between the communist and non-communist worlds was not appreciated and was allowed to impinge as little as possible on the arrangements. But, whilst the wartime allies were all founder members of the United Nations, it must always have been unlikely that the USSR would ratify the economic arrangements. The Bretton Woods agreements involved member nations depositing gold and dollar reserves on the basis of which the Bank and the Fund would be operated. For instance, in the case of the IMF, whilst 'the greater part of a member's subscription could be paid in its own currency . . . each member had to pay in gold 25 per cent of its quota or 10 per cent of its net official holding of gold and dollars, whichever was the less' (Ashworth 1975: 274). The two main planners were John Maynard Keynes who favoured intervention and wanted the USA to bear the financial burden of the arrangements entirely, and Harry Dexter White, an anti-interventionist who preferred and achieved a more modest fund with partial but majority participation from his country (Dimbleby and Reynolds 1988: 166). However, the dollar was the only really stable currency after the war and the United States, by far the biggest depositor initially, so that the World Bank and IMF were established in neighbouring buildings in Washington, DC, where, by convention, the president of the World Bank is an American and the president of the IMF, a European. The alliance between the Soviet Union and the other two powers had been contingent on the war and did not extend to the pooling of financial resources afterwards. In any case for the USSR to have taken a major role would have required a conjunction of state planning with the capitalist-oriented policies of the World Bank and the IMF.

In the United Nations, the participants were anxious to avoid the failures which had become associated with the League of Nations after the First World War. It was to be a forum of nation-states to which any independent nation could apply to join and, in accordance with its first principle of sovereign equality, all would have an equal vote in the General Assembly. Nevertheless, this basic democratic ideal was compromised by the creation of the Security Council oriented to the global military order, ostensibly as an overriding safeguard against the disturbance of the balance of power. The UN Security Council includes the right of veto for any of its members and therefore the right of one nation's interests over those of the organization as a whole. The permanent membership consists of the USA, the USSR, Britain, France and China and there are six non-permanent members elected from the General Assembly for terms of two years. China was included at the insistence of the USA to counteract British colonial influence in the Far East, but it became an embarrassment after Mao Zedong's successful communist takeover in 1949.

By 1947 the United States' leadership had been converted to the idea of the Soviet Union as a global threat (Kennedy 1988: 371). Churchill had been voted out of office in 1945 but it was, nevertheless, mainly he who in an unofficial capacity persuaded Roosevelt's successor, President Harry S. Truman, that the USA had underestimated the need for its participation in post-war Europe, although it was still some time before the American people accepted it (Dimbleby and Reynolds 1988: 170–1). Additionally, the first British Labour government with a secure majority in the House of Commons was, despite its socialist principles, also wary of expansionist plans on the part of the USSR. So when Churchill on a private visit to the USA in March 1946 spoke of an 'iron curtain' being lowered from 'Stettin in the Baltic to Trieste in the Adriatic', the Cold War lines were drawn (see figure 8).

Against a background of superpower politics and the global military order, the United Nations has had a variety of roles. During a Soviet boycott of the Security Council over the question of Maoist China's permanent membership, the USA and its big-power allies actually styled themselves as UN forces in the Korean War, when in the end their main opponent was not communist North Korea but China itself! However, since the UN's intervention in the brutal Congo civil war of 1960 the forces bearing its insignia have come either from neutral countries like Ireland or Sweden or from the Third World. But the United Nations perhaps received its biggest boost in 1990 when reaction to Saddam Hussein's Iraqi annexation of Kuwait produced the clearest UN resolution yet, backed unanimously by the Security Council, for the use of military force by the big powers in their own name.

At a more mundane level, the United Nations might be considered to have most practical benefit for the Third World. These countries constitute a majority in the General Assembly and this has produced a succession of resolutions directed at the ideal of a more equitable and just world. Occasionally, the big powers have been made to take notice or else have found it convenient to solve problems by resort to UN resolutions. There is also its symbolic value. In March 1990 the Republic of Namibia finally gained independence from South Africa after a long struggle and it was the Secretary General of the United Nations, Javier Perez de Cuellar, who presided at the swearing in ceremony of Namibia's first president, Sam Nujoma. The continuing existence of the United Nations Organization, its ideals and its international connections has proved to be a factor in the institutional reproduction of the contemporary inter-societal system.

The Bretton Woods arrangements

Although technically linked to it through the Economic and Social Council, the Bretton Woods arrangements are realistically in a different category to the United Nations. Whereas the UN General

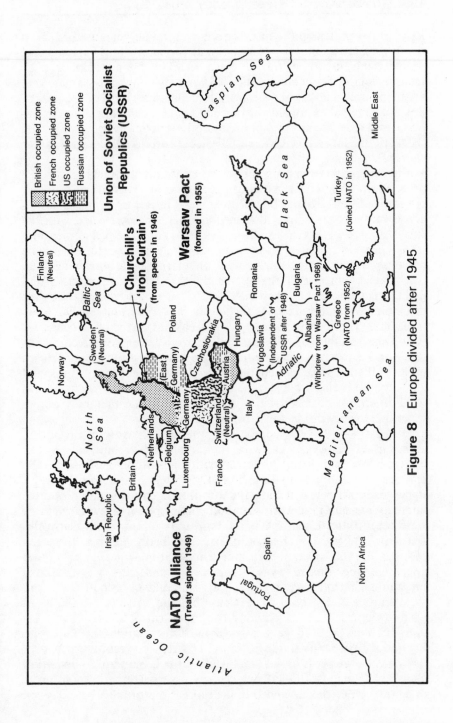

Figure 8 Europe divided after 1945

Assembly operates on the basis of one nation one vote, the boards of the World Bank and the International Monetary Fund incorporate voting rights in proportion to the amount of finance deposited by member countries. Therefore, the USA has always had the largest vote with not only the biggest deposits but also, until 1971, a currency linked to the value of gold. Britain made the second largest contribution until the 'economic miracles' of Germany and Japan, and recovery in France too, enabled these countries to command a bigger slice of international finance and more votes. The creation of the World Bank was an opportunity to structure international finance on lines alternative to the existing orthodoxy of the capitalist world-economy (Brett 1985: 74). But it has nevertheless remained a conservative body, mainly due to underfinancing connected with the USA's adherence to market principles and avoidance of interventionist policies. By the same token, the shortage of resources has been counteracted by the encouragement of international borrowing from commercial banks with the World Bank providing pilot loans and acting as guarantor (Ashworth 1975: 275). This also accords with the principles of modernization theory in the sense that World Bank policy has supplied finance for public-sector infrastructure to promote conditions suitable for self-sustaining private-sector investment. Thus the World Bank may be seen to operate fairly clearly within Western class (capitalist) society's separation of polity and economy, translated globally into nation-state system and capitalist world-economy. World Bank finance is given to nation-states in order that they may attract investment through the capitalist world-economy.

Initially, World Bank lending was intended to assist in the reconstruction of Europe, but even then the USA's contribution was parsimonious with many American politicians of the opinion that the end of the war represented the end of the commitment. Americans at home had prospered during the hostilities, enjoying an economic boom as a result of the war effort, and public opinion showed that they were not inclined to share their good fortune with the rest of the world. But with the growing realization of how badly Europe had been devastated, and of how real the threat from the Soviet Union appeared, the finance was stepped up and the Marshall Aid programme introduced in 1948. This was offered to both East and West Europe in the post-war division but the Soviet Union rejected what it regarded as an obvious capitalist 'carrot' (Kennedy 1988: 376–7). Marshall Aid gave rise to the Organization for European Economic Co-operation (OEEC) and in 1961, with recovery achieved, this became the Paris-based Organization for Economic Co-operation and Development (OECD), which acts as an economic monitoring organization for the advanced industrial nations of the West. Of even greater significance was a parallel development, the foundation of a customs union and a coal and steel community within continental Europe which, with the Treaty of Rome in 1957, gave rise to the European Economic Community (EEC). This is dedicated to economic and political union within Europe and, beginning with a core of six countries not at first including Britain, the membership has gradually been increased to the present level. With greater emphasis on political union it is now known simply as the European Community (EC) and there is much further expansion in prospect from the 'outer seven' European Free Trade Association (EFTA) countries and from the former state socialist countries of Eastern Europe.

In the wider world, with the granting of constitutional independence to the European colonies from 1947 onwards, there arose a whole new range of demands upon the World Bank for economic aid to 'developing countries'. In 1956 the International Finance Corporation was set up as an investing agency for this purpose, but still the funds were never large enough. For the poorest countries, larger resources were provided from 1960 by the International Development Association and loans are on easier terms with less rigorous standards of creditworthiness (Ashworth 1975: 276). There are also a number of UN regional economic commissions and loosely connected regional banks modelled on the World Bank, principally the African, Asian and Inter-American Development Banks. These sources of development assistance are normally referred to under the heading of multilateral aid, signifying that the finance comes from more than one country. Realistically, however, financed at the levels they have been, the World Bank and its associates could never hope to satisfy the growing demands of the Third World, even at the level of pump-priming exercises for free-market investment. Consequently, a supplementary series of national development agencies were set up by the industrialized countries, leading examples of which are the US Agency for International Development (AID), the British Overseas Development Administration (ODA) and the German Ministry for Economic Co-operation. These sources are known generally as bilateral aid but the channels are extremely varied and not necessarily focused entirely on any one government agency.

Moreover, the promise of aid can quite clearly operate as a useful instrument of diplomacy and as an indirect means to boost exports for the donor country through the attachment of conditions to loans. An important and overriding point, and a reminder that they operate within the capitalist world-economy, is that aid from 'official' agencies is seldom a gift but normally has to be repaid with interest, often at the full market rate. It is the voluntary agencies or non-government organizations (NGOs), such as Christian Aid, Oxfam, the Save the

Children Fund, etc., which dispense aid as a gift and they depend for their finance upon public subscription. Consequently, their mode of operation is different because, as non-government agencies, they can, to some extent, bypass government bureaucracy in the recipient country to install and supervise their own projects. There is a clear implication here that aid through official channels is often slow, inefficiently applied and even diluted through the relatively high levels of endemic corruption that tend to exist in the Third World.

The International Monetary Fund was intended to do a different job. Stated simply, whilst the World Bank granted development loans, the IMF was intended to maintain stability in international exchange by providing relief for weak currencies and preventing collapses of confidence which might precipitate a 'domino effect' internationally. Nevertheless, over the years the distinction between the two has become blurred as international finance has become increasingly complex. Eventually, even the USA found it increasingly difficult to maintain, virtually single-handedly, the underwriting of international exchange, and during the late 1960s the US government's Pearson Commission investigated the problem. Its report sealed the fate of the Bretton Woods arrangements as they were originally conceived, and the end of dollar–gold convertibility was announced by US President Richard Nixon in 1971. International finance was as a result plunged into a new phase of floating exchange rates, which have in fact pertained ever since (see chapter 10). The IMF was forced to change its mode of operating and a notable outcome was the establishment of Special Drawing Rights (SDRs) to member states. Brett (1985: 121) suggests that these were intended to operate as an extra form of international money created by political agreement which would constitute a form of intervention in the capitalist world-economy. But, amidst the economic turmoil of the 1970s and 1980s, these rights have formed only a tiny proportion of all international exchanges, and international finance has increasingly come directly from the private-sector money markets and therefore the commercial banks (see also chapter 10).

Perhaps the most important point to grasp from the operation of the IMF is that, as with the World Bank, its assistance comes only with conditions. In other words, any interventions that the IMF makes are aimed at what, through its policies, it interprets as misguided amongst the economic problems of its 'clients'. Like the World Bank, it might have had a more imaginative and more expansive role in the world-economy, but its major shareholders, the advanced industrial nations, have been unwilling to provide sufficient funds for the IMF to offer anything other than limited, short-term financing (Brett 1985: 72). Governments which draw upon its resources have been required to submit their economic plans for approval and when these have not conformed to established IMF norms, modifications have normally been required. Brett argues that because of the nature of IMF financing, such modifications tend to take the form of reductions in consumption rather than increases in investment. Even a big power may have demands put upon it in this way, as when sterling required support in the mid 1970s, and Britain's Labour government of the time was made to change some aspects of its predominantly interventionist policies. The Bretton Woods economic orthodoxy has been enforced in such cases precisely because it is seen as 'economic reality' in a world-economy based upon the capitalist economic mechanism. Furthermore it is entirely in keeping with the principles of modernization theory that these organizations should provide finance for the kind of public sector-infrastructure that is seen to 'modernize' society and produce incentives for 'achievement' through-private sector enterprise.

Finally, this section would be incomplete without mention of the missing third arm of what was intended to be a triumvirate of global economic organizations. The proposed International Trade Organization (ITO) never came into being despite the fact that agreement was reached in principle at the Havana Conference on Trade and Employment in 1948. In the original Bretton Woods arrangements it was intended that the ITO should monitor and where necessary intervene in international trade to undertake the removal of discriminatory structures, especially those in the form of European colonial preferences which annoyed the US government so much. Ashworth (1975: 278) is of the opinion that the ITO was unacceptable to the European colonial powers because its proposed introduction was not gradual enough. The USA wanted change right away but the Europeans, releasing their colonies only with reluctance, argued that they had to have time to adjust. After independence the former colonies themselves might have benefited from an organization set up to combat protectionism by Europeans, especially since the extraction of minerals and cash crops forms the basis of their economy. It is further revealing of the complexities of the capitalist world-economy that an arrangement which might have benefited the Third World would probably have disadvantaged Europe but favoured the USA. By 1950, however, attempts to float the ITO had been abandoned in the face of US insistence on market policies against European determination to include intervention (Brett 1985: 75). In its place there has been a series of conferences devoted to General Agreements on Tariffs and Trade which, Bailey (1989: 4) observed, 'is not a UN-related agency but could become one if an appropriate organization were created to administer the Agreement'. At GATT conferences there have been genuine attempts to provide a measure of relief for Third World countries against protectionism amongst the industrialized nations. Progress has often been in response to initiatives launched by individual statesmen or governments, as with the 'Kennedy round' of tariff cutting between 1964 to 1967, proposed by US President John F. Kennedy but negotiated after his assassination. The 1973–9 'Tokyo round' of negotiations produced a formal principle of preferential treatment in favour of and between developing countries as a 'permanent legal feature' (Brett 1985: 213). But a more recent series, the 'Uruguay round', ended more or less in deadlock in 1990.

The concept of 'unequal exchange' is significant here. The Third World has to import at market prices the technology and expertise which it lacks but is unable to produce itself. This can only be financed by selling cash crops and raw material commodities for hard currency, but the price obtained is determined by international commodity markets which are located in Western financial centres. These respond to economic pressures including patterns of mass consumption in the West, and in order to remain competitive the industrialized countries must obtain raw materials as cheaply as possible. Selective tariffs complete the picture by ensuring that only those Third World products which are of most advantage to the West can be imported at competitive prices, whilst other products attract heavier import duties. The result is a vicious circle whereby the Third World has little option but to sell its raw-material products relatively cheaply, but at the same time buy finished-product imports relatively expensively. In this lies the meaning of the term, unequal exchange, and GATT has been, at best, only partially effective against it. Ashworth (1975: 279) sums this up by suggesting that GATT policies could not produce results on their own without additional support for the shaky economies of the Third World countries whose trade GATT was intended to liberalize. In other words, if the World Bank had the determination and resources to intervene in the international economy then GATT might be more effective. But significant intervention has been anathema to Western financial leadership, and the avoidance of it is consistent with the separation of polity and economy in Western development. It has meant that whereas the aborted International Trade Organization or even the substitute GATT conferences might have acted as a moderating influence between First and Third Worlds, international trade has instead, been dominated by private-sector operations, particularly in the form of the transnational corporations.

Transnational corporations

Throughout this book my intention is to build up a picture of global institutions as structural forms which enable certain social, political and economic activities to take place, but restrain others. This is intended to address the one-sided approaches of modernization theory, with its optimistic view of development, and dependency theory, with its pessimistic view. Immanuel Wallerstein's historical analysis of the capitalist world-economy underlines the concept of core and periphery whilst drawing attention to the form of organization originally responsible for the transfer of resources from one to the other, the long-distance trading company. The celebrated examples of the Dutch *Vereenigde Oost-Indische Compagnie* and the British East India Company were described in part II, but there were several other less prominent examples operating out of other European states. These were not only trading companies, but instruments of empire. These organizations enabled certain developments in social, political and economic institutions to take place whilst constraining Western society and its colonies to ways of operating which became institutionalized over time.

After the Industrial Revolution, however, the emphasis in economic activity was moved from trade to manufacturing and, with advancing technology, the growth of manufacturing organization can be traced through from small workshops to factories and on to large plants. The initial principle of increased scale in manufacturing can be illustrated by innovations in the spinning of yarn for textiles such as Arkwright's 'water-frame' (patented in 1769) and Crompton's 'mule' (1779). These could not be accommodated in existing domestic workshops and required purpose-built factories (Mathias 1969). Moreover, with the widespread adoption of mass production during the early twentieth century, the need for ever-larger plants and organizational structures to exploit international markets becomes obvious. As a means to amass capital for specific ventures some form or other of the joint-stock company had existed since the middle ages. There were for instance the Venetian *partes* or shares in the voyage of a trading galley (see chapters 4 and 6). But during the second half of the nineteenth century, the legal concept of limited liability was introduced whereby investors could not be held liable for debts incurred beyond the extent of their original investment or shareholding. The company with limited liability, has in its various forms, spread the burden of investment, made shareholding more attractive and, as a consequence, enabled greater concentrations of capital to be formed. On the basis of the popularity of this form of investment, markets in capital (stocks and shares) were created in all the industrialized countries. The resulting increase in business activity enabled a greater division of labour to take place with more specializations and economies of scale so that through a process of concentration some local companies grew into national companies and some of these developed into international companies.

In the twentieth-century capitalist world-economy based upon mass production, mass communication and mass consumption, further development has depended upon the aggregation and rationalization of commodity supply and market demand. It is in this process that the transnational corporation derives its rationale. The principle is that production is organized globally according to where supplies of raw material and labour and access to product markets can most advantageously be found. There are limitations to the physical location of raw materials and human populations and there are contrived limitations in the fiscal policies of nation-states which enforce duties, excises, tariffs and taxes on goods which cross their borders. However, as several observers have pointed out, where goods and finance cannot be transferred with a satisfactory return on capital through 'official' channels, transnational corporations are able to resort at least in part to 'transfer pricing' and other paper transactions through 'unofficial' channels within their own transnational structure (cf. Hoogvelt 1978: 85–8). John Scott (1979: 166) describes this as 'the discretionary pricing in intra-company transfers of goods and services with little regard for market criteria'. In other words, whenever it is confronted with difficulty in transferring profits normally, a transnational corporation may set prices at artificial levels for the transfer of goods between subsidiaries thus adjusting the flow of capital to achieve a similar objective. All transnational corporations are in a sense national corporations in that they have headquarters in one particular country. Profits must ultimately be remitted there for distribution to shareholders and there may be various kinds of regionalized investment flows too.

Strategic decisions emanate from these headquarters and in fact transnational corporations are generally characterized as having a three-tier decision-making structure, as follows:

International headquarters: strategic decisions.
Continental centres: decisions of coordination.
National branches: day-to-day decisions.

This type of company is in effect an international matrix of 'profit centres', each one being a segment of business activity coordinated into an overall plan for the global production and marketing of a range of products or services. Within this matrix of profit centres only a certain number may be expected or predicted to produce bad results, or fail completely, during any particular period and overall a successful financial outcome is made much more probable. In this way, rational calculation in the capitalist business organization, as identified by Max Weber (1978: 107–9), is further extended.

A transnational corporation may also use its divisional structure, interlocked with dependent suppliers and distributors, to take advantage of varying marketing conditions in different parts of the world. This principle can be applied to all commodities purchased, including labour, and to all products sold. For instance, where relatively high selling prices are supportable in a particular market supplies can be brought in from areas of high labour costs and, by the same principle, where competition is fiercest supplies can be brought in from areas where labour costs are low. So-called consumer-durable products with multiple components are not normally manufactured exclusively in any one country and typically transnational corporations engaged in mass production have established coordinated networks for the supply and assembly of components. Partially manufactured products are finally assembled at strategic points in a manufacturing network, which may come to resemble a globally dispersed production line. In this way, alternative component supply routes and centres of assembly may be built into the system so that problems of economy or labour relations in any one country need not bring global production to a halt.

An archetypal example of this is the motor-car manufacturing company established by Henry Ford. It was founded before the First World War on the basis of the mass production of a 'world-car', the Model 'T' Ford, which was assembled from identical sets of parts, wherever there was a market for it. Later, the simplicity of this arrangement was disrupted by different tastes and demands in different parts of the world. Ford of America concentrated on big cars for that continent, whilst Ford of Britain supplied the British Empire, and Ford of Germany, the mainland of Europe. But more recently, heightened competition, especially from Japanese car manufacturers, coupled with the need to cut costs and energy consumption, have made it desirable to bring back the world-car concept. Current Ford models are manufactured in basically the same form the world over and parts or even whole cars can be shipped about between Ford plants with relative ease, given advanced transport and communication methods. In an extreme example, which serves to highlight the principle, the price competition from Japanese companies in Scandinavia during the mid 1980s became so severe that it was confronted by importing into that market Ford Escorts assembled in Brazil with much lower labour costs. This illustrates perfectly an extended capacity for the division of labour through the transnational corporations. Furthermore, the globalization of production and even of production lines is another demonstration of changed time and space parameters through the global systems of an inter-societal system.

Nation and nationalism in a nation-state system

The material presented in this chapter so far illustrates the concentration and growth of scale in social, political and economic institutions during the second half of the twentieth century, with distinct global systems providing the over-arching structures of the contemporary world. The nation-state system consists primarily of conjunctions of social and political activity anchored within specific territorial borders, whilst major conjunctions in the capitalist world-economy are the transnational corporations as free-floating amalgamations of productive or service activity. This is not to say that nation-states are completely excluded from economic activity. They do intervene in some areas as well as attempting to coordinate and regulate the economy within the confines of their territorial borders, but this is virtually always subject to constraints imposed through the broader workings of the capitalist world-economy. Nor is it to say that transnational corporations do not influence political activity for, just as clearly, one of the most powerful enabling factors in the fortunes of nation-state government is the participation of transnational corporations in the economy. Nevertheless, the separation of political institutions (public-sector) from economic institutions (private-sector) characterizes the way in which the capitalist economic mechanism has been harnessed in the growth of the Western nation-states. This arrangement has served to keep public citizenship rights in the polity insulated from private ownership rights in the economy.

However, whilst the constitution of nation-states within the nation-state system implies precise formal definitions of nationality, these do not necessarily coincide with their citizen's own ideas of nation and nationhood. Nation-states are quite clearly institutionalized arrangements for the control and administration of populations within clearly defined territories but separately the term, nation, may have connotations of primordial ethnic origins. Moreover, definitions of nationalism formally established as part of the make-up of a nation-state will not necessarily fit in with people's subjective notions of their origins and group identity. As a consequence of this, alternative and minority feelings of nationalism are a prominent feature of contemporary society and they are often nurtured and propagated by organizations antithetical to the legitimated authority of nation-state government. Therefore, there is a need to consider nationalism as a separate institution.

In *The Ethnic Origins of Nations*, Anthony D. Smith (1986) rejects one-sidedness in the definition of nationhood either as a 'modernist' theory, in which the formation of nations is attributed to broad changes contingent upon the development of industrial capitalism, or as a 'primordialist' and 'perennialist' theory in which it is viewed as the naturally produced extension of kinship. Of the 'modernists', Ernest Gellner (1983) sees nationalism particularly as part of the process of 'Westernization', whilst Clifford Geertz (1963) has suggested that in modern industrial societies nationalist sentiments have in various ways replaced community sentiments as part of the individual's primordial need for ontological security. Smith advocates the use of the term, *ethnie* or ethnic community, to describe origins traced back to ethnic roots, and attributes the existence of modern nations to processes of reconstruction by elite groups on the basis of perceived 'myths, memories, values and symbols' from the past. *Ethnie*, then becomes a term for collective cultural units and sentiments derived from previous eras (Smith 1986: 13), upon which Western culture has had an eroding effect, whilst an effective definition of modern nationalism should include continuity that transcends the sociologist's conventional dichotomy between traditional (agrarian) and modern (industrial) societies. Anthony Giddens believes that a multi-dimensional approach is necessary for an adequate understanding of nationalism in the face of tendencies to conflate separate and discrete aspects, particularly in the literature of modernization theory which 'was prone to assimilate the concepts of nation-state and nationalism' (1981: 191). He specifies that an adequate account of nationalism in the context of the Western nation-state and citizenship needs to illuminate its political character, ideological characteristics, psychological dynamics and symbolic content rather than accentuate any one of these exclusively (1985: 215–16).

Nationalism, then, is to a great extent a matter of the construction of national identity for political ends and it involves the manipulation of sentiments and symbolic contents. But, whilst certain claims to nationhood are based upon genuine and pure ethnic foundations, others are just as certainly the subject of contrived and contemporary aspirations. More difficult to disentangle, however, are those instances when ideas of ancient ethnic origins are reincarnated to reinforce contemporary political movements. Here the distinction between historical precedent and present-day expedient may be difficult to discern, particularly when concrete evidence is scarce. Ethnicity is a long-term anthropological process and deductively the further one delves into the distant past the more ethnic strains will converge upon each other. Therefore the terms, nation and nationhood, remain problematic concepts implying by definition notions of unbroken continuity existing in the context of modernity and the nation-state. Nationalism, by contrast, has a pragmatic connotation and the propagation of nationalism and nationalist movements may be traced to clearly defined periods of history and in this way 'outbreaks' of nationalism are linked to specific combinations of social, political and economic events.

In cases where nationalism has been used to form or regenerate a nation-state and influence the course of its historical progress, most writers have observed its 'janus-faced' nature. As Karl Deutsch (1969) asserted, nationalism can be developed as a movement to provide democratic rights generally, but it can equally be developed to restrict rights to particular national or ethnic groups. Like all social institutions it is a force for both enablement and constraint. In fact, the more one examines the historical detail of the establishment of nationalism the more one finds exclusivist tendencies. In what is one of the most notorious examples, the government of Nazi Germany came to be constituted by a fiercely nationalistic politico-military movement which mobilized popular support and even participation to pursue the notion of *lebensraum* for a brutally exclusive conception of the 'master race'. But there are many lesser examples and, as mentioned in chapter 4, we should not lose sight of the fact that even such an archetypal liberal–democratic document as the American Declaration of Independence in its provisions for 'equal citizenship' initially excluded, in practice, women, slaves and several ethnic groups (Karst 1989). The history of the West over the past two centuries has demonstrated that society does not proceed along an evolutionary pathway but in directions determined by human agency which is just as capable of regression and reaction in terms of liberal–democratic ideals as it is of progress. An obvious but important implication of this is that good government includes a caveat to the effect that democracy is never automatically guaranteed, and that, particularly in a global system of separately governed nation-states, vigilance against the 'janus faced' nature of nationalism must be maintained.

Reflections: economic concentration and political diversity

In this and earlier chapters I have emphasized that the development and spread of the nation-state was accompanied by the intensification of a capitalist world-economy. Each are manifestations of the rise of the West and the development of an inter-societal system. The nation-state system reflects the fact that in capitalist societies social and political institutions remain in the public sector, whilst the capitalist world-economy reflects the fact that economic institutions remain for the most part in the private sector. The second half of the twentieth century has witnessed the acceleration of economic concentration particularly in the form of transnational corporations. These operate across the borders of nation-states and use the world-economy to best advantage in terms of the capitalist ideal of the pursuit of economic efficiency and wealth creation. However, whilst they are transnational in terms of their operations they remain national in terms of capital accumulation and flows of capital. Each has a home country and for the majority this is the USA, but for virtually all it is the capitalist West with the addition over the past few decades of Japan and a few other newly industrializing countries (NICs). Consequently, there is a great deal of inequality in the distribution of their benefits and much uneven development in the world as a result. This uneven progress has usually been portrayed in terms of developed and developing worlds, but beyond these simplistic and sweeping distinctions economic concentration also creates distinctive zones of relative wealth and deprivation within the borders of nation-states. It is not just a question of the location of industry but also of the concentration of investment and of capital accumulation. The principle of 'core' and 'periphery', whilst not unproblematic (see chapter 2), can be applied to all parts and all levels of the capitalist world-economy.

The final issue in this chapter is the problematic relationship between nationalist identity, defined ethnically and/or politically, and levels of economic concentration. One of the most effective stimulants for oppositional nationalism is economic exploitation. This played a part in the American revolution whereby the people of the United States sought to free themselves and their country not only from political domination but also from economic exploitation by Britain. Comparable considerations have been present in all anti-colonial movements and are also factors in alternative nationalism ranged against the nation-state from within. Separatist movements represent peripheral or oppositional nationalism involving the demand for the division of the constituted political unit. These movements harness, principally, motives of a political nature, but virtually always there is awareness of economic deprivation, too. For instance, the Basque people have a long tradition of ethnic separation but, nevertheless, became incorporated as part of the modernization process into the Spanish nation-state. During the mid twentieth century, resistance to that incorporation became translated through the civil war during the Franco regime into an acute awareness of economic discrimination. In response, the current separatist movement has in many ways idealized the notion of Basque nationality and the goal of economic self-sufficiency is a powerful accompaniment to the political aspirations. Spain has now joined the European Community and as a result there are potentially three levels to the debate: the supra-national, the national and the intra-national. This may be a general pointer for the future, and it is perhaps significant that as the EC advances to economic and political unity, there are movements of peripheral nationalism which seek to destabilize and decentralize its component nation-states. This phenomenon is not, of course, confined to the West for, as the Soviet Union's liberalization process has continued, irresistible demands for independence have arisen from most of its Soviet republics. Meanwhile, in Eastern Europe, independence from Soviet domination has only lead to more demands from ethnic minorities, as for instance the pressure from ethnic Hungarians in Romania after the removal of the Ceaucescu dictatorship. This may be taken as a manifestation of people's determination to structure their own societies in the face of increasing concentration and the global institutions of an inter-societal system, which, in a book orientated towards structuration theory, is a suitable moment to conclude this chapter.

8

The Soviet Union and the Second World: State Socialism as an Alternative Pathway of Development

The strategic wartime discussions between Roosevelt, Churchill and Stalin and the outcome of the Second World War presented the Soviet Union with the chance to build a *cordon sanitaire* along its Western borders. At the beginning of the war Stalin had obtained from Hitler, as part of their temporary pact, the Baltic republics of Estonia, Latvia and Lithuania. Then, during the course of the war, the Soviet Union seized part of northern Iran to add to its Islamic republics which were formerly part of the tsarist empire. Finally, the Red Army's advance into Berlin and beyond assured the Soviet Union of a position of dominance in Eastern Europe. These historical developments produced a number of societies in which the institutions of Soviet state socialism were reproduced, but to understand properly the model on which they were based we need to consider the formation of the Soviet Union itself as an isolated state socialist country in a world almost consistently hostile to it. Arguably the establishment of state socialism as a concrete form of socialist society has more to do with historical expedience than the application of historical materialist principles, yet the Soviet Union is the original example of long-term, large-scale socialist institutions in practice.

The creation of state socialism

It is often recounted that Marx's three best hopes for a full-scale socialist revolution were: Britain because it was the first industrial nation; France because of its revolutionary pedigree; and Germany because the first Marxist political party was founded there. Indeed the Sozialdemokratische Partei Deutschlands (SPD), developed largely through Karl Kautsky's interpretation of 'scientific' Marxism, to a great extent provided the model for the organization of socialist politics and trade unions throughout northern Europe, including Russia. By 1912 it had 110 representatives in the Reichstag but in 1914 the possibility of a workers' 'international' arising from these successful beginnings hinged on the question of whether the European working class would refuse to fight against each other in the First World War. But, despite the efforts of the Spartacist splinter group which included the Russian emigre, Rosa Luxemburg, even the majority of the leadership of the SPD supported the German government in the war, and the social democratic parties in effect embarked upon a course of compromise to enter government via the ballot box. Instead of remaining the agents of Marx's international socialist ideals they became effectively contained within the existing political framework of the nation-state. Meanwhile, in Russia, events were taking a different course. As John Hall (1986: 11) puts it, whereas Marx 'was essentially democratic and rather naive about power relations, [Lenin] was elitist and thoroughly in tune with the harsher realities of power'. This is reflected in the development of Soviet state socialist institutions as alternatives to those of Western liberal–democratic capitalism.

In February 1917 Russia was at war with Germany and the tsarist administration had broken down in the face of unrest. Yet the provisional government formed in its place was at first led by non-socialists, as Theda Skocpol (1979: 208) points out. Only in April of that year did the Mensheviks (those social democrats opposed to Lenin's breakaway from the German mass-movement model in 1903) join the coalition along with some other socialists. They held to the 'scientific socialist' belief that since Russia was only relatively recently freed from feudalism it needed to develop capitalism before it could move on to socialism. However, this government's term in office was short because it lacked support even amongst the working-class which, in any case, was a tiny minority in Russia at the time. Meanwhile, the revolutionary Marxists, or Bolsheviks, eschewed the coalition and were building up support in soldiers' and workmen's councils called 'soviets'. Their leader, Vladimir Illyich Ulyanov, known to us as Lenin, returned from exile, and on 25 October 1917 seized power in Petrograd (before 1914 called St Petersburg, and later Leningrad). But the failure of the concept of an international socialist working class meant that the Marxist society which the revolutionaries set about building would, in effect be one nation-state, isolated within an existing inter-societal system through its withdrawal from the capitalist world-economy. Indeed the name Soviet Union signifies socialism in one country and it is this isolation which explains the high priority attached to the principle of support for foreign socialist movements in the Soviet communist party's formal constitution. This has been a significant factor in Western suspicions, imagined and real, of Soviet expansionism ever since the revolution and especially in relation to the NATO–Warsaw Pact confrontation after the Second World War.

The October Revolution was actually a politico-military coup during an uprising that had already begun, and it finally split the already demoralized Russian army. So an early move on the part of the new leadership had to be a peace settlement with Germany – reached in March 1918, with the loss of some territory from the old tsarist empire. After that, the real threat came from the White armies which were counter-revolutionary groups led by the officer corps, and supported by men and arms from several Western countries. The defeat of these called for an expanded Red Army, which also provided an extended means of coercion in establishing a centralized state amongst Russia's sprawling territories. The *Cheka* or secret police, later to be called the KGB, also dates from this period as the nucleus of a comprehensive system of surveillance in a highly centralized party–state system. This was the period referred to as 'war communism' and it has been estimated that it cost several million lives, the first of a series of huge losses during the development of Soviet society. The constituent assembly of government was disbanded and a party-dominated state system established which, it should be emphasized, has proved to be the model for all countries following in these footsteps of socialist revolution.

The main task confronting Lenin and the communist party leadership was one of organization over a huge geographical area, containing a large, ethnically varied and widely dispersed population, when the administrative capacity of the party was, in fact, minimal. This question could not be resolved overnight, and in the meantime it was important that the momentum of revolutionary change was maintained by whatever draconian methods were necessary. However, once created, the institutions of surveillance and control proved difficult to dispense with in the face of a continuing series of fundamental problems. When the White armies had been defeated, the inertia and hostility of the peasantry had to be faced. They made up the vast majority of the population but played little part in the revolution and had little understanding of it other than that they had been encouraged to seize land from landlords and rich farmers. After the emancipation of the serfs in 1861, the tsars had borrowed capital from abroad in order to improve agriculture but this was not an option open to the new leadership. Moreover, since the revolution was based upon the Marxist principle of a workers' rebellion against capitalism, the highest priority was attached to the transformation of the Soviet Union into an industrial power capable of sustaining socialism in a world that remained dominated by capitalism.

After Lenin's death in 1924, Stalin and his supporters took over the leadership, stepped up the priority of economic growth through industrialization and enlarged the party–state mechanism, with trade unions, social services and agriculture all becoming its instruments. David Lane (1978: 66–7) points out that in the face of disastrous economic decline resulting from the period of 'war communism', the first of the five-year plans (1928–33) achieved an extraordinary level of economic growth estimated as about 15 per cent, which was unprecedented, even in capitalist countries. But this plan also involved the enforced organization of rural peasants and twenty-five million private farms were reduced to a quarter of a million collectives without any immediate improvement in productivity (Hall 1986: 194). The grain harvest in 1933 actually produced five million tons less than in 1928, but the share taken by the state for industrial workers was doubled, such was the priority attached to the support of urban industrialization. The collectivization of agriculture was seen merely as an intermediate measure until all land could be brought under the direct control of the Ministry of Agriculture, but because of the scale of the undertaking the process was necessarily a long one. It could only be achieved with a high level of coercion – the 'terror' as it has been referred to – and the cost in human life to the peasantry was perhaps as high as five million.

Industrial workers have been regarded as the vanguard of the socialist society but economic growth was concentrated in energy extraction, producer technology and basic production rather than in consumer goods for the workers. These priorities have resulted in the high proportions of labour-intensive industry and agricultural labour which are still clearly visible in the Soviet Union. There has been no free market for labour because under centralized planning, wage rates and bonuses have been manipulated in order to maintain employment patterns within the parameters of the national plan and to avoid unemployment. Adam Westoby (1981: 346–53) suggests that the result of this, interpreted in Marx's own terms, in that 'the worker's estranged labour stands against him, not as capital but as the possession and instrument of the state'. Whether or not this is accepted, the Soviet labour process has allowed the USSR to rival the USA in armaments and space technology, so producing the two superpowers of the post-war global military order, whilst providing no competition in terms of consumption patterns and broad standards of living. Each system is geared to the accumulation of wealth and power but the organization and distribution is very different.

Westoby goes further, to suggest that Soviet society contains both socialist and capitalist elements. Central planning (the socialist element) exists at the same time as commodity circulation (the capitalist element) in a situation of dependence between the two, but the former prevents the latter from reaching levels that are commonplace in the West. The inadequacy of production and the imbalances in its organization are often due to bureaucratic mismanagement and what Westoby refers to as 'the hypertrophy of the state'. Under capitalism, value is realized and distributed through market mechanisms, whereas under state socialism it is realized through central planning and distributed mainly back into production. In one respect the relative efficiency of either the capitalist or the state socialist system remains open to debate since both have demonstrated that they can achieve technological advances and enormous military power. But only capitalism has produced high levels of distribution in consumer goods, and, on this basis, the contrast between the West and the Soviet Union has obviously been a critical factor in the social and political movement towards *glasnost, perestroika* and the fundamental changes which have taken place in the Soviet Union and Eastern Europe from 1989 onwards. In the mid 1980s, Howard Davis and Richard Scase (1985: 86) suggested that a leading question must be, 'How long can rapid growth be sustained ... before low living standards generate serious social discontent?' The events of the Gorbachev era, involving the introduction of the market economy, would seem to provide the answer. This illustrates that, even in the most rigidly surveilled social institutions, people have the capacity to make a difference in the course of their day-to-day social interactions and that this can amount to the most dramatic episodes of social change. By mid 1991 a coup by communist hardliners against the reforms in the Soviet Union was doomed to failure almost as soon as it had begun.

Society without the market mechanism: the monolithic planned economy

In capitalist society the principal economic mechanism is the market upon which all aspects of business enterprise are based. In the development of Western civilization this has proved to be a very dynamic form, providing substantial wealth creation within the structure of a capitalist world-economy. In principle, the market mechanism is applied to all commodities, including labour, and economic decisions are taken according to the fluctuations of market prices subject to trends of supply and demand. When this form of economic organization is dispensed with, as it was in the Soviet Union from 1917, something has to take its place as a basis upon which economic decisions are made and production is carried on. In a society dedicated to the initial building of socialism, the leadership and organization, according to Marxist theory, is provided by the 'dictatorship of the proletariat' but the precise working of this is something which Marx never adequately explained. In the Soviet Union the revolution was carried through by a vanguard party claiming to represent the working class, and the outcome was highly centralized party–state organization. In whatever direction state administration was extended, throughout the social structure into industry and agriculture, the communist party ensured that its representatives were installed in order to guard against divergence from political objectives. In Marxist theory the state structure is supposed eventually to wither away as production is made to satisfy human needs instead of responding to the capitalist market mechanism, but this was something else not clearly explained in Marx's writings.

David Lane and Felicity O'Dell (1978), using factory administration as an example, have depicted the basic structure of organization in the Soviet Union as three-cornered and this can be visualized as in figure 9. The state administration is at one corner, the communist party political organization at the second, and the trade union movement, *Trud*, at the third. This format has applied at all levels from the central administration in Moscow, through the administration of the republics and their regions, down to the factory, state farm or other type of organization. In other words, in the Soviet Union the state has been ubiquitous in the form of a bureaucratic hierachy, but equally the party has been omnipresent as an ideological watchdog. Wherever an element of social, political or economic organization exists it has been locked into a huge hierarchical and bureaucratic network and, as a crucial element of the party–state system, the representatives of the communist party have been connected in parallel through a shadow hierarchy of party membership. Therefore, with the party ruthlessly maintaining a monopoly of political power, its ideology has been hegemonic in the state bureaucracy. The third element, the trade union organization, has operated not as a challenge to management, as in the West, but as a mechanism for the distribution of housing and social welfare benefits according to state policies. As Davis and Scase (1985: 95–6) have pointed out, 'neither the party nor the trade union in the Soviet factory has a direct parallel in the West'. Party members have always been present to ensure that nothing has displaced the ideological goals which have, in official terms, unproblematically represented the interests of workers and society at large. In this way, the oppositional role of trade unions was removed in what was seen,

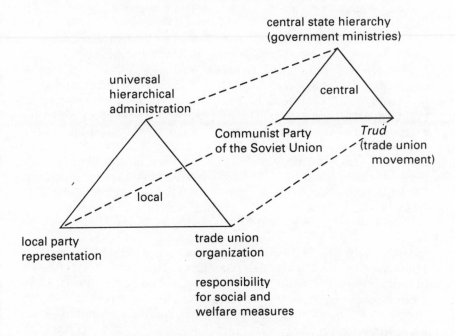

central state hierarchy
(government ministries)

universal
hierarchical
administration

central

Communist Party
of the Soviet Union

Trud
(trade union
movement)

local

local party
representation

trade union
organization

responsibility
for social and
welfare measures

Figure 9   Simple diagram of administrative format in the Soviet
Union depicting local representation linked to central
hierarchy (after Lane and O'Dell 1978)

in terms of Marxist ideology, as a non-antagonistic relationship
between employer and employee.

The structure of Soviet state organization has, therefore, been,
above all, monolithic. The term, Union of Soviet Socialist Republics
(USSR), refers to a collection of separate republics each subordinated
via the party–state network to Moscow. These republics contain a
variety of ethnic groupings, some from the old tsarist Muscovite
empire which derived its orthodox Christianity from Byzantium (see
chapter 4). From the fifteenth century, under such leaders as Ivan the
Great (1440–1505) and Peter the Great (1672–1725), the empire
expanded eastwards to cover the whole of central Asia and it includes
Islamic areas captured from the Ottoman Empire during that period.
Other possessions were acquired during the Second World War,
including, notably, the Baltic states of Estonia, Latvia and Lithuania.
Each republic has had a 'national' party organization but each has
been vetted and controlled from Moscow and, in practice, throughout
this huge territory of more than 250 million people, an attempt has
been made to run an enormous planned society.

In the desperate circumstances immediately after the revolution, the leadership under Lenin was forced to make compromises in which certain sectors of the economy were allowed to carry on responding to market forces. There followed from this the debate over Nikolai Bukharin's proposed 'market socialism' and Leon Trotsky's system of complete central planning. Stalin at first supported Bukharin opportunistically, but when he came to power in 1924 he adopted central planning, according to Hall (1986: 193), in 'a spirit all of his own'. From that time, the residual market mechanism was eschewed and the economy planned through a series of huge ministries. Principally, there was Gosplan, the All Union State Planning Committee with extensive regional subsidiaries; Gostsen which fixed prices in place of the market mechanism; and Stroibank, the investment bank for industry (Davis and Scase 1985: 93). For this reason the Soviet economy has often been called a 'command economy' and it was the sheer size of the undertaking that lead to the glaring inflexibilities, shortages, lack of coordination, corruption and wastage. Reports have been legion of Soviet enterprises having to employ unofficial *tolkachi* (full-time 'fixers') to chase up supply shortages and overcome them by whatever means appeared necessary (cf. Westoby 1981: 331). A complex official institutional structure was routinely reproduced, but the people involved proved adept at creating and reproducing unofficial institutions too. Additionally, such things as production figures were frequently falsified to fit in with state plans and, therefore, official statistics were often misleading and sometimes very far from the truth. This scale and pattern of organization applied not only to industry and agriculture but also to education, health and other state services. When all this is taken into account, therefore, references to the Soviet Union as a 'great experiment' assume their full meaning. It has been perhaps not so much an experiment in socialism as in large-scale centralized organization or, in Bruno Rizzi's (1985) terms, 'bureaucratic collectivism'. The obvious question arises as to whether socialism necessarily implies increased bureaucracy, as Max Weber predicted, but it is one that may never be answered conclusively in conceptual terms. However, the wholesale changes which took place in the Soviet Union and Eastern Europe from 1989 onwards may well be interpreted as an answer in practical terms.

In such a monolithic structure, officially dedicated to the building of a form of socialism which the mass of the population did not necessarily understand or desire, it was essential to maintain routinized practices of surveillance through a structure institutionalized throughout society and dedicated to ideological goals. In the Soviet Union the communist party organization placed members at all levels of society and with its de facto policing arm, the KGB, carried out the role assiduously. Allowance must be made for the tendency in Western reporting to emphasize the negative aspects of Soviet society, but Stalin's notorious 'Great Purge' of 1936–8 accounted for 70 per cent arrested or shot from the Central Committee elected in 1934 (Hall 1986: 194). This and the operation of the *gulag* labour camps have been fairly obviously only the more extreme examples of sanctions in a regime of vigorous and routinized surveillance of the subject population.

However, as with the *tolkachi* fixers in Soviet industry, so with the wider society, people as human agents created and maintained their 'unofficial' but equally institutionalized ways of dealing with such a frustrating and potentially draconian social system. The Soviet Union provides a further and rather different illustration of the capacity of people when they are viewed as agents in the day-to-day reproduction of society. Under the extreme inequalities of power that have pertained in the Soviet Union this has amounted to a range of outcomes including the maintenance of the status quo, but in the light of the changes that have taken place since 1989 it should also be seen in terms of broad social change. Economic crises may have prompted the party leadership from the top to permit forms of institutional change during the 1980s but the readiness of the Russian people to modify the routines of day-to-day life and admit all kinds of different institutional practices should not be neglected. Witness the speedy take-up during the early 1990s of all kinds of religious sects in place of the enforced atheism of the recent past.

The Soviet Union as a model for others: the extension of a Second World

The Soviet Union has served as a model for the subsequent establishment of other socialist societies. Those of Eastern Europe brought under the control of the Soviet Union as part of the Yalta agreement in 1944 can be unproblematically called 'Soviet-type societies' (Davis and Scase 1985: 109). However, the central importance of the party–state structure was still evident in Yugoslavia until the death of its post-war leader, Josip Tito, despite his successful political break with Moscow and opting out of the Soviet bloc. Furthermore, it is apparent in countries such as China, North Korea, Cuba, Vietnam and several other Third World examples, where Marxist regimes have come to power (see figure 10). Their histories and pathways of development are obviously different, but they face the same basic problem of providing a planned alternative to the capitalist economic mechanism. In principle, this is addressed by taking the Western model of the state with its responsibility for social and

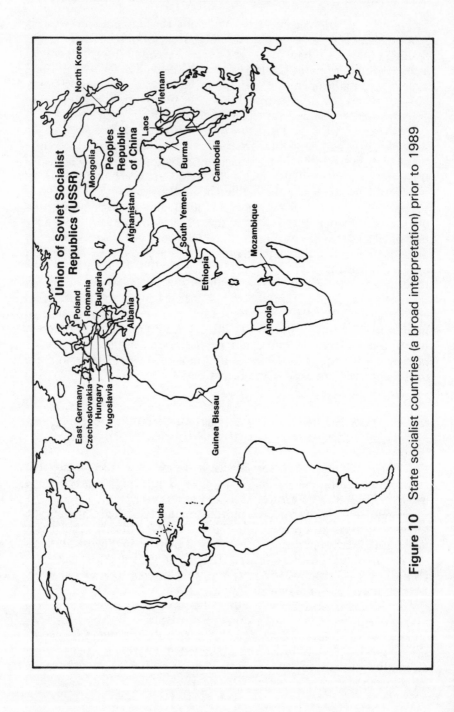

Figure 10 State socialist countries (a broad interpretation) prior to 1989

political institutions and extending that responsibility into economic institutions. The allocation process then becomes, in formal terms at least, based upon the needs of the people with use values given priority over exchange values, in accordance with Marxist principles. But the responsibility for achieving this goal is taken up by the communist party through the establishment and control of a highly centralized state structure and, thus, the party–state format becomes the modus operandi in both the guardianship of socialist ideology and the planning of the economy.

As an illustration of the practical dimension to socialist revolution, however, the case of Cuba in 1959 contains many ingredients which illustrate how the structuring of post–revolutionary institutions is carried out against a background of international relations and the global military order. The Cuban revolution was first and foremost a nationalist revolution against the tyrannical Batista dictatorship, but Fidel Castro's politico-military leadership was aided by Marxist, tacticians such as Ernesto Che Guevara, who, as a result of his principles and his actions, became a folk hero throughout Latin American revolutionary politics. Given the isolation in which the Communist Party of the Soviet Union was founded, socialist revolution in Cuba automatically qualified that country for economic and, potentially, military support, but it was the geographical location close to the coastline of the USA that made it especially sensitive. This brought events into the arena of global politics and strategically Cuba almost became a Soviet military base in the Cold War confrontation with the USA. As part of its retaliation the USA organized a trade embargo amongst its allies, and itself ceased buying Cuban sugar, the cash crop on which the Cuban economy had depended since Spanish colonial times. Not surprisingly, the Russians stepped in and subsequently maintained their buying price at a level substantially higher than the commodity price for sugar on world markets (Carciofi 1983: 207). At the same time, the Cuban economy was effectively committed to sugar production and the disposal of the crop to the USSR. Ironically, therefore, American reaction to the situation, based upon well instituted fears about the spread of communism in Latin America, contributed to making Cuba a Soviet ally. This confrontation between the USA and the USSR produced the Cuban Missile Crisis of 1962 which brought the world probably closer to nuclear war than it has ever been before or since (cf. Abel 1969). What might have been only a nationalist revolution was transformed into state socialism and Cuba became a member of the Council for Mutual Economic Assistance (CMEA or 'Comecon'). This is the Soviet bloc's economic community formed as an alternative to the West's Bretton Woods arrangements and specializing in commodity barter arrangements which have been of great help to a cash-crop economy like Cuba's. The USSR not only maintained a highly favourable price for Cuban sugar but also traded it for strategically important oil supplies. In return, troops from Cuba have since been deployed in various Third World revolutionary wars when it would have been politically unacceptable for Russian troops to be present.

For theorists and ideologists, the Cuban revolution served to extend the debate, which began with the Russian Revolution, as to whether a socialist revolution can take place in a country where industrial capitalism has not been developed. Marx's writings provide valuable critique of the development of the capitalist labour process, but his theory of social change based upon historical materialism presents a linear pathway to socialism. In each 'epoch', the relations of production are supposed to be developed to the full before revolutionary transition to the next stage can take place. In Russia, however, the capitalist industrial epoch had only recently begun when the revolution took place, and in Cuba it was completely absent in terms of broad employment patterns. Therefore, the question remains as to how the transition to socialism may be expected to take place successfully. Chapter 2 described the arguments of Latin American economists that the colonial phase was capitalist and therefore brought societies such as Cuba into the capitalist ambit, albeit in a dependent role. Also included was discussion of dependency theory and the concept of the capitalist world-economy in which the Western nations form the core (or metropolis) and the Third World, the periphery (or satellites). These ideas have been labelled 'neo-Marxist' by orthodox Marxists because in the analysis of capitalist exploitation they emphasize the core–periphery division on an equal basis to the quintessential class division. In terms of dependency theory, therefore, the absence of a properly formed working class in the Third World is no barrier to revolution if it is accepted that, through colonialism, these parts of the world have been rendered into a dependent position within the capitalist world-economy. The clear implication is that Third World countries are open to socialist revolution on Marxist principles without the prerequisite of capitalist industrialization. On the other hand, the experience of Cuba, as an example of the state socialist pathway of development, would seem to suggest a case of economic dependency upon the Soviet Union. Without the latter's support for its cash crop, sugar, and in the absence of any viable alternative buyer, Cuba's economy would surely have collapsed, as it may well do now that the post-1989 Soviet Union is no longer interested in maintaining such dependent relationships. During the 32nd anniversary in 1991 of the Cuban revolution, observers noted that Jose Marti, a nineteenth-century non-Marxist Cuban patriot, had been raised in status as nationalism was revived to counteract the decline of Marxism–Leninism. At approximately the same time, Angola and Mozambique announced moves away from the Soviet model and even the most isolated example, North Korea, has entered the first tentative negotiations with capitalist South Korea over reunification. Of the others, China appears to be the main bastion of Marxist–Leninist orthodoxy, displaying some determination whilst the 'old guard' of communist leadership remains alive, as the Tian An Men Square massacre indicated. Even in China, however, economic pressures have prompted the political leadership to relax economic restrictions and so it may be only a matter of time before the state withdraws substantially from the economy and allows full links with the capitalist world-economy.

Reflections: the maintenance of socialism?

In the late twentieth century it is unlikely that any credence can be attached to the maintenance of socialism in the orthodox terms of historical materialism. In the West, the social democratic and labour parties have found it impossible to maintain consistent majority support in elections whilst in the Soviet bloc the state socialist regimes have been maintained only with massive surveillance of the population and repression of opposition. When this has been relaxed huge demands for democracy have emerged. Moreover, all state socialist societies have produced inequalities and there is much evidence to support the arguments of Milovan Djilas (1966) or David Lane (1971) that the communist party elite had in effect taken the place of a capitalist elite in terms of access to privileged lifestyles. Furthermore, the ability of party members to influence the education system in favour of their children contributed to the reproduction of such an elite and to the maintenance of what would otherwise be regarded as bourgeois family patterns. Westoby (1981: 307–310) confirms the privileges of party membership and the luxurious lifestyles of communist leaders, a factor which became clear during the deposing of East European political leaders during 1989–90.

The counter-argument to this is that, in the Western case, the resilience of capitalism can be attributed to the effective maintenance of a 'dominant ideology' by an established and entrenched elite (cf. Abercrombie et al. 1980). This is taken to represent a much less extreme means of compulsion than in the Soviet Union, but one no less successful. Nevertheless it might reasonably be asked what advantages, if any, the state socialist societies have produced. Consideration must certainly be given to the distribution of welfare benefits which, from limited resources, has been impressive. Data from Cuba supports the argument that in such things as education, health service, gender equality, etc., advances have been made that are superior to those in neighbouring capitalist Latin American countries at a comparable level of development (cf. Kidron and Segal 1981: 44–50; Donahue 1986). These benefits are as much attributable to the elimination of the capitalist market mechanism in favour of mono-lithic planning as are the overall economic shortcomings of the state socialist model.

As the twentieth century draws to a close the Soviet Union has begun to liberalize after periods characterized by tyranny under Josef Stalin and corruption under Nikita Kruschev or Leonid Brezhnev. During the period of Kruschev's leadership a declaration was made that Soviet society had officially progressed from socialism to com-munism, but that seems part of a forlorn dream now. Subsequently policies of *perestroika* and *glasnost* have been introduced under a new style of leadership by Mikhail Gorbachev and during 1989 and 1990 the principle of monopoly political control was removed by commu-nists parties throughout the Soviet Union and Eastern Europe. Throughout the 1980s there had obviously been mounting economic problems, made worse by the institutionalized falsification that had become a feature of Soviet industry, and in May 1990 there came the official announcement that the Soviet union was abandoning mono-lithic economic planning and introducing the market mechanism into its economy. By May 1991 there was talk of a 'Grand Bargain' by which, in return for massive investment from the West, the Soviet parliament would for the first time allow wholly owned foreign firms to operate in the Soviet Union. It will be some time before the effects can be determined, but presumably in the long run it will mean direct links between the Soviet economy and the capitalist world-economy. It is revealing to consider Hall's (1986: 198) observation, made four or five years before, that the industrialization process in the USSR had enabled upward mobility to take place, so creating expectations in the society which at some point had to be met. Similarly, Davis and Scase (1985: 86) asked how long economic growth could be sustained, directed so overwhelmingly into industrial and military technology, before low living standards generated serious social discontent that even the Soviet party–state system could not contain. At the same time, Hall (p. 204) was able to express quite reasonable expectations against the emergence of parliamentary systems in Eastern Europe.

Thus it was justifiably with some amazement that, during the latter half of 1989, the world witnessed via the mass communications media of the global information system, the first tentative steps to democracy as they actually took place in Poland, Czechoslovakia, Hungary, East

Germany and Romania. Denied sustenance from Moscow, communist party regimes that had hitherto appeared well entrenched were swept aside virtually overnight following persistent mass demonstrations of dissatisfaction that had obviously been harboured for years (cf. Rothschild 1989). As part of this process, that supreme symbol of the Cold War, the Berlin Wall, was officially breached. Following this, the discovery of corruption and privilege on such a huge scale was seen to shock even hardened senior army officers in the countries involved and, although the long term outcome will not be apparent for some time, the further discrediting of state socialist systems seems likely. In 1989 the European Community, at its annual summit, responded to a French initiative and announced that it was setting up a European Bank for Reconstruction and Development with the precise purpose of helping to finance Eastern Europe's transition from state socialism. Such events will undoubtedly bring about a massive reassessment of socialism worldwide, and direct attention to limitations in Marx's writings at source. Westoby (1981: 346) argues that Soviet state socialist society contained both socialist and capitalist elements in the juxtaposition of centralized planning with commodity circulation but that the former prevented the latter from reaching the whole population. Marxist theory hinges on historical materialism and as such is economistic and seriously deficient in social and politico-military terms. As Hall (1986: 196) points out, this is mainly because 'Marx considered that the sole source of evil in human affairs resulted from economic exploitation by social class' and 'in consequence he had little conception of the need for restraints to be placed upon power.' Marx's writings produced brilliant insights into the development of capitalism and industrial society but historical materialism does not constitute an acceptable formula for the understanding of social change. In the case of the Russian Revolution, Lenin's theories were adopted to redress some of these deficiencies, but arguably the efficacy of this did not last far beyond the revolution. Massive compromises had to made with capitalist principles during the period of 'war communism' and 'war economy' and then with authoritarian rule and terror under Stalin's obsessive industrialization programmes. The writings of neither Marx nor Lenin contain theory capable of addressing the historical developments of these periods. The main contradictions in the state socialist societies are, firstly, between egalitarian principles and rigid hierarchical institutions and, secondly, between the socialization of production and the absence of democracy (Davis and Scase 1985: 87). Where socialism in any consistent form has been sustained it has been at the cost either of individual freedoms or of far-reaching compromises with the otherwise reviled capitalist system.

9

The Indentification of the Third World and the Recognition of Dependency

In chapter 6, I described how the European countries embarked upon successive phases of colonialism from the sixteenth century. The Portuguese and Spanish at first notionally divided the world up between themselves with the Treaty of Tordesillas in 1494 and they remained dominant in South America. Elsewhere their colonial activities were subsequently eclipsed first by the Dutch and then by the French and the British, with the latter emerging unsurpassed in the nineteenth century. It is important to consider that the occupation of territory by Europeans was spread out over more than three centuries in a number of fairly distinct episodes, with the final 'scramble for Africa' taking place during the closing decades of the nineteenth century. There was some further revision of colonial holdings after the First World War when Germany forfeited its colonies and the collapse of the Ottoman Empire provided extra inroads into the Middle East. Only the major powers of Russia, China and Japan with their own empires, plus a few 'buffer zones' between European colonial territories such as Siam (now Thailand), remained unoccupied by Europeans during these centuries and even they were not immune from the demands of European trade.

The reversal of colonialism and the attaining of constitutional independence was equally long drawn out. The United States of America made the initial break from European domination with the Declaration of Independence in 1776 and other white-settler colonies in Latin America, Australasia, Canada and South Africa followed their lead during the century or so afterwards. Therefore, for these parts of the world the European colonial episode was over before it had begun for most of the interior of Africa and with exception of Latin America the white-settler colonies have not become part of the Third World.

Subsequently, pressure for the end of colonialism in Asia, Africa and the Caribbean increased during the 1930s but was delayed by the exigencies of the Second World War. Afterwards, the call for independence could not be ignored for very long especially as the American leadership was insistent on the end of colonialism as part of a post-war reconstruction programme (see chapter 7). India, the 'jewel in the crown' of the British Empire, became independent in 1947 and Dutch Indonesia, in 1949. Others followed suite throughout the world (see figure 11), especially during the 1960s which the United Nations duly acclaimed as the first 'decade of development'.

In some cases there was reluctance and the process could be a violent and painful one. France spearheaded the resistance to the spread of communism in Asia by determining to retain its colonies in Indo-China as a bastion against Chinese communism, a task later taken over by the USA in Vietnam. Malaya was successfully defended against communist guerillas by the British army, before gaining independence with a pro-Western government in 1957. French settlers did not want to give up their privileged existence in Algeria, and British settlers were reluctant to surrender their considerable advantages in the good farming areas of Kenya and Rhodesia. The Portuguese dictatorship eschewed all calls for independence and held on to its African colonies of Angola, Guinea and Mozambique right up to the end of the 1970s. The thing that all of these resistant cases have in common is that they gave rise to savage guerilla wars in which the Western country's resolve was finally ground down and the typical outcome was Marxist government – in several cases linked strongly with the Soviet Union.

Constitutional independence and economic dependence

Even for those 'emergent nations' which had gained their constitutional independence peacefully, political separation proved to be no guarantee of socio-economic progress. This is of course the prime argument in dependency theory, derived from the original *dependencia* observations of the Economic Commission for Latin America (ECLA) as described in chapter 2. The propagation of the unequal exchange concept, low-priced raw materials from the developing countries for high-priced manufactured goods from the industrialized countries, in fact led to the founding in 1964 of the United Nations Commission for Trade and Development (UNCTAD), a move associated with Raul Prebisch, the ECLA economist. This UN agency became a focus for the economic grievances of the developing countries

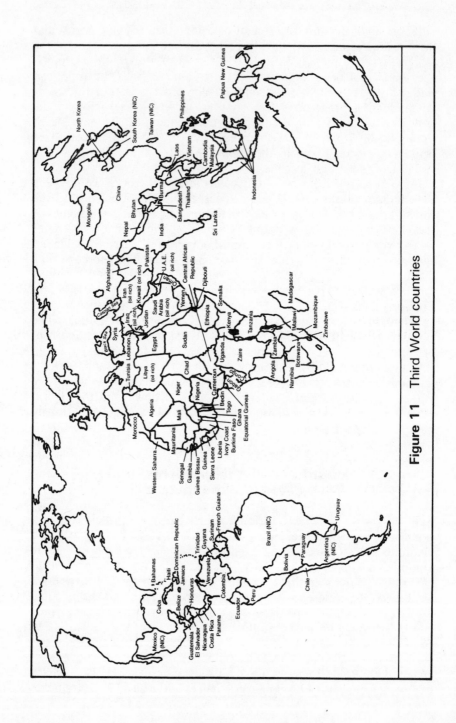

Figure 11 Third World countries

and has connections with the conferences of the General Agreement of Tariffs and Trade (GATT), although the latter is more clearly dominated by the advanced industrial countries. UNCTAD is also associated with the politically motivated Non-Aligned Movement through the founding of its economic wing, the Group of 77 which is dedicated to economic co-operation between Third World countries.

The adoption of the dependency theory argument initially involved developing countries in attempts to break out of unequal exchange through the policy of import substitution industrialization (ISI). This entails the establishment within these countries of industry capable of producing locally the very items which otherwise cost so dearly in Western hard-currency earned laboriously from low-priced raw materials production. However, there was resistance to this from those people who actually benefited from raw material exports, the traditional and conservative land-owning oligarchies left over from colonialism (see chapter 6) and now pursuing their interests in the newly constituted post-colonial state. Ian Roxborough (1979: 31) observes that the principle of independent development through ISI was adopted for a while not only by the US government through its foreign policy towards Latin America but also, ironically, by the post-revolutionary Cuban government which during the early 1960s was the primary thorn in the side of the Kennedy administration. Both parties anticipated, but from very different perpectives, that the whole of Latin America was likely to follow Cuba's Marxist revolution and the USA wanted to introduce capitalist industrialization as a safeguard against communism. Cuba needed it urgently as a protection against the US-led economic blockade but, as things turned out, both parties had to change their policy when it was discovered that Cuba's revolution was a special case. Therefore, the USA's initial stand against traditional land-owning oligarchies as impediments to modernization was reversed, particularly in view of their resistance to the elected Marxist regime in Chile after 1971. Meanwhile, Cuba's political isolation pushed it towards a resumption of the sugar-led economy with the support of the Soviet Union (see chapter 8).

In general, import substitution was unsuccessful. With slender resources any switching of emphasis from cash-crop production tended to create a rapid reduction in foreign exchange earnings to the detriment of all imports including the very production technology on which industrialization programmes depended. Even the ECLA economists came to realize that ISI only created new dependencies. As Roxborough (1979: 32–3) puts it, 'The crucial fact that, for many underdeveloped countries, the export sector functioned as a quasi-capital goods sector, had been entirely neglected.' Tariff barriers imposed to protect indigenous industry from imported finished goods also served to stimulate the setting up of local assembly plants by foreign companies intent on maintaining their export sales. ECLA had, in fact, welcomed foreign investment all along but was concerned that the technology it brought was on a scale too large and therefore inappropriate for the relatively small markets of the developing countries. Despite the existence of regional organizations such as ECLA or the foundation of boarder structures such as UNCTAD and the Group of 77, it has remained an elusive goal to obtain the extensive implementation of regional agreements in order to promote exchange between developing countries and therefore extend protected markets for their products.

The alternative for developing countries is to welcome all foreign investment, but this tends to produce awkward internal divisions between regions that benefit and others that are left out. It is in such internal divisions, as well as those between developed and developing countries, that the full meaning of the core and periphery concept in dependency theory can be found and also that of Samir Amin's (1974) 'disarticulation of economy within developing societies'. In Brazil, for instance, ISI was abandoned in favour of the conscious establishment of a high-income and consumption zone involving not more than 20 per cent of the population and leaving the remaining 80 per cent as an underemployed reserve-labour zone on very low wages. The industrialized zone is, of course, linked directly to the capitalist world-economy and the reserve-labour zone is 'disarticulated' from it. The operation of such a policy requires government to be authoritarian in order to maintain social order when large and visible inequalities in standards of living are created. It also involves capitulation to overseas investment by transnational corporations which are geared up for capital-intensive, mass-consumption production, and so add to the marginalization of the poorest sectors of the Third World.

Whether in the form of import substitution industrialization (ISI) or unrestricted foreign investment, the choice of an economic model for a developing country is not made in a vacuum and there are social and political as well as economic outcomes. For instance, economic decisions which are protective of ISI can have the unintended consequence of producing an internally overvalued currency which is inflationary and disadvantages exports, especially of basic foreign exchange earning cash crops and minerals. Not uncommonly in the short history of the Third World, the result of this has been economic instability accompanied by the erosion of popular support for fledgling government, creating conditions for civil unrest and the risk of a politico-military coup. For example, Richard Nations (1975) describes how Pakistan was identified as a 'showcase' developing country by the Western powers during the 1960s and so attracted massive economic support, especially from the USA. This support was forthcoming under the general modernization policy of encouraging capitalist industrialization, but in this case there was also Pakistan's strategic military location bordering the Soviet Union and China. Pakistan, 'the Homeland of Islam in the Indian sub-continent', was, in fact, split artificially into two 'wings' separated by more than a thousand miles of territory belonging to its potentially hostile neighbour India. This was the result of the hurried partition of Pakistan from India in the face of mounting Hindu–Islam violence during the granting of independence to the former British Raj in 1947. It is a vivid example of the arbitrary territorial definition of some post-colonial states and the difficulty of creating a self-conscious new nation in the face of earlier colonial decisions, ethnic and religious tensions and the sheer urgency of independence granting.

In the case of Pakistan, the building of the post-colonial state included a Western-inspired modernization programme involving protection for embryonic manufacturing industry but it was almost exclusively to the advantage of a Gujerati and Punjabi elite entrenched in the western 'wing' of the country. Their advantage was considerably at the expense of Bengali peasants in the eastern 'wing' who were the producers of jute, a cash crop which had earned foreign exchange since colonial times. In other words, the emerging and mainly Gujerati business elite in West Pakistan enjoyed a form of client relationship with the predominantly Punjabi government as part of which fiscal policies were operated in favour of manufacturing industry and, ostensibly, in the interests of a modernization programme. Foreign exchange earnings from the jute produced in East Pakistan were artificially undervalued by the government and the difference syphoned off in hard currency to support manufacturing industry in West Pakistan. This caused an overvaluation of the currency and inflation in the economy which, when it became public knowledge, provided fuel for existing feelings of disadvantage amongst the Bengali peasants in East Pakistan. Mounting discontent amongst these people was organized through the Awami League into vigorous political protest, but even victory at the ballot box amongst the larger East Pakistani population was ignored by the well-entrenched government based in West Pakistan. During post-election negotiations, ostensibly over the Awami League's participation in government, the army was moved in secretly from West Pakistan to ensure that the Mukti Bahini Bengali guerillas would be rendered ineffective other than in the more remote areas. The civil war of 1971 involved, tragically, the virtual genocide of the Bengali intelligentsia and political activists in East Pakistan by the government-controlled Pakistani army. Too late for these victims, the atrocities were quickly brought to an end upon the intervention of a superior army from India in response to the international outcry. However, the final act was a bizarre illustration of some of the unintended consequences of colonial institutions. After the Pakistani surrender the senior officers of both armies, who had in common their training either at Sandhurst, the elite British officer school, or at replicas of it established during colonialism, could be seen socializing as though after a sporting event (Ali 1975: 310).

The response of the US and British governments was now to switch their support away from the Pakistani government so that the Bengalis of the eastern 'wing' were able to secede from Pakistan and form the separate state of Bangladesh. Unfortunately, the economic price of freedom was high and, with the virtual collapse of the Jute industry, Bangladesh has since remained consistently one of the poorest countries in the world. This has undoubtedly contributed to its vulnerability to recurrent and widespread flooding with great loss of life during cyclones such as those of May 1991. Meanwhile Pakistan has veered back and forth between civilian government and military dictatorship, but eventually regained access to strategic aid from the USA, following the Soviet Union's abortive intervention in neighbouring Afghanistan in December 1979. However, Pakistan remains politically unstable and during the 1980s appeared from time to time to be on the verge of dismantling its secular state in favour of a system of Islamic principles modelled, presumably, upon Iran. This seems an even more likely outcome for the 1990s.

State and nation in the Third World

It is useful to examine the recruitment of indigenous people to form administrative strata in the European colonies, since some of these went on to become the elites who transformed the colonies into constitutionally independent nation-states. At first the only education available to indigenous people in the colonies was provided by missionaries whose main objective was the provision of literacy for religious teaching with conversion as the end purpose. However, as the colonies grew in size and complexity more ambitious educational institutions were established so that the supply of ex-patriate administrators, which was limited and expensive, could be supplemented with locally recruited and educated colonial servants. It was amongst these groups that the future leaders of independence movements first came into contact with the legal and constitutional practices of

Western culture, and their education and socialization in European institutions was of great significance in their role as the founding presidents of the post-colonial emergent nations. The welding of people into post-colonial national identities, within inherited colonial territorial borders, proved to be one of the greatest problems to face these heads of state, since the emergent nations which they led into constitutional independence did not neatly coincide with pre-existing tribal, ethnic and religious divisions.

In his book, *State and Nation in the Third World*, Anthony D. Smith (1983: 39–58) provides a useful approach to the issue of colonial nationalism and state formation by reference to five 'phases and types' in the recent history of Africa. These illustrate the different manifestations of nationalism in relation firstly to initial anti-colonial resistance, then to the generation of educated strata from the local population and finally to the post-colonial elites charged with state formation. This framework has the advantage of juxtaposing ethnic influences with colonial influences and so shedding some light on the complexities built into post-colonial nation-states or, as some observers have it, state-nations:

1   The first phase of nationalism is that manifested in 'primary resistance movements to European incursion'. This refers to the resistance by tribal groups to the invasions of the Europeans during the late nineteenth century, all of which were eventually overcome through the use of vastly superior military technology. The Zulu in South Africa and the Ashanti in West Africa are good examples of tribal nationalism which existed then and also has re-emerged against very different political backgrounds during the contemporary period.

2   The second phase of 'so-called millennial protest movements against colonial rule' is less important for present purposes and less well known. It refers to instances of 'messianic' movements predicting that the apocalypse would be visited upon the Europeans for the sins of colonialism, and Smith cites the primary case of Kimbanguism amongst the BaKongo in the Belgian Congo. It is an example of religious ideas invoked to provide a focus of spiritual resistance against the deprivations of the extremely harsh colonial rule maintained in the Belgian Congo, but it has ethnic nationalist connotations too.

3   Perhaps the most important phase is the period of gestation and adaptation of 'a new urban strata'. This took place during the first half of the twentieth century when educated colonial subjects operating partially within the colonial framwork began to use European institutions, such as education, the legal system and the

free press, to articulate the grievances of a new urban strata. It demonstrates clearly how the reproduction of Western institutions by colonial subjects had enabling and constraining effects for them. It enabled them to confront the colonists formally through the medium of Western institutions, but it constrained the outcome to constitutional independence based heavily upon those same Western institutions. The independence movements may have involved tribal loyalties but the affiliation was with nationalism in the form of European institutions rather than the tribal structure itself.

4   Smith's fourth phase is that of the 'rise of nationalism' and 'nationalist agitation for self-rule'. After the Second World War these independence movements found their leaders and in the post-war world order independence became no longer just an inspiration but a real possibility. Good examples are Kwame Nkrumah in the Gold Coast (later Ghana), Patrice Lumumba in the Congo (later Zaire), Jomo Kenyatta in Kenya and Leopold Senghor in Senegal. These all became the first presidents of their respective countries.

5   The final phase is 'the adoption of social programmes for the masses by nationalism'. This is the stage at which these new leaderships faced the task of building emergent nations, using the Western model of the nation-state but with the restriction of having to conform to inherited colonial territorial boundaries usually containing uncomfortable mixtures of tribal, ethnic and religious identity. Virtually the entire modern map of Africa was drawn up at the Congress of Berlin of 1884–5, a gathering convened to mediate diplomatically in the 'scamble for Africa'. This was the final fling of European colonialism during the later stages of nineteenth-century industrialization when the participants were acutely aware of the need for access to physical resources and new markets for products.

The borders decided upon at the Congress of Berlin have survived for the most part as the geo-political territorial definitions of today. This is because the proto-state infrastructures for the post-colonial period were formed during colonialism in conditions detached from pre-colonial forms of society and connected through global institutions with the Western model of capitalist industrial society. The continuity is between the colonial and post-colonial periods and the emergent nations of Africa have depended for their socio-political integrity and economic viability upon infrastructures created during colonialism. For instance, in their constitutional independence these new nation-states have remained virtually entirely dependent upon the export of cash crops and minerals through the international commodity markets of the capitalist world-economy. This has remained the chief means of obtaining hard currency when their own fledging monetary systems command no significant international exchange value and capital formation for alternative industries is consequently difficult. The juxtaposition of different societal structures in this process of transition under colonialism is conceptualized here in terms of inter-societal systems, as outlined in chapter 3. Western society was already a global culture when it came into contact with African tribal society and the two different societal forms, with their very different time–space contexts, have since co-existed in an extremely unequal and uneasy relationship. The media of that relationship have been the global information system, the nation-state system, the capitalist world-economy and the global military order, all of which are dominated by Western society but have affected the other type of society.

In some cases this has resulted in tribal groupings being joined together in a new nation as in the case of the Hausa, Ibo, Yoruba and many smaller tribes in the large former British colony of Nigeria. At the time of colonization Britain was only really interested in the coastal strip but took possession of extensive northern territory simply to prevent it falling into the hands of the French. The whole was organized as a vast colonial federation. Since independence the government of the Federation of Nigeria has been faced with the task of forging a new Nigerian nationality and identity. This is a goal that was, for a while, riven by civil war when in 1967 the Ibo, on whose tribal lands oil reserves had been discovered, attempted to secede as the separate state of Biafra. The war was won by the Nigerian government with Western backing, and the Federation of Nigeria maintained intact, but its government has nevertheless continued to oscillate back and forth between liberal democracy and military dictatorship. In a number of Third World countries the military elite has been the harsh alternative when democratic government by a civilian post-colonial elite has broken down.

In other cases, people of the same tribal origin found themselves on different sides of colonial borders, since transformed into nation-state borders. For example the Togo people, also of West Africa, were initially colonized by Germany, but with defeat in the First World War this was forfeited. Togoland then became a League of Nations trustee territory and was divided as a protectorate between the British and the French. Today some Togolese live in Ghana and speak English, whilst other French-speaking Togolese make up the independent state of Togo. Those in Ghana are now encouraged to think of themselves as Ghanaian along with fellow citizens of Ashanti descent. Through the process of colonialism Togo tribal society was incorporated into nation-states of the Western model, but certain aspects of tribal society remain within the new format.

'Neo-colonialism'

Kwame Nkrumah was the inaugural president of Ghana, formerly known as the Gold Coast and Britain's first independent African colony. He is credited with the first substantial use of the term, neo-colonialism, observed in the following much-quoted phrase. 'The essence of neo-colonialism is that the state which is subject to it is, in theory, independent and has all the trappings of international sovereignty. In reality its economic system and thus its internal policy is directed from the outside.' (Nkrumah 1965: ix) The background to Nkrumah's rise to leadership in Ghana displays the essence of the idea, observed in earlier chapters, of colonial institutions used against the colonialists. He was educated at Achimota Teacher Training College which was established by the British to provide an educated class for the Gold Coast colony. But he used his educational advantage to travel first to the USA in 1935 and ten year's later to Britain, where he was influenced by pioneering black political activists from the colonies. When he returned to the Gold Coast, therefore, it was to pursue a political career and in 1949 he founded the Convention People's Party which was to take the colony to independence through party and trades union support. Crucial electoral successes came during the 1950s and in 1951, to the embarrassment of the British, Nkrumah moved to the presidential palace directly from a prison sentence as a political subversive.

As a 'pan-Africanist', Nkrumah saw Ghana's pioneering independence as only a first step in the destiny of the continent which he visualized as a politically and economically co-ordinated unit, a 'United States of Africa'. This plan has never materialized, however, and Nkrumah with other like-minded leaders had to reconcile himself to the more modest aspirations of the Organization for African Unity (OAU) which was founded in Addis Ababa in 1963. Beset by a range of political ideologies amongst its membership, ranging from the extreme right to the extreme left, it has never found the unity that it would require for political agreement and effective economic co-operation.

Despite its name, the Gold Coast's chief economic value to Britain was in plantation agriculture for the production of cocoa beans, a cash crop for the Western chocolate industry. The cocoa bean is a plant native to South America but as in the case of other cash crops, under colonialism production was transferred from continent to continent to satisfy the demands of markets in a developing inter-societal system. The cocoa plant reached West Africa during the nineteenth century and the economic plans for Ghana which Nkrumah inherited from the colonial administration included the maximum exploitation of this existing foreign-exchange earner. In line with Nkrumah's socialist principles, the National Development Company was set up in 1957 to take a share of the cocoa business and at the same time provide support for Nkrumah's political ambitions (Jones 1976: 183–4). In improving the infrastructure of the industry and the national economy, the government arranged the building of huge storage hoppers for cocoa beans by the harbour at Tema. The idea was that the supply of the commodity could be controlled whenever necessary to coincide with favourable world market prices for cocoa.

Like many other former colonies, Ghana found itself dependent on this one commodity for almost two-thirds of its exports and, consequently, for the hard-currency earnings necessary for any imports or foreign exchange dealings. The situation was especially acute, because in searching for a form of pan-African socialism, Nkrumah had tended to make Ghana appear ideologically unsound to Britain and the USA, so that there were problems over development assistance. Ghana's fledgling currency, the *cedi*, had little or no value on the world's currency markets and so it was a fundamental principle that Ghana needed to earn sterling or dollars to be able to make purchases from abroad. The plan for cocoa earnings, however, was a failure. The world price for cocoa had been consistently high during the mid 1950s as the nation prepared for independence, but it fell in 1961 and remained at a low level for most of the decade, precisely at the time when Ghana was committed to expensive development plans. This was compounded by the fact that the cocoa beans did not store successfully for any length of time in the country's extremely humid climate. It was a fate that beset other cocoa-led economies in the Ivory Coast, Nigeria and Colombia (Jones 1976: 319). In 1966, Nkrumah was deposed whilst pursuing his internationalist ambitions as a member of a peace mission to Vietnam. By 1969 the cocoa bean storage hoppers, and an expensive and prestigious congress centre for the Organization for African Unity, were virtually abandoned – poignant memorials to some of the failings of independent Africa's first decade of development.

There are many factors in this example which illustrate the perils faced by Third World countries in their attempts at economic development. First and foremost are the considerable advantages held by the transnational corporations which have grown to dominate global resource procurement, manufacturing and trade during the twentieth century. Barbara Dinham and Colin Hines (1983: 34) estimated that in the case of cocoa, four companies: Cadbury-Schweppes, Gill and Duffus, Nestle, and Rowntree controlled 60 to 80 per cent of world sales of the cash crop, and since then Cadbury's have taken over Rowntree. There are perhaps four areas in which transnational corporations enjoy significant advantages in their dealing with the Third World. They have privileged access to:

1   Western capital.
2   Expertise gained through long-term activity.
3   State-of-the-art technology for the efficient processing of commodities.
4   Membership of established worldwide distribution networks.

In these areas, Third World countries suffer severe disadvantages unless they can earn or borrow sufficient foreign exchange to be able to buy the technology and expertise from the West. They might finance the training of their own personnel, which is a long-term project, but even then they will have to keep up with technological advances and ultimately compete with Western transnational corporations for mass consumption markets. Access to large-scale markets is crucial for the economies of scale to apply, and Third World markets remain small in terms of purchasing power. Moreover, the developing countries have been singularly unsuccessful at forming regional blocs to combine their resources into more effective competition for the West.

Ever since their constitutional independence the developing countries have been urged to diversify away from dependence upon the cash crops and mineral exports which they inherited from colonialism. But that is a risky business involving a move away from proven foreign-exchange earnings attached to existing links with world markets and areas of expertise in which limited resources have been concentrated. Moreover, if developing countries seek the obvious remedy of moving along the production chain into processing and manufacturing where profits are higher, they tend to find progress difficult due, firstly, to technological difficulties and, secondly, to import tariffs which protect Western manufacturers from outside competition. Thus, even if a Third World country succeeds in obtaining the capital, technology and expertise required to become a manufacturer rather than a raw material producer, the chances are that its prospects will still not be good.

Another gifted African independence leader was Julius Nyerere in Tanzania, whose administration introduced a characteristically African type of rural cooperative socialism, the Ujamaa villages. The nation-state of Tanzania was formed as a union of the colonial Tanganyika Territory (originally German then British) with Zanzibar island (a British-influenced Islamic Swahili sultanate and former Portuguese trading post). Coffee was a main cash-crop, comprising a little over one-third of export earnings, and soon after independence the government was keen to capitalize upon it. Instead of selling coffee beans at raw material commodity prices, the plan was to process them into a finished product which, potentially, could yield much higher levels of foreign exchange earnings. As a reflection of the earlier colonial past, German engineers were engaged to supervise the building of a plant to produce instant coffee powder. However, the Tanzanians came up against some basic problems, and the dependence of the Third World upon Western expertise was brought sharply into relief. Construction work was delayed several years beyond the original schedule, and, by the time it was commissioned, the Tanzanian plant was outdated from the start. Furthermore, when it could not be made to operate properly, a second set of German engineers had to be called in to advise. There was little the Tanzanians could do about this because they lacked both the technological skills to intervene themselves and the legal power to penalize the consultant engineers for any shortcomings. Finally, when the plant was at last, brought into production, marketing was a problem. They had to compete with the world leaders in instant coffee, the American transnational corporation, General Foods, with Maxwell House, and their Swiss rivals, Nestle, with Nescafe. Therefore, although the Tanzanians at last had their own brand of instant coffee, Africafe, they still faced the ignominy of having to call in experts from Nestle to advise on marketing plans. The outcome has been that distribution, even in other African countries, has not been impressive, and in Europe or North America, where Nestle's and General Foods's major markets lie, it can only be found in stores especially set up to market Third World products. As a consequence, the plant has never worked at more than half capacity and the whole exercise, far from being a major source of foreign-exchange earnings, has been an expensive drain on Tanzania's finances. For another account of this episode see Barbara Dinham and Colin Hines (1983: 67–8) who suggest that there was reluctance on the part of both the German engineers and the Swiss marketing management to make the venture successful.

Nkrumah's term, 'neo-colonialism', encapsulates very effectively the frustrations of the emergent nations of the Third World as they attempted with great vigour and optimism to take up the economic challenges of constitutional independence. During the 1960s, the UN's first 'decade of development', an overall economic growth target of 5 per cent was achieved with a little to spare at 5.5 per cent according to UN statistics. But that is an aggregate figure and when calculated on a per capita basis the apparent growth becomes minimal or even non-existent in terms of concrete benefits to the mass of the population. As an arbitrary goal achieved, it masks failures such as those described above, which were tremendous blows to national self-confidence at a time when encouragement was sorely needed.

Development aid

The plight of the Third World in seeking to develop along the broad lines laid out for it by Western economic planners has to be viewed against the background of the Bretton Woods global economic arrangements. The World Bank was set up initially to confront economic reconstruction after the Second World War by stimulating the renewal of private-sector investment in the advanced nations, but two decades later with the end of colonialism much of its attention had been transferred to the Third World. The bank normally operates on straightforward commercial lines in terms of creditworthiness and interest payments and there are two extensions to its format that illustrate its engagement with developing countries. In 1956 the International Finance Corporation was set up as an off-shoot that was an investment rather than a lending agency, but it lacked sufficient funding to make a real impact. Further to this, 1960 saw the foundation of the International Development Association to provide 'soft loans' for the poorest of the developing countries, at lower interest rates and with easier creditworthiness requirements. This was given a proportionally higher level of funding than its predecessors but still never enough for the huge potential demand in the Third World. In accordance with Western economic orthodoxy, World Bank policy has been to avoid substantial intervention and to act merely as a primer for private-sector finance. This is the principle of the capitalist world-economy in practice, Western development policies and modernization theory. The position is further complicated by the fact that most of the other agencies of the United Nations have budgets, and two notable examples engaged in economic development are the United Nationals Industrial Development Organization (UNIDO) and the United Nations Food and Agriculture Organization (UNFAO). The controversial nature of some of these activities is illustrated by the fact that UNFAO was heavily criticized during the 1970s for working too closely with participating transnational corporations in its Industrial Co-operative Programme (ICP), which, as a result, was excluded from FAO and UN activities (cf. George 1986: 214). Elsewhere, the European Community (EC) has an aid agency separate from those of its member-nations and the Organization for Economic Co-operation and Development (OECD) maintains its Development Assistance Committee.

These types of assistance are termed multilateral aid but the organizations described above are by no means the only ones set up to promote development. Most of the Western countries maintain their own 'bilateral' agencies which of course may be used for political and diplomatic reasons as well as for purposes of economic development. In the case of the USA there is the Agency for International Development (AID) and it is generally known by its 'hands across the sea' emblem which has to appear on any item supplied or financed by it. In Britain the equivalent is the Overseas Development Administration (ODA), in West Germany it is the Ministry for Economic Co-operation, and other countries have less clearly defined agencies for aid disbursement. With their outstanding economic recovery after the Second World War both Germany and Japan have become substantial providers of aid and, according to the OECD's Development Assistance Committee, were by 1988, respectively, the second and fourth largest lenders after the USA. Outside the Western world, the Soviet Union has tended to concentrate on large-scale construction projects in countries that have courted its assistance, such as the construction of the Aswan High Dam on the Nile. This was during Egypt's alignment with the USSR, under the leadership of President Nasser, a figure of great influence in the Third World after Egypt's seizure of the Suez Canal and survival in the face of British and French reprisals that lacked US approval. Saudi Arabia and some other Islamic Arab countries have used their oil wealth to provide aid but this is predominantly directed at other Islamic countries. Virtually all of the aid generated is in the form of loans and not outright gifts. However, in the case of the Soviet Union there have been exchanges of commodities and with Islamic countries, where the charging of interest is proscribed by the religion, the alternative is for the creditor nation to take a financial stake in the project financed.

All of these are termed 'official' aid agencies, whether multilateral or bilateral, but there are also the 'unofficial' agencies or non-government organizations (NGOs) which obtain their funds through public subscription on a voluntary basis and, therefore, normally grant aid as a gift. These NGOs usually involve their own officials in the supervision of development programmes in order to avoid the potential inefficiencies associated with government schemes in the Third World. However, 'unofficial' aid can never match the amounts of money involved in official schemes administered through government channels.

Last but not least, is private-sector aid, where the commercial banks are involved directly in loans to the Third World. In a free-market capitalist system the banks are always involved directly or indirectly, and with limited funds the World Bank has often acted as a coordinator between commercial banks and developing countries. However, large quantities of so-called 'petro-dollars' became available for overseas investment during the late 1970s as a result of the dramatic escalation in oil prices which followed the 1973 oil crisis precipitated by the Arab–Israeli war (see chapters 10 and 12). Third World countries which appeared to exhibit promising signs of development then became new prospects for investment loans from the commercial banks. Ankie Hoogvelt (1982: 51–3) observes that 'middle-income countries', such as Brazil, attracted private-sector loans whilst there was increased pressure to channel 'official' (public-sector) loans to the 'low-income countries', such as most of Africa. This was not a philanthropic move but was undertaken in the belief that prospects in the newly industrializing countries (NICs) were good and, therefore, that it was a reasonable investment. In this way, loans from the money market overtook other forms of industrial investment and supplier credit as the largest form of private-sector finance for the Third World (Hoogvelt 1982: 51).

Unfortunately, the economic forecasts which formed the basis for these private-sector loans proved to be over-optimistic. The global economic recession of the early 1980s brought increased credit charges across the board which effectively cancelled out the economic advantages achieved, not only by developing countries but also by some of the especially targeted newly industrializing countries (NICs). Their export earnings slumped after they had generally shown increases with the general upturn in commodity prices which followed the 1973 oil crisis, whilst the cost of their imports rose as the advanced industrial countries retrenched to defend themselves from the recession. The result was that the repayment of many loans became virtually impossible and it was difficult enough to keep up with the payment of escalating interest charges. The amounts outstanding to the Western banks grew as further loans had to be negotiated just to meet existing interest payments on original loans which were on too large a scale to be waived without damage to the whole financial system. Hoogvelt (1982: 55) suggests that short-term deposits in the Western banks had been used to finance long-term loans in developing countries so that, in the economic downturn, huge financial pressures were created. The position became so bad by the mid 1980s that graphs could be plotted showing the scale of interest payments to the West overtaking the level of export earnings of the developing countries. In effect, a net flow of wealth from the Third World to the

West was created. This broad phenomenon has been referred to as the 'debt trap' and in the end such loans have had to be drastically rescheduled, written off (where possible without damaging Western finance) or else made the subject of debt-conversion schemes. 'Debt-for-equity swaps' have been the most common form of such conversion schemes and they normally involve the lending bank in a financial stake in the capital of the borrower nation. Unfortunately, this tends only to extend dependency and in the World Bank's Development Report for 1987, debt for equity swaps were summarized as follows:

> Debt conversion would be a more appropriate term, since conversion of external debt instruments into domestic obligations can take place not only for foreign direct investment purposes, but also for more general purposes by residents or nonresidents of the debtor country. In essence, a foreign investor wishing to buy assets in a debtor country can, through a debt-equity swap, obtain local currency at a discount. The foreign investor, in effect, obtains a rebate on the purchase of the currency equivalent to the discount on the loan less the transactions cost of the debt-equity swap. (World Bank 1987: 22)

Since 1989 the World Bank has introduced two new acronyms: SIMICs denoting severely-indebted middle-income countries and SILICs, severely-indebted low-income countries. The problems of the SIMICs have been tackled by the Brady Initiative which is intended to enable concerted action for the first time from the commercial banks supported by IMF, World Bank and OECD government funds towards such countries as Brazil, Mexico, etc. Whilst the problems of the SILICs have been addressed with IMF short-term programmes known as the Structural Adjustment Facility (SAF) and the Enhanced Structural Adjustment Facility (ESAF). However, a number of important debtor countries are not covered and the programmes continue to be under-funded with much of the finance not new but diverted from other schemes which must consequently suffer (Overseas Development Institute 1990).

It is not surprising, therefore, that dependency theorists have written off aid as yet another means by which Western countries maintain their hold over developing countries. In fact, as David Harrison (1988: 174) points out, outright condemnation of aid comes from writers of both the left (cf. Hayter 1981) and the right (cf. Bauer 1984). Peter Bauer is a monetarist advocate of market forces and he argues that aid stifles whatever entrepreneurial spirit exists in Third World countries. There is evidence in favour of this view, as in the dramatic example of emergency supplies rushed to Ethiopia and Sudan in the face of famine. To some extent, this has undermined local trading structures in food and other basic items and caused them to collapse.

There are grounds for arguing that aid to the Third World is modernization theory operationalized. Official aid agreements always have conditions written into them which can be expected to conform to whatever version of capitalist economics is considered orthodox in the West at the time. During the 1960s Keynesian policies prevailed, whilst during the early 1980s monetarism became dominant but the structure through which these principles are applied is that of the capitalist world-economy. This structure overlaps and interconnects with that of nation-state system and global military order especially given sophisticated global communications, all of which form dimensions to the overall late twentieth-century inter-societal system. The granting of aid by the West is a part of international relations and Third World countries which aligned themselves with the Soviet Union and the state socialist model of society were for the most part excluded. For these reasons, Western aid to the Third World and, indeed, Western-sponsored international economic development in general may be appropriately referred to in terms of a 'World Bank orthodoxy'. The Bretton Woods arrangements in their original form may have expired in 1971 but World Bank policy remains institutionalized at the core of Western development policy. Furthermore, the political integrity of the West was structured to depend upon the reproduction of private-sector capitalist institutions and the defence of this against the apparent threat of Soviet state socialism. Arguably this premise carries with it the necessary application of modernization to the Third World in order to entrench the capitalist system there as far as possible. In Western foreign policy, therefore, neglect of modernization in the Third World was equated with risking the expansion of the Soviet Union's sphere of influence and the spread of state socialism. Thus development aid has been as much a politico-military device as an economic one.

Reservoirs of disposable labour

A recent feature of the inter-societal system especially in terms of world-economy has been the globalization of production, which was described in chapter 7 in connection with transnational corporations. A major role in this for the Third World has been the provision of 'export processing zones' or 'free trade zones' which are areas of land, usually adjacent to an air or sea port, set aside as a form of industrial estate exclusively for foreign investment or joint ventures between overseas and local companies. Michael Barratt Brown (1982: 153–6) describes, for instance, how the Sri Lankan government took a large advertisement in the British *Financial Times* to publicize their 'well-educated' labour force, available to investors through the Greater Colombo Economic Commission. Such an advertisement by a Third World country in Western 'quality' newspapers is not an isolated occurrence. Most workers travel in and out of the zones on a daily basis, but others have to be recruited at a distance and, therefore, often live in hostel accommodation adjacent to the zone. Not all Third World countries have populations educated sufficiently in the Western manner to be easily assimilated into industrial organization, but many are striving to put themselves into that position. The number of export-processing zones in the Third World was not more than a handful in the early 1960s but by the end of the 1980s there were estimated to be between 150 and 200 scattered about the world. In the absence of more substantial forms of economic investment this represents an attainable and viable, if exploitative, means of alleviating under-employment in Third World countries. Local politicians have quite openly referred to the Sri Lankan zone as a place set aside from the country's sovereign territory where the 'robber barons' of capitalism can come and take advantage of cheap labour (cf. Barratt Brown 1982: 153–71).

Manufacturing activities within these zones are normally exempt from the payment of taxes and import duties or, alternatively, these are levied at highly preferential rates in order to make investment as attractive as possible. Practically the only advantage to the host country is employment and the rates of pay may be as little as one-twentieth of those paid in the West. But it does mean work for sections of the population that would otherwise be unemployed or underemployed. Many such enterprises tend to be of a relatively short-term nature, however, and they also tend to employ the most vulnerable labour. A high proportion of this is typically made up of young women who might otherwise be employed only by their families without pay, in the traditional economic and social structure, until such time as they can be married off.

In Third World countries with export processing zones, therefore, there exists a large reservoir of labour which is increasingly at the disposal of transnational corporations or firms in partnership with them or making up their service networks. It has become one of the tasks of sociology, therefore, to examine the nature of employment in these sectors of the international labour market (cf. Mitter 1986, Fuentes and Ehrenreich 1987). The main reason for the use of such labour is low costs and consequently the question of exploitation arises. Typically, there is a high degree of surveillance with workers checked in and out of the zones by security staff provided by the host government. Thus it is relatively easy to ensure that trade unions are excluded and that union activists do not retain employment. Indeed, the 'problem-free' aspect of labour in the zones is one of the things emphasized by host governments in the promotion of the zones to Western employers (cf. Barratt Brown 1982: 153).

Since export-processing zones tend to be used by light industries with easily transportable technology, movement from one site to another and potentially from one part of the world to another is relatively easy. Consequently, there are grounds for arguing that an international market in manufacturing sites has been developed and that these sites form the most labour-intensive sections of some 'global production lines'. All kinds of assembly work can be located in export-processing zones, given the low cost of labour, and some of the tasks involved are basic and the investment minimal. For instance, sales promotion companies send large batches of brochures and other promotional material to be collated and put into envelopes before being shipped back to Europe or North America for mass mailing. At a slightly higher level of involvement, textile companies which nowadays use computer-assisted design and cutting of fabric, still require garments to be sewn, and even allowing for the investment in electric sewing machines, the cost of such work in an export-processing zone is much lower than in the West. Much of the mass marketing of fashion clothes at low prices in Western shops would not be possible without resort to such techniques (Mitter 1986). Perhaps the most extreme example of flexibility in the use of such sites is in the case of the Mexican *maquilas* or *maquiladores* which are located just over the border from the USA. United States' firms can get work done at these locations at a fraction of US labour costs, whilst their managements can continue to enjoy the benefits of life in the USA by commuting daily across the border. There have even been cases in which industrial relations problems have arisen in reaction to exploitation, but the US company has been able to transfer relatively easily to another site along the border. In fact, there has been competition between border towns in Mexico when local government has been anxious to provide employment for the native population.

It would be a mistake to think that all people in all Third World countries fulfil the criteria for entry into this labour market. Some degree of education or socialization into Western work patterns is necessary for even the most basic and repetitive kinds of industrialized work to be carried out satisfactorily. Nevertheless, there exist underemployed people in large numbers, with some education but little hope of any advance in living standards in the immediate future other than to provide this type of exploited work. Such people are typically faced with the choice of this or no work at all. Therefore it seems that export-processing zones go to make up what has been referred to as the 'bargain basements' of the new international division of labour.

Reflections

The transnational corporations are organizations which buy raw materials for processing from all parts of the world-economy including the Third World and increasingly they buy labour on the same basis. Under colonialism the Third World countries served as suppliers of raw materials and labour from the time of the slave trade and the plantation system. These countries find themselves in a similar position today as they did formerly – on different terms, but disadvantageous ones, nevertheless. The transnational corporations are also the producers and purveyors of mass communication services and mass consumer products to a global market. During the colonial period people in Third World countries were introduced to Western culture and so they too have become consumers, albeit at much lower levels of purchasing power. The persistence of this has been referred to as 'cultural imperialism' and 'media imperialism' (cf. Lee 1980) and, in this sense, the transnational corporations are capable of subverting the cultural integrity of nation-states through the homogenization of culture. These tendencies are reminiscent of the images portrayed by Clark Kerr et al.'s (1960) concept of the 'logic of industrialism' driving the different societies of the world to 'convergence' and by Marshall McLuhan's (1964) 'global village' of media and product consumers. The 'commodification of social existence' is a concern taken up by writers such as Georg Lukacs (cf. Haug 1986) and Herbert Marcuse (1964). But the Third World countries participate in mass consumption at a disadvantage because of 'unequal exchange'.

One of the ways in which Third World countries might break out of the unequal exchange predicament is to trade amongst themselves, but in this they have been conspicuously unsuccessful. Part of the reason lies in the lack of capital, expertise and technology but another factor lies in the political problems which constitute a barrier to mutual cooperation within the Third World. The Group of 77, an economic spin-off from the Non-Aligned Movement, and regional organizations, such as the Organization for African Unity (OAU), have never enjoyed much success because of their members' widely varying political ideologies, extending from Marxism to examine right-wing politics. Therefore, Third World countries have co-operated neither politically nor economically and statistics continue to show that by far the greater part of the Third World's trade is directly with the advanced industrial countries. This takes place through the structure of the inter-societal system with its dimensions of communication, nation-states, world-economy and military order as the overarching institutions which connect our day-to-day lives of Western consumption with those of Third World deprivation.

Part IV

THE WORLD TOWARDS THE END OF THE TWENTIETH CENTURY

Part III was devoted to the definition of three 'worlds' in popular terminology after the Second World War and now, in Part IV, I shall discuss the situation as the twentieth century draws to a close. The West of course remains the source of the liberal–democratic model of society but during the twentieth century there have been many setbacks to the belief so characteristic of the nineteenth century in Western progress, the potential of science and of human beings over their environment. As suggested in chapter 4 and taken up further in chapter 7, the world wars with their terrible weapons, the reversals in economic depression and the realization of damage to the physical environment have all contributed to a decline of Western confidence. During the 1980s, the whole world felt the effects of a downturn in the capitalist world-economy which was referred to as a 'recession' in preference to the term 'depression' as applied to the 1930s, but the developed welfare systems of Western states were more effective in camouflaging the resultant social problems this time. Nevertheless, large numbers of people became unemployed and therefore unable to join in the otherwise slowed but continued increase in living standards. With the use of more sophisticated investment techniques and electronic technology at the 'nerve centres' of London, New York, Tokyo, etc., the world's capital and commodity markets were better equipped to weather the storms of financial instability that accompanied the recession. On 'black monday', 19 October 1987, twice as much value was lost from Western stock markets as on the previous record one-day fall of the Great Crash on Wall Street in 1929, yet the financial system was able to absorb it much more effectively. Generally, the 1980s were referred to as 'a time of change'.

Tokyo is included now as a major centre of the capitalist world-economy. It is probably the fastest growing and most vigorous of the financial centres, and yet, at the end of the Second World War, Japan was a defeated power shattered by the first use of nuclear weapons. Like Germany, Japan transformed itself from vanquished nation through an 'economic miracle' to become one of the world's leading manufacturing countries. I shall examine the proposition that the legacy of Confucian philosophy in East Asian history is a form of 'post-Confucianism' which has presented the area with an ostensibly liberal–democratic but, in fact, rather authoritarian form of capitalist society. This has produced, so the argument goes, a labour force socialized into norms of group cohesion and loyalty that fit in very well with the requirements of modern manufacturing industry.

I shall also address 'Islamism', which is the title preferred by Islamic people for the resurgence of Islam but often referred to in the West as 'Islamic fundamentalism'. The attempt to construct a society with institutions based upon the teachings of the Prophet Muhammad, as set out in the Qur'an, has seen its fullest flowering in Iran after 1979 but the tendency is apparent in several other Islamic countries too. Such developments are a reaction against the pervasiveness of Western civilization which, after the collapse of the Ottoman Empire in 1918, asserted its interests more freely throughout Islamic areas especially in connection with oil production. More recently it has become an irony of history that Islam should be not only the West's main energy source but also a powerful form of resistance to Western ideologies both capitalist and socialist. The Islamic countries have become more than a source of energy for Western and Japanese industry, however, because reliance on very substantial earnings from oil have involved them inextricably in the capitalist world-economy, notwithstanding recent attempts to interpret the situation through the teachings of the Qur'an.

10

Contemporary Western Development: Liberal–Democratic Capitalism through Crises but Re-affirmed

In part II of this book, 'The rise of Western civilization', I addressed the processes by which Europeans developed a belief in their superiority over the other peoples of the Earth. Achievements in arts, science and technology gave Europeans confidence that the global environment was theirs to develop without limits to the process, and a general term for the philosophy emanating from these developments is 'positivism'. Western self-confidence was sustained by notions of liberty enshrined in the liberal–democratic model of the nation-state, and communicated through an inter-societal system in which the West was politically and militarily dominant. The system was supported in concrete terms first by merchant capitalism and then by industrial capitalism, two forms of an economic mechanism with great effectiveness for wealth creation on a global scale, but centred on the West. Yet, despite all of this, the confident hopes for the future of Western civilization have received some shattering blows during the twentieth century. World wars, nuclear weapons and environmental damage are only the most notable factors to undermine confidence in Western culture and modernization giving rise to such manifestations of doubt as 'counter cultures' or the 'post-modern movement'. The period seen in these terms might be seen as beginning with the twentieth century and the eclipsing of Europe by the USA as the focus of power in Western civilization.

The USA at the centre of an inter-societal system

As early as 1901 an English aristocrat and journalist, Wilfrid Scawen Blunt, published a book called *The Americanization of the World*, a theme since take up by countless others (Roberts 1985: 373). The rise of the USA was largely a matter of continuing 'modernization' involving a strand of liberal democracy begun with the Declaration of Independence and drawing from the spirit of the French Revolution, British liberalism and other European sources. In physical terms, the United States' initial expansionism was internal and westwards, but by 1890 the State Department had announced officially that the 'frontier' no longer existed and from then on progress came in two ways. Firstly, in a society where mass participation was constitutionally assured, enormous economic growth was achieved through the pioneering of institutions of mass production, mass communication and mass consumption. A social structure was created that was at the same time enabling, in terms of a broadening range of opportunities created, and constraining in terms of the racist after-effects of slavery and the ruthless exploitation of successive waves of immigrants. Secondly, there was the external expansion of the United States' activities, not as a colonial power in the accepted sense, but as a politico-military and economic power of such scale that ultimately only global systems could accommodate it.

The USA's twentieth-century economic expansion virtually begins with the transnational corporation because, not unlike Britain in the late nineteenth century, its most important exports were whole packages of production techniques. At the turn of the twentieth century Frederick Winslow Taylor identified 'scientific management', against a background of advances in metal-cutting, and out of this came the 'time and motion' principles of workstudy, broadly aimed at formally separating the management and the execution of work for the greater efficiency of industry. Other people could have done what Taylor did but his success was in ensuring that his ideas were listened to against opposition, even from the US Congress. During the same period Henry Ford realized that, although profit could be made from manufacturing expensive hand-built cars, much more money could be made from producing large quantities of a car that almost anyone could afford. This result of this was 'Fordism' or monolithic mass-production technology taking maximum advantage of the economies of scale. It became a cornerstone of consumerism and 'the American dream' from which the combined principles of Taylorism and Fordism were used to set up global manufacturing empires. Companies such as Ford and Hoover, with mass production perfected, were not long in setting up plants in Europe and elsewhere so that the direction of innovation was reversed. When railways were first built during the nineteenth century, British technology was exported worldwide but when the London 'Tube' was laid out at the beginning of the twentieth century it was extensively with American electrical technology. Britain had chosen to put resources into empire and finance rather than into the technology of a 'second industrial revolution' during the late nineteenth century and as a consequence it was disadvantaged in the subsequent crucial development of synthetic chemicals, electrical energy and the internal combustion engine (cf. Barnett 1972, Weiner 1981).

The first blow to American self-confidence in this process of industrial growth was the Great Crash of Wall Street in 1929 and the ensuing economic depression. Yet even this may be seen as a manifestation of mass participation because greater numbers of people than ever before had been speculating in stocks and shares and other forms of popular investment. There was much to be gained and the entire process of finance capitalism was over-extended leading to a complete but temporary collapse of the system. However, one of the indirect results of this was that in its interplay with events American social theory entered a process of teleological development. Like the American political leadership, it remained inexorably optimistic and dedicated to the positivistic idea that industrial capitalism incorporated the potential to deal with these and all other social, political and economic problems. The post-war 'orthodox consensus' which was so influential in sociology, was the result of interplay between American social theory, government policy and events during the period of Roosevelt's 'New Deal' and the subsequent industrial recovery during the Second World War. The way out of economic and politico-military crises was seen exclusively in terms of industrial capitalism and, in the light of the events in Russia after 1917, the avoidance at all costs of anything resembling socialism. Marxism was completely eschewed in the USA and, although at first there was mixed reaction, events proved that German National Socialism (Nazism) had to be confronted too. The USA entered the Second World War as a result of Japanese imperialism and the attack on Pearl Harbour, but it was always agreed between Churchill and Roosevelt that Nazi Germany would need to be defeated first.

The 'Americanization of the world', then, involves a model of industrial capitalist society especially in terms of an idealized conception of mass-participation. Almost anyone can drink a bottle of Coca-Cola or eat a McDonald's hamburger or even buy a General Motors or Ford car. Each of these examples is a contribution to the symbolism of Americanized Western culture which has been so pervasive throughout the world. Each involves the application of technology to mass production, of professional management to business organization and of marketing principles to mass communication and mass consumption, together the hallmarks of twentieth-century American economic success.

Despite the disruption of the two world wars and because of them in terms of technological advancement, the rate of economic expansion in Western society has been phenomenal since the focus of the inter-societal system was transferred to the USA. Global economic concentration has produced unprecedented material standards of living in the advanced industrial societies, but it has required the continued exploitation of disadvantaged people especially in the Third World. In real terms, salaries and wages have risen in the West whilst the price of the staple necessities of life has fallen, thus leaving surplus spending capacity for new consumer products. In North America and Western Europe, the number of people working in manufacturing industry (the secondary sector) has been surpassed by the number working in service industries (the tertiary sector). The nineteenth-century agricultural and industrial revolutions reduced the number of workers in the extractive industries (primary sector) and these now represent less than 5 per cent of the workforce in the West. Since the Second World War, the service industries account for more than 50 per cent and this has led to the use of phrases such as 'the post-industrial society' and 'the service economy' (Bell 1973; Touraine 1974). These concepts are clear examples of Western ethnocentrism because the capacity for such change depends upon an inter-societal system in which the vast majority of people elsewhere are engaged in agriculture or, increasingly, manufacturing as the new international division of labour enables this to be extended.

The USA's loss of hegemony

During the late 1960s the US government's Pearson Commission carried out an examination of the USA's role and responsibilities as underwriter to an expanding world-economy. The outcome was President Richard Nixon's decision in August 1971 to end free dollar–gold convertibility and, therefore, the US currency's role as anchor to global financial exchange. Before this, exchange rates had been fixed and subject only to periodic change but ever since they have been subject to market forces and the fluctuations that are now monitored and reported continually from the financial centres. Furthermore, in 1976 the articles of agreement of the International Monetary Fund (IMF) were changed to eliminate the role of gold from the international monetary system (Brett 1985: 129). It was the end of the Bretton Woods arrangements as envisaged in 1944, depending upon the strength of the US dollar, just as until 1931 the world's monetary system had depended upon a 'gold standard' backed by both British and American reserves. In his concept of a capitalist world-economy Wallerstein (1979: 29–31) sets British's outright hegemony between 1815 and 1873 and that of the United States between 1945 and 1965, but each was extremely powerful in the years adjacent to these relatively short periods.

In 1973, the first of the oil crises arose when, in retaliation for Western support of Israel in the Arab–Israeli wars, the Arab-dominated Organization of Petroleum Exporting Countries (OPEC) restricted the supply of crude oil without warning, so that its price quadrupled virtually overnight. The significant thing was that Saudi Arabia, a leading member of OPEC but until then an unproblematic ally of the West, played a central role with a 10 per cent reduction of its own oil supply and a total embargo on oil for the USA, the Netherlands and Denmark singled out as special culprits (Mansfield 1985: 485–6). There was a further sudden increase of price in 1979 upon the change of government in Iran and the effects were dramatic for the West, the world's largest consumers of energy. The market prices of most other basic commodities fluctuated enormously to the particular detriment of Third World economies dependent upon the production of one or two cash crops. Some of these countries at first saw their fortunes rise, and so embarked upon investment pro-grammes, only to suffer impoverishment later when foreign earnings took a downturn. Those who borrowed their way out of the ensuing financial crisis were later faced with escalating interest rates and the so-called 'debt trap'. A notable result of this economic turbulence was the further enlarging and entrenching of transnational corporations during a period in which many firms were so weakened financially that they became ripe for takeover. As economic concentration took place, accelerated changes to the international division of labour occurred too. Some industries 'migrated' from Europe and North America to other parts of the world, especially to East Asia, Brazil and Mexico which were dubbed by economists as 'newly industrializing countries' (NICs). The results of these developments have been referred to as a 'new international division of labour' (cf. Frobel et al. 1980).

A contributory factor to the United States's loss of hegemony in the world-economy was the high cost of waging the Vietnam War which, by the early 1970s, had substantially increased a trading deficit begun during the previous decade. This vividly illustrates the interconnec-tions between nation-states, world-economy and global military order against a background of industrialized warfare. The USA's involve-ment in Vietnam was aimed at stemming the spread of Soviet and Chinese influence in South-East Asia but the economic cost was very high, with concern about casualties forcing the ratio of munitions costs to troop losses further than in any previous conflict. Nevertheless, the fatalities amongst young American males still increasingly aroused

American public opinion against the war. The enormous financial cost and the apparent futility of a war against ideologically committed guerilla fighters can be linked to the growing sophistication of weapons coupled with their increasing mass production and wider availability. The USA spent its huge war budget on state-of-the-art weaponry and maximum security for troops on the ground, involving comprehensive superiority in quality and quantity of supplies. Yet, like the Vietminh against the French in the 1950s, the Vietcong guerillas were able to deploy considerable firepower in positions often unanticipated by the US forces. The blanket bombing of cities in North Vietnam involved an aggregate tonnage greater than that used by all participants in the Second World War. Vast expanses of terrain were chemically defoliated, yet the Vietnamese social structure survived and the Vietcong continued to fight.

The realization came for the Americans in Vietnam, as it came later for the Portuguese in Angola and Mozambique, the white Rhodesians in Zimbabwe and the Russians in Afghanistan, that guerilla wars against determined and dedicated opposition cannot be won short of using techniques that are unacceptable to public opinion or dangerous to the global balance of power. In conditions where two superpowers maintain global strategic objectives and where sophisticated weapons are mass produced, arms are likely to be made available to guerilla fighters. This casts doubts upon the concept of the monopoly of violence as a cornerstone to the Western model of the state, but there have been very few serious military challenges to authority in the archetypal Western nation-states. Coups d'etat have occurred mainly in less stable post-colonial countries where full advantage has been taken of the increased availability of mass-produced arms.

The post-war global military order was until the late 1980s unequivocally centred on the confrontation between the NATO and Warsaw Pact alliances and the international relations of 'nuclear diplomacy' have involved nation-states on a worldwide scale in alignment with either of these two superpower blocs. Historically, the 'pax Britannica' of the nineteenth century may be seen to have been replaced by the 'pax Americana' of the twentieth. According to Ronald Steel (1977: 134), by 1970 'the United States had more than 1,000,000 soldiers in 30 countries, was a member of four regional defense alliances and an active participant in a fifth, had mutual defence treaties with 42 nations, was a member of 53 international organizations, and was furnishing military or economic aid to nearly 100 nations across the face of the globe'.

International relations, then, has until recently involved two major military groupings with a balance of interests extending into the Third World. Initially it was seen as straightforwardly a matter of global military power, but the setbacks faced by the USA in Vietnam and by the USSR in Afghanistan showed that the proliferation of 'conventional' armaments and the practice of guerilla warfare could make possible the successful challenging of military hegemony. In 1990, the Iraqi invasion of Kuwait under the leadership of Saddam Hussein raised the spectre of new military powers challenging the West with nuclear and chemical weapons, at a time when the NATO–Warsaw Pact confrontation was in decline. In the Gulf War of early 1991, the advanced military technology of the USA and its allies proved vastly superior and reversed the doubts raised previously during the Vietnam war, although contrary reports questioned the absolute efficacy of the new weapons beyond the favourable reporting arranged by the military. The industrialization of warfare through the mass production of sophisticated armaments has not only provided an extra dimension to industrial production but has also enabled more and more nation-states and other groupings, including guerilla and 'liberation' forces, to play a part in international relations and the overall balance of power. Now, exclusively, the superpowers possess extensive nuclear arsenals with global delivery systems and access to the most advanced of the non-nuclear armament systems.

Recession in the world-economy and mass unemployment in Western society

During the 1970s, currency and oil crises led to stark reactions in capitalist market mechanisms and created levels of inflation which were unprecedented in the Western economies. A rate of inflation up to 5 per cent is considered normal and acceptable but during the 1970s some Western countries, Britain in particular, experienced levels escalating to between 20 and 30 per cent. This was accompanied by a dramatic slowing down in economic growth, although it was less apparent in the post-war 'economic miracles' of West Germany and Japan. Towards the end of the decade, unemployment rates in Europe and North America began to rise and exhibit some new evidence of the dimensions to the inter-societal system. There *was* economic stagnation but there was also the increasing 'migration' to other parts of the world of older industries, principally textiles, steel making, shipbuilding and to some extent motor-vehicle manufacturing. Additionally, sections of the newer electronics industry were from the beginning located outside of the West in newly industrializing countries (NICs). These events marked the onset of a global recession which was not to bottom out until the mid 1980s and with the combination of economic stagnation and inflation an ugly new word, 'stagflation', was in common use for a while. The accelerated running down of older industries coupled with rising unemployment put a whole new slant on the concept of 'post-industrial society' in the West!

It is interesting to look at sociological reactions to inflation and crisis, at the time, in Britain, which appeared hardest hit of the major powers. John Goldthorpe (1978: 196) suggested that inflation was the result of '(i) the decay of the status order; (ii) the realization of citizenship; and (iii) the emergence of a "mature" working class'. His critics accused him of assuming that nothing could be done about inflation and his reply was that the social scientist should not try to see into the future but merely attempt to interpret the facts. This was perhaps wise counsel when it is considered that Andrew Gamble and Paul Walton (1976: 201) suggested that, as an outcome in Britain, 'An authoritarian regime would need to suppress unions and free elections but at the same time, to ensure its own stability, it would need to maintain relatively full employment.' In fact, without anything like such draconian measures people adjusted in their day-to-day lives to very high levels of unemployment and social institutions were reproduced without great disruption. With hindsight it is easy to be critical and there is no doubt that at the time the economic situation appeared bad enough for extreme outcomes not to be precluded.

Perhaps the main reason for the lack of dramatic reaction to economic downturn was sweeping changes in political allegiances in the West which were reflected in peoples day-to-day attitudes to events. The economic recession of the late 1970s and early 1980s was accompanied by a generally recognized political swing to the right in the advanced industrial nations. In 1979 Margaret Thatcher was swept to victory in the British general election on a pledge to 'restore old values' and reduce the high levels of unemployment, which were attributed to the outgoing Labour government's failure to come to terms with industrial decline and its relationship with the trade unions. Two years later Ronald Reagan was inaugurated as the fortieth president of the USA, according to Dimbleby and Reynolds (1988: 303), 'determined that his country should "walk tall" once more, after the drift and self-doubt of the 1970s'. These observers go on to say:

> For both leaders the central tenet of their faith was 'freedom', which, they believed, was endangered at home and abroad. The enemy within was seen as big-spending, Keynesian government which throttled enterprise and stifled self-reliance. They wanted the freedom of the individual increased at the expense of the encroaching state. Abroad, they believed that communist Russia posed a threat to freedom and that the West, deluded by detente, had become complacent about the danger. They doubted that an accommodation could be reached with the Soviet

Union on the basis of mutual self-interest and argued that negotiation
could only take place from a position of much greater military strength.
(pp. 304–5)

This involved a reaffirmation of the 'special relationship' between
Britain and the USA, which had tended to lapse during the 1970s, and
it became a central feature of the Western alliance. It tended to
interfere with Britain's relationship with its EC partners, which Mrs
Thatcher did not find easy in any case, but there were swings to the
right in several other parts of Western Europe too.

The resurgence of right-wing politics as propagated by Reagan and
Thatcher lasted through the 1980s mainly due to the successful
projection of credibility for such policies in the search for economic
recovery. Keynesianism, which had held sway since the 1930s,
followed the Bretton Woods arrangements into oblivion, and its place
was taken by the monetarism of Milton Friedman and F. A. Hayek
with its emphasis on minimum state intervention. However, Western
societies continued to endure mass unemployment, particularly
amongst the young, as older inefficient industries ceased to be
subsidized and were allowed to collapse. Certain sections of the
working class suffered huge traumas as, in vain, they mounted
campaigns to prevents cuts and closures in the industries where they
worked. The migration of basic steel production caused decline in steel
towns along the Ohio River in the USA; in South Wales and the north
of England; in northern France, Belgium and the Ruhr Valley of
Germany. In shipbuilding, the same countries suffered, plus Sweden,
which had created the most modern shipyards and working practices
in the world. In textiles, the southern states of the USA, the north of
England and the eastern Netherlands were some notable sufferers. The
migration of employment was not restricted to old industries,
however, because in new phases of electronics development, involving
microprocessors, much of the routine manufacturing from the outset
went to newly industrializing countries (NICs), especially in East Asia.
This denied the West a source of potential renewal for manufacturing
industry, but ensured that labour costs were kept low and that the
electronics industry remained buoyant.

With mass-produced electronic products it is possible to operate
both a global division of labour and worldwide production lines. Basic
developments in microprocessor technology can be carried out at
research and development concentrations, as in California's so called
'Silicon Valley', where the resulting microprocessor configurations are
etched on to wafer-thin 'chips' of silicon or alternative materials.
Then the labour-intensive part of the manufacturing process, which
is the microscopically-aided wiring up of the 'chip' to its practical

application, may be performed wherever suitable labour can be recruited at lowest cost. This has tended to be in East Asia where plentiful supplies of young female labour are available for the purpose (cf. Mitter 1986, Fuentes and Ehrenreich 1987). Final touches may be added in the USA and Europe where much of the demand for such products continues to exist, but people in Japan and the newly industrializing countries of East Asia have become enthusiastic consumers too. This constitutes, truly, a form of global production line (cf. Henderson 1989).

With rising standards of living and the extension of consumer demand, the international division of labour has changed dramatically and long-standing industries have to a great extent been transferred from Europe and North America to other parts of the world where wages and other costs are lower. Major directions of such transfers have been from North America to Latin America, from Northern Europe to Southern Europe and from the West in general to East Asia. From the 1960s onwards, Japan has consistently captured a large part of the world's production of motorcars, motorcycles, cameras and electronic equipment, when before this time it produced relatively little. These and new industries, especially in electronics, have spread throughout East Asia initially to serve Japanese and Western manufacturing interests but since showing indications of independent economic growth too. The so-called 'four little tigers' – Hong Kong, Singapore, South Korea and Taiwan – and others, will be considered later.

As a consequence of these changes, where manufacturing firms remained located in the West or chose to locate new plant there, they faced more intense competition. In the 'migrating' industries, mentioned above, firms staying in the West were forced to keep labour costs down and thus 'dual labour markets' were created, involving a secondary category of low-paid, temporary and part-time workers (cf. Doeringer and Piore 1971). In other cases, extremely low paid 'out-working' (working at home) became a feature of employment, particularly amongst immigrant groups (cf. Mitter 1986, Phizacklea 1990). In these cases, workers are not normally unionized and so they have much less control of conditions and terms of pay by comparison with permanent full-time workers whose membership of trade unions offers protection.

Reflections: the new international division of labour

The term, new international division of labour (Frobel et al. 1980), has been used in previous chapters to refer to the significant restructuring of manufacturing resources in an inter-societal system. This involves the transfer of manufacturing industries from one part of the world to another and the setting up of industry in parts of the world where there was previously little or none. These changes are not part of any overall plan but take place as a result of competition through the market mechanism inherent in capitalism. There are many exceptions to the classic economic principle but, other things being equal, competition drives manufacturers to supply their products at the most competitive prices.

Workers in the industrial countries, however, have in the long term created and reproduced institutionalized ways of resisting decreases and, in fact, bargaining for increased wages. This has attracted employers to productivity deals, often connected with the introduction of more advanced and productive technology, in order to become more competitive. Harry Braverman (1974) drew fresh attention to the 'de-skilling of labour' and the debate surrounding his work examined extensively the use of mechanization and automation in manufacturing, not only to keep down labour costs through increased productivity but also to control labour through changes in work discipline and organization. Workers as human agents have consistently resisted such measures and as a result have played a considerable part in the shaping of industrial organization (cf. Littler 1982; Thompson 1983). Richard Edwards (1979) has suggested that business firms and in particular the transnational corporations have used considerable ingenuity to maintain control over labour, using techniques of:

1 Simple control (supervision by foremen).
2 Technical control (assembly-line production, in which the pace and continuity is set through the technology).
3 Bureaucratic control (innovative organizational forms with worker incentives designed into them).

Nevertheless, there is another way to reduce production costs which avoids, in the short term at least, both incremental increases in the price of labour and the institutionalized conflict of Western industrial relations. This involves the employment of labour in areas of the world unaffected by Western trade unions or industrial relations procedures. An alternative to the further manipulation of Western labour is the the re-location of industry where labour has not been organized and is sufficiently desperate for work to accept inferior pay and conditions. The juxtaposing of Western conditions of work with the potential to exploit Third World labour places the achievements of Western labour in a different perspective if employment costs are raised sufficiently to price Western workers out of a global market for labour. This is an important implication. The Third World offers a huge potential reservoir of reserve labour with low expectations of pay or welfare benefits. This is especially significant if we accept another consequence of 'de-skilling' to be the transportability of advanced manufacturing technology into which, effectively, skills have been designed and incorporated. Advanced technology requiring high levels of skill to design but only moderate levels to operate can be installed wherever the cost of labour is advantageous.

The new international division of labour (cf. Frobel et al. 1980) represents a further phase of development through the global institutions of the inter-societal system in which further advances in the time and space distanciation of Western culture are demonstrated. Global transport and communications enable products to be manufactured in almost any location yet marketed worldwide, although distribution is still heavily skewed towards the richest consumer markets of North America, Europe and Japan. The modern electronics industry based upon the microprocessor is archetypal of new global manufacturing arrangements but they are not necessarily restricted to electronics. The manufacturing of textiles represents the oldest mechanized industry, and since the basic technology had been perfected by the end of the nineteenth century, production facilities are easily reproduced and eminently transportable, so that manufacturing sites can be established wherever cheap labour is available. In the West, chains of fashion shops, operated by large companies and located in centres of population, depend upon co-ordinated networks of manufacturing facilities. Some of these operate on a large scale to manufacture basic items and some produce small production runs for garments of ephemeral appeal. The use of computers makes it easier to transfer new designs into fabric-cutting machinery and also to control diversified and disparate sources of supply. However, the linking of computers to the making up of garments has so far proved more difficult and this is where low-cost female labour in 'secondary labour markets' is employed, both in the West and in the Third World (Mitter 1986; Fuentes and Ehrenreich 1987; Phizacklea 1990). It requires a minimal investment to set up a small workshop equipped with electric sewing-machines and yet such a unit is very effective in maintaining product variety.

Developments such as these can be linked with the trend to so-called 'corporate raider capitalism' in the financial centres of the world-economy. The principle at stake is the further extension of the market mechanism into capital ownership. The trading success of business firms is linked to the market value of their stocks and shares and, consequently a variety of models have been devised to produce the most effective investment portfolios. The ideal company then becomes a legal package of marketing arrangements for a range of products and services actually produced in a variety of physical locations. In business competition, takeovers and mergers occur at a level removed from physical manufacturing resources and in an idealized enterprise such resources can be acquired and dispensed with as appropriate for the imperatives of the investment portfolio. Thus the 'corporate raider' is a successful business leader pursuing optimum share valuation, far removed from the classical capitalist entrepreneur with a paternalistic orientation towards manufacturing and workers. To some extent, the financially oriented model has already replaced the classical capitalist model in the wealth creation of the advanced industrial countries (cf. Spybey 1984).

A further development is the transition from 'Fordist' to 'post-Fordist' manufacturing systems. It was described earlier how Henry Ford pioneered mass production by means of the production line. Post-Fordist manufacturing was pioneered by the Japanese in order to break away from the inflexibilities of this system. New approaches to stock control, made possible by the introduction of computers and enhanced forms of transport and communication, have enabled much greater flexibilities to be applied to the manufacturing process. This has two main advantages. Firstly, the range of products is not only more attractive to the customer but also more adaptable to progressively planned modification and obsolescence. This is clear from any examination of the fast changing ranges of Japanese-produced cars, motorcycles or electronic products. Secondly, the technique for the coordination of component supplies, known as *kanban*, which translates as 'just in time', results in less capital tied up in stockholding when components are programmed by computer to come together at the point of assembly at just the right time (cf. Eccleston 1989: 35–7).

The introduction of more flexible approaches to manufacturing coupled with the exploitation of cheap labour in Third World countries has revolutionized the supply of consumer products. New markets for such things as home computers or personal stereos are satisfied in this way. It may be discerned, however, that, with global production, another capitalist market is created. This is a market in manufacturing sites and, in extreme cases, certain firms in certain industries have found it attractive to move their factories at relatively frequent intervals. When labour costs rise or when labour organization poses a consistent threat, the leaders of this trend have pursued the advantage of moving relatively portable installations to 'virgin' employment sites. There could never be an inexhaustible supply of these but there is still a large number of Third World countries which suffer from a lack of economic development sufficiently to co-operate with such proposals.

The new international division of labour, therefore, involves the transfer of manufacturing industry from the West and latterly even from Japan. It is transferred to the newly industrializing countries (NICs) of East Asia and Latin America and also to 'export processing zones' which less fortunate Third World countries have set up in order to try and attract industrial development. What this indicates for the West is that much of the unemployment which accompanied the economic recession of the early 1980s is structural and linked to the new international division of labour rather than merely contingent upon the recession. It is also part of the trend in the West towards 'the service economy' whereby more of the workforce is employed in service (tertiary) industries than in manufacturing (secondary) or, much less still, in agriculture and the other extractive (primary) industries.

11

Development in the East: Japan and the Newly Industrializing Countries of East Asia

As Nigel Harris (1987: 9) observes, there is debate over which countries should be labelled 'newly industrializing', but all accounts include the so called 'four little tigers' of East Asia (see figure 12). Hong Kong, Singapore, South Korea and Taiwan all have direct or indirect connections with the earlier rise of Japan as a major industrial power and this will be explored here. However, Japan is unequivocally a different case, involving wholly independent, internally generated development. Additionally amongst the countries recognized as newly industrializing there are the Latin American examples of Brazil, Mexico and possibly Argentina. India, too, is sometimes included, but it is a very large, mixed and less clearly defined case. In Immanuel Wallerstein's (1974) terms, these newly industrializing countries are interpreted as part of the capitalist world-economy's semi-periphery, along with the northern Mediterranean countries and, more problematically, the Soviet bloc of state socialist countries. However, in the newly industrializing countries there is substantive and growing evidence of indigenous investment alongside foreign investment, which qualifies as self-sustaining growth, even in terms of Walt Rostow's model of 'stages of economic growth'. One illustration is the South Korean *chaebol* or industrial conglomerate, Samsung, which was in July 1990 estimated by the American business magazine, *Fortune*, to be the twentieth largest corporation in the world in terms of cash turnover per annum. This puts it amongst the giant transnational corporations, and it is not the only non-Japanese East Asian company that has grown so dynamically in the age of mass-produced high-technology consumer products. It is not intended that this point should be seen as a vindication of modernization theory, the discrediting of which was addressed extensively in chapter 2, but that

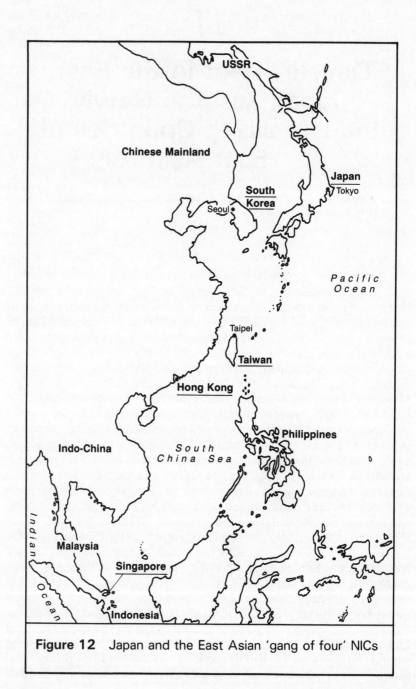

Figure 12 Japan and the East Asian 'gang of four' NICs

some of Rostow's principles may be attributable to particular cases
rather than as he suggests, general ones. I shall now explore some of
the specificities of the East Asian newly industrializing countries and
their connections with Japan.

The Post-Confucian hypothesis in East Asian development

Levels of capitalist expansion in East Asia that are clearly independent
of Western development have given rise to speculation that a different
form of capitalism exists there. Peter L. Berger (1987), in his
retrospective overview, refers to East Asia as 'a second case' of the
growth of capitalism. The model for East Asian industrial success is
quite obviously Japan, but similar kinds of development on a smaller
scale now exist in Hong Kong, Singapore, South Korea and Taiwan.
According to Anthony Giddens (1985: 273), Japan comes under the
category of a 'modernizing state' that managed to achieve modernization internally without the help of outside powers. Theda Skocpol
(1979: 100–5) argues that the lack of a land-owning aristocracy during
the Tokugawa feudal shoganate was a crucial factor. This allowed the
samurai, formerly a warrior and then an administrative group, to carry
out the modernization process after the 1868 coup when the *shogan*
was replaced as head of state by an emperor. South Korea and Taiwan
were both colonies of Japan during the first half of the twentieth
century and as in all cases of colonialism this can be held to account
for some changes to their social structure. But, more recently, both
enjoyed considerable military and economic support from the USA in
the global military order as bastions of capitalism in an area seen as
vulnerable to the spread of communism. That type of support became
a problem diplomatically after the USA's detente with China in the
early 1970s, but by that time the development process in South Korea
and Taiwan was well underway. By contrast, Hong Kong and
Singapore were formerly entrepot ports of the British Empire in its
trade with China and the Far East, both of which have since converted
successfully into manufacturing locations. Hong Kong remains a
British colony until 1997 when it is scheduled to transfer constitutionally to the People's Republic of China and will no doubt add
significantly to that country's capitalist liberalization process. Hong
Kong has for a long time benefited from its position as an unofficial
outlet on to the world market for goods manufactured in China, often
indistinguishable from those mass produced within its own small
territory. Undoubtedly, all four of these newly industrializing countries have benefited from their special connections with the USA and

Britain in the inter-societal system, but the chief interest here is with their capacity for dynamic industrial progress.

One reason for the success of Hong Kong, Singapore, South Korea and Taiwan is that they are examples of successful 'post-Confucian' societies. China, the birthplace of Confucius, is a state socialist power excluded from this consideration of the newly industrializing countries. But the areas bordering China are historically imbued with Confucianism, too, and it has been taken seriously as a factor in their development. For instance, the Japanese writer, Yasusuke Murakami (1986: 229–30), who differentiates Japan from other societies of the 'China periphery type', nevertheless assumes the generality of post-Confucian influence throughout the area. The Taiwanese economist, Yuan-Li Wu (1985: 122–3), addresses the issue of 'practical and selective application of Confucianism' and more cautiously the question of 'whether Confucian ethics truly constitute a driving force in Sinic societies like Singapore, Hong Kong and ... Taiwan'. From the Western point of view, Dennis John Gayle (1986: 109), points to the familial nexus between citizenry and government in Singapore's success as an industrial city-state with its dependence upon a political culture and societal value orientation in which the single most important factor is Confucianism and the reproduction of Confucian institutions.

Herman Kahn's (1979) proposal of a 'post-Confucian hypothesis' posited that the success of business firms in East Asia can be explained by reference to key traits shared by members of these organizations and attributable to their upbringing within the Confucian tradition. In its classical sense, a Confucian upbringing involves a central concern for the correct and courteous execution of the individual's duties, especially as they involve the family, based upon a profound respect for social conventions. The main elements are ritual, order, service and the meritocratic achievement of these virtues, derived from Confucius's notion of *chun-tzu* or nobility of character as realized practically and historically in the Chinese mandarinate. As Michael Mann (1986: 343) points out, 'For Confucius nobility of character was not private but social. Expressed by culture, etiquette, and ritual, it could be learned and taught. Thus a hereditary nobility was insufficient [in Confucius's conception of the desirable social order].' This last sentence, however, tends to suggest a functionalist explanation for the existence of the mandarins which would mask their political origins. They were the elite servants of the emperor who actively maintained for themselves a monopoly of literacy and therefore of state record-keeping and surveillance in a class-divided society. This can be linked with the imperial patrimonialism of traditional Chinese culture, which was, above all, a profoundly anti-individualistic ethos.

It is, therefore, the Confucian principles of collectivism rather than individualism, and merit rather than ascription that are reproduced in 'post-Confucian' form as an explanation for work-group productivity and industrial success throughout contemporary East Asia. In this book the principle of the duality of structure is emphasized whereby regular social practices in their day-to-day reproduction constitute the structure of society, which may then be seen as distanciated in time and space.

The post-Confucian hypothesis begs the question of why Confucian principles might now be seen as a catalyst for industrial capitalism in East Asia, when in classical China they were considered an impediment to progress. Max Weber's view was that the failure to develop scientific rationality and capitalist economics adequately under classical Chinese philosophy was connected with the explanation for their subsequent and successful maturation instead in north-western Europe under the Protestant ethic. There is, in fact, more to the subsequent capitalist industrialization process in East Asia than the post-Confucian thesis alone. For instance, in Stewart Clegg et al. (1990), it is suggested that Confucian principles of collectivism and merit may serve as part of the explanation for successful industrial relations and management in East Asia, but that explanation for the equally important dimensions of innovation and marketing would seem to lie elsewhere. The flexibility of manufacturing techniques in East Asia is the definitive example of 'post-Fordism', contrasted earlier with the rather inflexible mass production of 'Fordism'. Post-Fordist consumerism in the advanced industrial nations, involving a wider choice of product, is propagated through the attractiveness of notions of individualism, even if those notions are mainly illusory given the nature of consumerism. East Asian manufacturers have been particularly successful at identifying market niches at which to aim their flexible production runs, as any examination of their 'consumer durable' products will reveal. The complexity of production ranges and brevity of life of particular variations lend themselves to notions of individualism in consumption and to planned obsolescence in manufacturing and marketing. In this way, flexibility of product has successfully provided a broadening of demand, but people in East Asia are just as enthusiastic in the consumption of these individualized products as people in the West. Thus, there are grounds for scepticism over the appropriateness of the post-Confucian principle of collectivism, at least when it is applied to consumption patterns in contemporary East Asian societies.

As a counter-argument, it may be suggested that East Asian industrial organization, on the one hand, and the marketing success of East Asian products, on the other, may be entirely separate categories.

Certainly the urban centres of Japan, Hong Kong, Singapore, South Korea and Taiwan are today as fashionable and consumer-orientated as their equivalents in the West. But, at the same time, these are societies containing much greater social inequalities. The familiar model of post-war Japanese industrial organization made up of loyal and well rewarded workers who are members of supportive 'enterprise unions', is one that is not representative of the entire Japanese industrial scene let alone that of other East Asian countries which have sought to emulate it. It is clear that the privileged class of consumer-orientated people subjected to Western culture, which undoubtedly exists in these societies, is counteracted by a class of less privileged people and even an underclass of immigrants from other East Asian countries. Thus, although the post-Confucian hypothesis may be unacceptable in exactly the form proposed by Kahn, there is, nevertheless, evidence of a high degree of social control which contributes to an ordered and pliable labour force in manufacturing industry.

Work groups and industrial relations in Japan

There is as yet insufficient material available in English to carry out anything other than an extremely cursory review of work groups in Hong Kong, Singapore, South Korea and Taiwan. But, in order to shed light on the post-Confucian hypothesis, we may examine the plentiful evidence for Japan in more detail. A common approach to Japanese work groups by Western authors is through a preoccupation with the Japanese propensity for participation in group decision making without any apparent relinquishment of group hierarchies (cf. Ketcham 1987). The precedent for this social characteristic is the *ie* which originates from a type of peasant group formed to assert land rights in Japanese society when it was administered by the *samurai*. Therefore, any explanation of 'groupism' in Japanese industry owes something to the *samurai* legacy as well as to Confucianism. This is likely to be the case with any society of the China periphery type since Confucianism is a philosophy which over a long period has been reproduced in a wide range of regular social practices. In the case of Japan the *ie* is all the more significant since the *samurai* were instrumental in the country's modernization. In sociological terms the *ie* as a primary group in social organization has brought into modern Japanese society and work practices the importance of the functional quality of the individual in a small group. The homogeneity of group membership based upon functional qualities is, in certain respects, more significant in Japan than kin, class or status (Murakami 1984,

1986: 230). This renders more complex the simple connection between cohesiveness in Japanese work groups and the ethos of familial duty, but the emphasis remains on anti-individualism and the importance of the group, attributable to a combination of Confucianism and the *samurai*–society group ethic.

A different approach, however, emphasizes hierarchical authoritarian control in the explanation of 'groupism' (cf. Sugimoto 1986; Sugimoto and Mouer 1985). This identifies a mistake on the part of Western observers which is attributable to their examination only of privileged sections of the workforce where long-term employment, enterprise unions and consensus are the norms. Other sections of the workforce, it is claimed, lack such benefits and face a much more problematic relationship with employers. In this way a broad 'culture of consent' is mistakenly attributed to traditional 'groupism' when, for a large proportion of the workforce, it is really the result of authoritarian social control by an elite, nowadays legitimated by the outstanding success of Japanese industry. The history of Japanese industrial relations, both before and after the Second World War, is revealing (cf. Gordon 1985). Initially, with the acceleration of industrialization during the approach to the war, the formation of an industrial working class from a recalcitrant peasantry was as much a subject of conflict as in any other example of the industrialization process. Coercion was the means used, involving legislation, surveillance by police and sometimes violence on the part of employers. After the war, in the confusion of defeat, the socialist and communist parties quickly organized a large proportion of the workforce and attempted to co-ordinate the introduction of workers' control. By then there were different politico-military imperatives, and it was the American forces of occupation under General MacArthur which cracked down on this new trade union movement. Priority was attached to the familiar Western priority of 'stemming the tide of communism' in South-East Asia in the light of events in China. Many suspected activists were expelled from projects regarded as strategic to Japan's economic recovery and, ironically, it was the US military administration which imposed the neat pattern of enterprise unionism onto strategic businesses during the occupation. As an unintentional conseqence, therefore, it was ensured that model industrial relations arrangements would contribute extensive industrial peace to the 'economic miracle' of post-war Japan.

Enterprise unions are an integral part of the 'company world' which characterizes the powerful nucleus of contemporary Japanese industry. Such unions involve internal labour markets which offer lifetime employment and seniority wage systems to selected employees, but this is not characteristic of all Japanese industry. The 'company world' employees, projected in some accounts as typical, make up less than one-third of Japan's total industrial workforce. The remaining two-thirds consist of a complex mixture of members of breakaway left-wing unions and workers subject to varying degrees of exploitation in a range of small and medium-sized firms which often act as sub-contractors to the big-name companies (Eccleston 1989: 33–8). John Junkerman (1987: 131–44) contrasts the advanced technology and working environment of the Nippon Kokan steelworks, on an artificially created island in Tokyo Bay, with the overcrowding and environmental pollution of the industry which services it in the city of Kawasaki on the mainland. There, a wide belt of hundreds of firms, some established early in this century and rebuilt after the devastation of the Second World War, employ less fortunate workers including a ghetto of Korean immigrants, a legacy from the imperial period of the 1930s and 1940s, (cf. Eccleston 1989: 197–9). This is the less attractive and less publicized side of Japanese industrial success. The steelworks is a model admired and envied by visitors from North America and Europe but the rest is comparable with industrial exploitation anywhere.

Industrial relations in Japan, therefore, is anything but straightforward. Alongside the enterprise-union core, and sometimes eating into it, are the chronic labour disputes in those companies which have to deal with more than one union. The more difficult situations often involve an enterprise union and a 'breakaway' union formed as a result of some past labour dispute. Some of the flexibility that is characteristic of the Japanese system is derived from an ease of recruitment and dismissal amongst the plethora of sub-contracting firms, themselves often sub-contracting in turn to even smaller workshops. Many workers are employed either on a seasonal basis from the agrarian sector, an institution continually reproduced in Japan since its earliest industrialization, or else they are part-time out-workers and typically housewives. The average wage of a Japanese male worker has been approximately double that of a female in recent years, and the broad notion of a secondary labour market, as described in the last chapter, seems to have currency in Japan as much as it does in the West. Union organization in these sectors is problematic and payment is usually by piece-rate with wages at a fraction of those applying under core enterprise-union conditions. In all industrialized countries sub-contracting is more prevalent than it may appear, and in the archetypal motor industries of North America and Europe as much as 50 per cent of the work may be contracted out, but in Japan the figure is as high as 75 per cent. Sub-contracting networks are, however, strongly dominated by the principal firm which can maintain its show-piece plant, employing mainly core workers, whilst depending upon a support network of secondary labour-market workers.

Undoubtedly, the union structure in Japan is changing. Since 1987 the independent unions in the private sector, with the exception of the few associated with the Japanese Communist Party, have been unified under an umbrella organization called Rengo (the National Federation of Private Sector Unions). Through this the socialist and social-democratic parties are eventually, but not speedily, expected to achieve a greater degree of unity against the ruling Liberal Democratic Party which during the late 1980s began to suffer a series of electoral setbacks. Nevertheless, for core workers in Japanese industry, control continues to be exercised through the 'job-for-life' loyalty ethos associated with Confucianism. Individuals are carefully screened upon recruitment, and training is specific to the firm and its methods of operating. As a result an internal labour market is created which offers prescribed career pathways guaranteeing employment, but not neces-sarily advancement. Core workers are the ones relied upon to maintain productivity levels, especially through the application of innovatory electronics-based technology and the crucial quality controls that have been such a key factor in the continuing success of Japanese products. These efforts are backed up by the highest levels of non-military research and development expenditure in the world. There are as many industrial robots in operation in Japan as in the rest of the world put together.

The control of labour in Japan, through institutionalized primary and secondary labour markets, would therefore appear to be as strong an element in the Japanese industrial and economic success story as post-Confucianism or *samurai* culture. Group harmony is evident in industrial organization, as it is in Japanese society in general, but it appears to complement forms of control characteristic of industrial work organization anywhere. It seems, therefore, that traditional social practices have been combined with more recent ones in the repro-duction of contemporary social institutions as they apply to Japanese industry. This is normal in the development of any society and is consistent with the concept of an inter-societal system presented throughout this book. Pervasive Western institutions – segmented labour markets – have come into contact with traditional indigenous institutions in the guise of Confucianism and *samurai* culture, and as a result of such complementary forms the control of work is especially authoritarian in Japan and in other East Asian countries. This manifests itself in other areas of society too. In South Korea, for instance, the well publicized confrontations between students and police serve to illustrate the institutionalized elitism of the society. South Korean students are, in the Confucian tradition of the society, exercising the right as scholars to criticize authority when others would not dare and they do so with significantly higher status in the social structure than their riot policemen adversaries. For these reasons the term 'authoritarian democratic capitalism' has been used to describe not only the Japanese system but also that of its East Asian neighbours: Hong Kong, Singapore, South Korea and Taiwan (cf. Clegg et al. 1990). It is the authoritarian nature of the employment relationship which seems most appropriate to distinguish East Asian capitalism from the original Western liberal–democratic model.

The success of East Asian capitalism

It is useful here to review the contents of this chapter. Japan is obviously an exceptional case and since its military defeat in 1945 has, with initial support from the USA, risen to become the world's outstanding industrial nation in terms of manufacturing innovation and economic growth. In particular, military protection by the United States and consequent lack of large-scale defence expenditure has allowed capital to be directed by Japan's renowned and interventionist Ministry of International Trade and Industry (MITI) into innovatory industrial development whilst the value of the yen was for a long time kept artificially low to encourage exports. As such, it is the only country outside Europe and the former European settler colonies of North American and Australasia to become a member of the Organization for Economic Co-operation and Development (OECD) and of the inner elite known as G7 countries – Britain, Canada, France, Germany, Italy, Japan and the USA (see figure 13). Membership of these groups is an unequivocal sign of acceptance amongst the advanced industrial nations, yet that distinction now seems the least of Japan's accolades. According to Paul Kennedy (1988: 467), in 1951 Japan's gross national product was one-third of Britain's and one-twentieth of the USA's but, with only 3 per cent of the world's population and 0.3 per cent of its land area, by 1981 it had grown to twice Britain's and one-half of the USA's. Embarrassingly for the USA, whose foreign debt escalated during Ronald Reagan's presidency in the 1980s, Japan has become its creditor to an extent in the region of US $500 billion in 1990 and that is expected to grow further. Japan is set apart therefore in a number of ways:

1   By its distinction as an internally 'modernizing' nation-state – it has developed to advanced industrial status independently of Western colonialism.

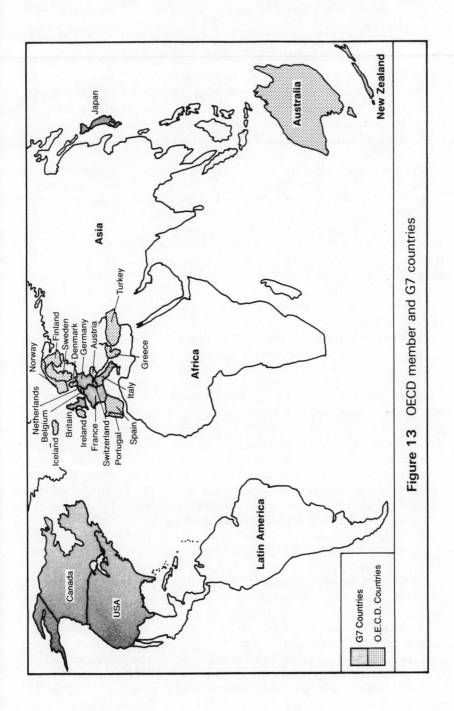

Figure 13 OECD member and G7 countries

2   By its remarkable success in the manufacturing of motor vehicles, electronics and other precision-engineered products.
3   By its new status as a major capital provider for the West.

The East Asian newly industrializing countries of Hong Kong, Singapore, South Korea and Taiwan have a variety of links past or present, either with Britain or the United States. But what they have in common with each other and with Japan as East Asian neighbours of China is a historical and geographical (time and space) association with Confucian philosophy. This serves as a partial explanation for their industrial success, but by no means a complete one. Indeed Hong Kong, Singapore and Taiwan are societies predominantly of Chinese people, whilst the Korean archipelago lies between China and Japan and has been colonized by both at various times in history. Japan and the 'four little tigers' have, in various ways, all served as allies of Western capitalism in the face of the establishment of Marxist regimes in China and North Korea after the Second World War. Resistance to Marxism can be connected to the reproduction of traditional elements in the cultures of these countries and significant amongst these are aspects of Confucian philosophy. It is not so much post-Confucianism as a broader authoritarianism in the social structure that is responsible for their industrial success. This authoritarianism is, however, served by Confucianism and takes deliberate and instrumental forms when reproduced in the industrialized institutions of these countries.

The success of East Asian newly industrializing countries (NICs), with their lower wages, has been sufficient to ensure that Japan itself has had to transfer manufacturing from the bottom end of the production spectrum, with which its early growth was achieved, into 'up-market' goods. But that appears only to have benefited Japan and thrust it into further competition or collaboration with the West, specifically in terms of new generations of product. Examples are new 'super-computers'; nuclear-power technology in conjunction with the American firm, Westinghouse; and energy-efficient aircraft for the 1990s with the Boeing Corporation (Kennedy 1988: 462–3). In November 1989 it was announced that the US government was withdrawing research funding for the next generation of high-definition television receivers which are of enormous consumer potential and with which American scientists had been in competition with the Japanese up to that point. Meanwhile, Japanese investment in the rest of East Asia has provided much of the momentum for the developments there, at the same time as providing Japan and the Western nations with new supplies of cheaper labour. In January 1991, Prime Minister Toshiki Kaifu announced the 'Kaifu doctrine' redefining Japan's role as Asia's economic superpower and laying the foundations for a new international order in the region. This involves Japan's emergence as head of a continental trading bloc to rival the USA and the EC in market size and economic power. Included in this initiative was the reaffirmation of links with China and the opening of new ties with North Korea, the most frigid of Cold War adversaries, but very advanced industrially. The prospect at some point in the future of Japanese industrial dynamism associated with a liberalized Chinese population of more than a billion potential consumers provides considerable food for thought in the context of Japan's proposed Asian trading bloc.

Reflections

Perhaps the most important consideration in connection with Japan and the East Asian newly industrializing countries is the extent to which they signify a process of social development and modernization. With Hong Kong, Singapore, South Korea and Taiwan there is evidence of labour shortages pushing up wages as economic development proceeds, even though trade union activity is relatively suppressed (Bienefeld 1981: 88). If this indicates that the process has penetrated the whole of the available working-age population then it is reasonable to assume that the average standard of living must rise as a response to the demand for labour. Equally, the experience in these countries shows evidence of independent capitalist accumulation. Yet these cases are of highly centralized states exercising repressive political power directly in the economic sphere, in contradiction of the Western liberal–democratic principle of separation between polity and economy. Geoff Lamb (1981: 107) argues that attempts to hold up South Korea and Taiwan (or Brazil) as examples of the free play of market forces in the Western mode are grotesque when 'they are among the more corporate, planned and dirigiste economies in the world'. Development in these areas is at a price, in terms of Western liberalism at least.

12

The Resurgence of Islam: an Alternative to Western Capitalism or State Socialism?

In this chapter I aim to address the resurgence of Islam during the 1980s and the extent to which this may be interpreted as a rejection of Western capitalism and Soviet state socialism. In this context 'Islamism', is a term acceptable to Muslims in preference to 'Islamic fundamentalism' or 'Islamic revival' which have been commonly used in the Western media. According to Nikki Keddie (1988: 15) Islamism refers 'to twentieth century movements for political Islam, usually aiming overtly or covertly at an Islamic state that would enforce at least some Islamic laws and customs, including those related to dress, sex segregation, and some economic measures and Qur'anic punishments'. The reproduction of Islamic institutions would be protected by the state in legislation, and in certain areas of day-to-day life, other institutions, such as those derived from Western culture, would be discouraged. Islamic culture was initially protected from the rise of Western civilization by the existence of successive Islamic empires and indeed, the direction of European maritime expansionism was originally determined by the need to circumvent their territories. This situation lasted to some extent until the First World War and the collapse of the Ottoman Empire. By this time the discovery of large quantities of oil in the Middle East had brought fresh interest from an industrialized West, and the Middle East was drawn into the inter-societal system of Western-dominated activities (see figure 14). Subsequently, the demand for oil continued to grow, with Westerners, and especially Americans, as the largest consumers, so that recent Islamic resurgence has taken place against the background of the world's largest oil reserves. As an added complication, some Islamic societies have flirted with the rejection of capitalism through socialism, usually in some form of association with the Soviet Union.

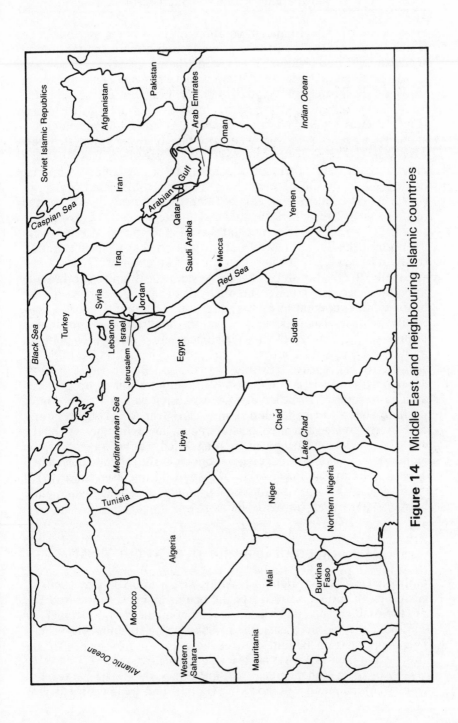

Figure 14 Middle East and neighbouring Islamic countries

However, since the Iranian revolution in 1979 there is a sense in which Islamism itself constitutes the rejection of both capitalism and socialism with the creation of renewed Islamic society.

Any attempt to understand Islamic development benefits from a study of the history of the religion. For instance, the present day Sunni–Shi'a schism underlines the importance since the early sixteenth century of Shi'a Islamic institutions amongst Persians (now Iranians), as contrasted with their minority following amongst Arabs. According to Malise Ruthven (1984: 222), it was the Safavids, a tribe originating in Azerbaijan (since, part of the Soviet Union), who first made Shi'a Islam the state ideology in Persia; whilst Peter Mansfield (1985: 34–5) confirms that this has constituted a key feature of the relationship between Persians and Arabs ever since. Yet, as Keddie (1988: 23) points out, in recent times even many Sunni Muslims were unaware of the Shi'a minority until it was brought to their attention by the mass media following the Iranian revolution of 1979.

Equally, the relationship between Western Christianity and Islam is important because conflict between them has been part of the historical development of each civilization. The foundation of Christianity precedes Islam by more than six hundred years, yet it was Islamic civilization which first developed into a large-scale politico-military empire with cultural exchanges and long-distance trade, in advance of European maritime expansion. But whereas Islam's development was as a land-based 'world-empire' made up of class-divided societies, Europe's maritime expansion was as a collection of separate states which developed into class (capitalist) societies and collectively created an inter-societal system involving the rest of the world. I shall continue by examining briefly some aspects of the foundation of Islam before going on to look at the separate but related question of Arab nationalism and Western oil interests. Since 1979, there is also the issue of the establishment of a reactionary Shi'a Islamic state in Iran (formerly Persia).

The origins of Islam: a rival to the West

At the time of Islam's origins, the Arabs were a group of tribal societies inhabiting the arid desert area of the peninsula between the Red Sea and the Arabian Gulf. Their peoples were nomadic warriors, traders or semi-nomadic pastoralists, hitherto subscribing to animistic beliefs. The fierce warrior Beduin are the best known for their itinerant lifestyle and their skill with horses which made for some very effective cavalry in Islam's phenomenal military expansion during the seventh century. Muhammad was born in AD 570 and in his fortieth year began to receive the word of Allah which has formed the teachings of Islam, principally set down in the Qur'an, the Islamic holy book, but also in the *hadiths* or traditions of the faith. At the time, Arabic was an oral language in tribal society, but subsequently the importance of Muhammad's teachings generated the spread of a written form. This served in the institutionalization of the religion and its culture with the role of priests, familiar to other cultures, as scribes and teachers in city-based class-divided society. These teachings together with Islamic law, the *Shari'a* which was derived from similar sources, contain patterns for all aspects of life including science and technology, with a decidedly environmental perspective (cf. Husaini 1980), and economic exchange with the prohibition of *riba* (the charging of interest). Therefore, in orthodox Islam the routine reproduction of religious institutions is closely connected with establishing a wide range of other day-to-day institutions. Ruthven (1984: 227) has thrown some light on this with the suggestion that if Christianity is the religion of love, then Islam is that of communality and justice.

Muhammad failed to nominate his successor, the *khalifa*, or, in Westernized form, caliph, and so his death led to conflict in which the succession went to Abu Bakr, the father of 'Aisha, Muhammad's youngest and favourite wife. His cousin, Ali ibn Abi Talib, despite his reputation for extreme piety was excluded and later when offered the caliphate declined on the grounds that the precedents set by Abu Bakr were unacceptable (Hiro 1988: 14). Nevertheless, Ali did become caliph upon the assassination of Uthman, the third to have held that office, but the succession was never resolved to the satisfaction of all. Ali himself was murdered, and throughout its history the caliphate has tended towards the qualities of hereditary leadership with dynasties intriguing and fighting for power (Ruthven 1984: 95–6). Its importance remained until modern times, however, and when the Turkish nationalist leader, Kemal Ataturk, took over from the Ottoman sultan in Istanbul and abolished the caliphate in March 1924, there were stubborn attempts by other Islamic countries to retain it (Hiro 1988: 108). This is indicative of the enduring reverence for the caliphate as a central institution of Islam and, although it has never been revived, there is, nevertheless, a sense in which the principle of Islamic spiritual leadership has relevance today. Regardless of the Sunni-Shi'a distinction the Iranian leader, Ayatollah Khomeini, was for many Muslims a renewed spiritual leader of a stature sufficient to fill an ontological void created through Western domination over many centuries.

It was the supporters of the original caliphate succession, in favour of Abu Bakr, who became known as Sunnis after the term, *Sunna*, meaning the Prophet's practice. Whilst the followers of Ali became known as Shi'as from the term, *Shi'at Ali*, meaning partisans of Ali. According to Hiro:

> Sunnis – or more specifically *Ahl al Sunna*, People of the Sunna, the Beaten Path or Tradition – who regard caliphs as fallible interpreters of the *Qur'an*, the Word of Allah ... Sunnis revere the Prophet and the four 'Rightly Guided' caliphs, whereas Shi'as venerate only the Prophet and Imam Ali, and Ali's descendants. (Hiro 1988: 18)

The four 'Rightly Guided caliphs' mentioned above include Ali as the fourth caliph, but the Shi'as believe that Ali should have succeeded Muhammad in the first place. He is considered never to have deviated from true Islamic practice and consequently Shi'as believe in the infallibility of the Imam, a Shi'a term for leaders in the lineage of Muhammad. The Iranian Shi'as are 'Twelver' Shi'as and believe in that number of true spiritual descendants of Ali including a Twelfth Hidden Imam who disappeared in the tenth century. In connection with this and the earlier point, Ruthven (1984: 225) suggests that 'Though [the Ayatollah] Khomeini never made any formal statement to the effect that he was the Hidden Imam, his tumultuous reception on his return from exile, and the fact the since he took over the leadership of the state he has been known to all his supporters as "the Imam"', point to the same conclusion', here referring to the 'latent eschatological expectations' of his supporters.

Arab nationalism in the nation-state system: Middle East oil resources in the capitalist world-economy

The disputes between Iran and other Islamic countries have been not so much concerned with the interpretation of Islamic teaching as about political conflict and the historic differences between Arabs and Persians. Islam has its origins amongst the Arabs, but as a world religion came to embrace a great number of other peoples. In the Middle East there have been effectively two focuses for resistance against Western domination: Islam the religion and Arab nationalism. In recent history the seeds of renewed Arab nationalism were sown during the nineteenth century in opposition to the Ottoman Empire. In the Crimean War the Ottoman Turks were allies of the British and French against the Russians, but by the First World War relationships had changed and the allied powers switched to supporting the Arab cause against the pro-German Turks. The exploits of Lawrence of Arabia are a well known episode in this sequence of events and he was successful in fomenting Arab revolt against Turkish forces to facilitate the entry of allied forces into the Middle East. With the completion of the Suez canal in 1869 and the resultant foreshortening of time–space relationships between East and West, the area had increased in importance as a very strategic link in the route to India and the Far East. But its value in the inter-societal system increased further with the development of the internal combustion engine and the consequent burgeoning demand for oil. In 1917 another element of British foreign policy, the Balfour Declaration, gave substance to the idea of a Jewish homeland in Palestine and only a few years later, with Palestine under British mandate from the League of Nations, the admission of Jewish immigrants began to provoke Arab resentment. Thus were created all the major ingredients of the Middle East question more or less as we recognize it today (cf. Fromkin 1991; Yapp 1991).

At the end of the First World War, the Ottoman Turks capitulated a little while before the Germans, and their Islamic empire was broken up by the allies. Kemal Ataturk used Turkish nationalism to salvage a Turkish nation-state from the wreckage, but the so-called 'Arab Rectangle' was designated as occupied territory and the new nation-states of Iraq, the Lebanon, Palestine, Syria and Transjordan were created under Western jurisdiction and to the Western model (cf. Mansfield 1985: 179). As in earlier examples of colonialism, state borders were set by Western nations but in this case they were sustained through a 'divide and rule' principle of military support for nominated rulers without reference to broader Arab interests. France obtained a League of Nations' mandate over the Levantine coastal strip comprising Lebanon and Syria, with some influence in Iraq in terms of oil supplies. The British mandate extended over Iraq, Palestine and Transjordan, at a time when the Anglo-Persian Oil Co. (now BP) were already extracting large quantities of oil in Persia (now Iran). This was the culmination of a series of concessions negotiated in favour of Britain, aided by the fall of the Russian government in 1917 and the Ottoman collapse in 1918 (cf. Shwadran 1973). In 1927 large oil fields were discovered in Iraq and there was also the important enclave of Kuwait which had been linked to Britain by a treaty since 1899. Under the terms of the mandate there were concessions for two British oil companies, two American and one French, all negotiated by Western businessmen with the new Iraqi ministers playing only a nominal role (Mansfield 1985: 199). Later, in 1938, major oil fields were discovered on the Arabian peninsula and the USA, feeling it had been rather squeezed out by Britain and France, cemented its interests with support for King Ibn Saud. After the Second World War, this huge Saudi Arabian concession became

Aramco (The Arabian American Oil Co.), a conglomerate which has included Standard Oil of California; Standard Oil of New Jersey, later known as Exxon, or Esso in Britain; Socony Vacuum, later Mobil; and the Texas Oil Company, later Texaco (cf. Nawwab et al. 1980). This illustrates the links between the developments of that time and the transnational oil companies of today which are amongst the largest corporations in the world. Britain and the USA shared other similar concessions in the Arabian Gulf, all of which became more important during and after the Second World War. Such a chain of events clearly constitutes the dividing up of rights to Middle East oil fields as part of an inter-societal system in which nation-states and transnational corporations are the dominant forms of organization.

Egypt has no extensive oil fields, but historically is an important centre of Islam. After Napoleon's expedition of 1798, it was ruled by Muhammad Ali virtually independently of the Ottoman Empire and there was considerable British and French participation from the middle of the nineteenth century. However, Egypt's involvement with the capitalist world-economy, through the operation of the Suez Canal and the growing of cotton as a cash crop, produced fluctuations in its economic fortunes (Ruthven 1984: 293). Western dominance continued and even when the country was unilaterally declared independent by Britain in 1936, the right was reserved to control vital imperial interests including, principally, the Suez Canal. According to Mansfield (1985: 208–11), this was a prescription for instability and during the 1920s the Muslim Brotherhood was founded in Cairo as an organization dedicated to campaigning for government on Qur'anic principles. Arguably, therefore, this movement was one of the precursors of contemporary Islamic revival and as such a significant focus in Middle East politics.

In Istanbul, the former centre of Islam and the Ottoman empire, the nation-state of Turkey was created amongst the sweeping changes which followed the First World War. The survival of the Turkish nation was led by Mustafa Kemal who took the name of Kemal Ataturk. He embarked upon a programme of vigorous Westernization and was, for instance, photographed ballroom-dancing with his daughter at her wedding reception, contrary to all Islamic tradition, in a self-conscious demonstration of 'modernization' (Roberts 1985: 393). The allies were anxious to avoid further conflict and allowed Turkey to be proclaimed a republic in 1923, although the nation-state so created also contained other nationalities such as Kurds. The following year, despite protests from various Islamic groups, the pan-Islamic caliphate was finally abolished after a not uninterrupted tradition of 1292 years (Hiro 1988: 56). Perhaps more significantly,

Turkish and Arab destinies were separated after more than four centuries (Mansfield 1985: 196).

By the Second World War the strategic importance of the Middle East was based unequivocally upon oil, and the first of the allied summits between Roosevelt, Churchill and Stalin was held at Tehran, drawing attention to the strategic global importance of the area. As in the First World War, the unification of the Arabs was in the Western allies' interests and the Arab League was set up as a political union under British auspices in 1944 (Mansfield 1985: 228). Ironically, by the end of the war the establishment of a Jewish settler colony in Palestine, at the insistence of the Americans but under British supervision, was a new factor to galvanize Arab nationalism. With the actual displacement of Palestinians, the propensity for conflict was immediate, but in 1947, no sooner was the partition of Palestine accepted by the newly formed United Nations than Britain washed its hands of the problem by suddenly relinquishing the mandate. This left the initiative to the Zionists who proclaimed the state of Israel in 1948, a signal to invade for Syria, Transjordan, Iraq and Egypt who were by then anxious to demonstrate not only their opposition to Israel but also their independence of the West. Thus, the first Arab–Israeli war was fought, and at its conclusion Israel occupied 80% of Palestine. Of the remainder, Egypt took the Gaza Strip and Transjordan absorbed the West Bank including Jerusalem to form the Hashemite Kingdom of Jordan (Mansfield 1985: 238). There were strong Islamic connections in this, for the Hashemites were an Arabian family who traced their ancestry back to Muhammad and who traditionally provided the Grand Sharif at Mecca. Before this they had harboured aspirations for a 'Greater Syria' embracing Syria, the Lebanon, Transjordan and Palestine which, as Mansfield (p. 224) points out, gives some indication of conflicting definitions as to what might constitute an Arab nation.

During this period the US government, with its powerful Jewish lobby, was consistent with its support for Israel in finance and armaments, whilst Egypt became the focus for opposition. Under the leadership of Colonel Gamal Abdul Nasser and the Free Officers movement, Egypt asserted its full independence from Britain and France in 1956 by seizing the Suez Canal. Nationalization of the canal prevailed, despite an invasion by British, French and Israeli forces, when the USA expressed its uncompromising disapproval in a clear confirmation of post-war US power and opposition to European colonialism. Nasser, although in conflict with the Muslim Brotherhood, spoke in terms of the coincidence of the Arab Circle, the African Circle and the Islamic Circle (Mansfield 1985: 246) and became a symbol of anti-Western struggle throughout the Third World. Under his charismatic leadership there was a fleeting glimpse of Arab unity when Egypt joined with Syria as the United Arab Republic (UAR) between 1958 and 1961 and, as a slight to the West, aligned themselves with the Soviet Union.

Meanwhile Saudi Arabia remained friendly with the West, mainly due to extensive oil connections with the USA and the revenues which they produced. Nevertheless, it gave extensive financial support to the poorer Arab states of Egypt, Jordan and Syria, especially when their common fortune was harsh defeat in an Israeli attack, the Six Day War of June 1967. In 1973, Egypt and Syria took the military initiative and the conflict was less one-sided but Israel still emerged unequivocally the victor. However, a devastating blow was delivered to the West when the 'oil weapon was unsheathed' and supplies generally were reduced by 5 per cent per month, with Saudi Arabia cutting back its output by 10 per cent. The Arab countries would have preferred a more selective reprisal to hit those countries which they perceived as more friendly to Israel, but the difficulty of policing supplies outside the Arab world was recognized. A total embargo was, however, imposed upon the USA, the Netherlands and Denmark, which were considered to be particularly hostile (Mansfield 1985: 485–6). As a result, the price of oil quadrupled in what amounted to a simultaneous demonstration of Arab, Islamic and, especially, OPEC interests against the West. It came only three years after the USA had terminated the Bretton Woods financial arrangements by ending automatic dollar–gold convertibility. The combined effects created havoc in commodity and currency markets alike, precipitating a hiatus in the world-economy, followed by recession.

On the side of conciliation, President Anwar Sadat, the successor to Nasser in Egypt, began his accord with Prime Minister Menachem Begin of Israel in 1978, and caused Egypt to be ostracized amongst the Arab nations, despite the fact that it had always borne the brunt of conflict with Israel. It cost the life of Sadat, who was assassinated by Islamic extremists in 1981, and his successor Hosni Mubarak has set about patiently repairing relationships. The headquarters of the Arab League were moved from Cairo to Tunis in 1978 when the accord with Israel was signed, but they were moved back again in 1990 in the face of Tunisia's support for Iraq over the invasion of Kuwait. The league has remained a focus for Arab economic cooperation and oil money has been used to assist Arab and other Islamic states, even if political union appears as distant as ever.

In 1979 the focus of events in the Middle East moved to Iran where the Pahlavi Shah's pro-Western and modernizing dynasty collapsed and gave way to the re-establishment of a Shi'a Islamic state, a much older Persian tradition. This late twentieth-century example has taken a form not acceptable to all Muslims but, nevertheless, represents the most complete example of Islamic resurgence and defiance of Western capitalism and Soviet state socialism alike.

The creation of an Islamic state in Iran after 1979

Prior to the First World War, the Ottoman sultan, Abdul Hamid II, had 'revived the ancient Islamic title of caliph by persuading the European powers that this gave him a quasi-papal spiritual authority over Muslims everywhere' (Ruthven 1984: 298–9). It was a hollow triumph for Islam, and mainly held advantages for Europeans in their politico-economic organization of the Middle East during the mid twentieth century. In the face of European power, the spiritual choice faced by Muslims was either to accept the inferiority of Islam or else the deviation of Islamic people from the true path of their faith. The latter was the only acceptable explanation, and indicated a need for spiritual renewal (Hiro 1988: 46). This might be seen as coming to full fruition in Iran in 1979, which inspired Muslim people everywhere regardless of sectarian differences.

Islam provides a comprehensive prescription for all aspects of life. As mentioned earlier, the provisions for this are mainly contained in the Qur'an, which every devout Muslim should know by heart, and if any matter cannot be settled by reference to this or the *hadiths* (traditions) then the matter becomes the task of learned Islamic priests. Thus, as with all religions, interpretation by the priesthood is a key factor in the teachings and it is in this light that some of the current controversies in Islam might be seen. Sunnis are tolerant of a lay political system working in parallel with the church, but the Shi'as regard their origins in terms of Ali's piety and eschewing of secular politics. In principle, they see no separation between sacred leadership and political government, and where the latter becomes central to the modern nation-state form, secular aspects of political and legal institutions are subject to ratification by the religious hierarchy. According to Ruthven (1984: 220), 'About 10 per cent of all Muslims are Shi'ites of the Imami (Twelver) faith. Most of them are concentrated in Iran and its peripheral territories – Pakistan and Afghanistan to the east, Soviet Turkmenistan and Azerbaijan to the north, Turkey, Iraq, Bahrain and the Saudi province of Hasa to the west.' Inasmuch as Islamic people respect piety, however, the lead taken by the Ayatollah Khomeini in Iran tends to have had some impact upon all.

Hiro (1988: 169) points out that, 'On his return from exile on 1 February 1979 Khomeini lost no time in dismantling the secular state he had inherited [from the Shah] and installing an Islamic one.' A referendum was held at the end of March on the question, 'Should Iran be an Islamic Republic?' The voting age was reduced from eighteen to sixteen, to reward youth for its part in the revolution, and an 89 per cent turnout produced a 98.2 per cent majority in favour. On the basis of this a new constitution was drawn up by the Islamic Revolutionary Council and revised by an Assembly of Experts. The latter was made up of learned priests but dominated by the Islamic Republican Party and so reflected the unity of religion and politics. In November of the same year the constitution was also put to the vote by referendum and it too received massive approval. Under these arrangements Iran became a Twelver Shi'a Islamic Republic in which other Islamic schools of thought would be accorded full respect. It remains something of a puzzle to Westerners that Islam can on one occasion appear so tolerant and on another so inflexible. Certainly, representative government is considered to be the core of an Islamic political system, a factor which the Iranian leadership is keen to contrast with the autocratic regime of Saudi Arabia, and there are many tiers to government, with a National Consultative Assembly (popularly known as the *Majlis*), provincial councils, municipal councils, city, neighbourhood, division and village councils. But all national decision making is vetted for compatibility with Islamic principles by six Islamic jurists selected originally by Khomeini. It is also checked against the constitution's general principles by these individuals plus six lawyers elected by the *Majlis*. These twelve people make up the Council of Guardians, whilst a separate Supreme Judicial Council is the highest legal authority responsible for the standards and criteria of the Supreme Court and its subordinate chambers (Hiro 1988: 174–5). Until his death all senior officials were appointed by Khomeini himself.

The post-revolutionary Iran which was created in this way might be considered a working example of an orthodox Islamic nation-state. What it represents is the implanting of Islamic institutions into the Western nation-state model in order that the needs of modern society and oil economy are not neglected in the course of Islamicization. In Iran all the chains of authority led to the Ayatollah Khomeini, and so it was written into the constitution that there had to be successors to fulfil his role. However, although there was never any question over the suitability of Khomeini as the spiritual leader, there was controversy over the principle of succession, and whether a suitable individual could in fact be found. Khomeini, himself, intervened with the argument that this was not something for a council to decide but rather a principle ordained by Allah, so the doctrine of *vilayat-e faqih* by which the successor would inherit the same powers became part of the constitution. The principle was tested in June 1989 when Khomeini died having nominated as his successor in spiritual leadership the hitherto president of Iran, Ali Khamenei, a lesser figure not from the ranks of the Grand Ayatollahs. Less than two months later, Hashemi Rafsanjani, the former speaker of the *Majlis*, was elected by referendum as the new president, but with significantly enhanced political powers. Subsequently, Rafsanjani has appeared to be attempting to distance the political presidency from the spiritual leadership, arranging the building of a new palace for Khamenei far from the centre of government in Tehran. Rafsanjani inherited huge economic problems, partially masked by substantial oil revenues despite the decline of these during the 1980s, and he has had to face general inefficiency. Much of this is associated with an excessively large state apparatus derived to a great extent from the long and fruitless war fought with the secular Ba'athist regime of neighbouring Iraq between 1980 and 1988 (cf. Halliday 1988: 40).

In overview, then, the events in Iran since 1979 amount to the establishment of an Islamic state with inbuilt infrastructure to subject all decision making to principles of Islamic theology. In this sense it has been truly an Islamic revolution although, as a thoroughgoing Shi'a example, many of the decisions taken have proved politically unacceptable to Sunni Islamic countries. For instance, Saudi Arabia has frequently been disapproving whilst wishing, as the home of the foremost Islamic shrines, to avoid anything that might be interpreted as an anti-Islamic stance. Conversely, the Saudi royal family has been heavily criticized by the Iranian leadership for religious laxity and its lavish lifestyle in contrast to the Ayatollah Khomeini's frugal existence. Incidents have been provoked, such as at Medina in 1982, when the Saudis were accused of beating Iranian pilgrims during the course of their *Hajj* (pilgrimage) to Mecca. Iran's problematic relationships with other Islamic countries are often hard to understand for Westerners, notably in the case of the long and bitter war with Iraq. Both of these countries have a majority of Shi'as in their population but Iraq has been governed by a Ba'athist party under the leadership of President Saddam Hussein. Briefly stated, Ba'athism stands, in principle, for pan-Arab nationalism, the removal of foreign influences and socialism as a way of rebuilding Arab society. Apart from this, Iraq is an Arab country whilst Iran is Persian and historically, this has been a distinction bitterly maintained. Beyond the Middle East in other non-Arab countries, such as Pakistan and Bangladesh, the state has been partially Islamicized and even in multi-faith Nigeria, Islamicization has been mooted by its large Muslim population in the north. Much of this can be attributed to the spiritual model and the political potential projected from Iran by the Ayatollah Khomeini.

Reflections: an alternative to Western capitalism and state socialism?

The fall of the pro-Western Pahlavi dynasty in Iran, which coincided with the declaration of an Islamic republic, represented a great disappointment to the Middle East foreign policy of the USA. The last Shah, Muhammad Reza Pahlavi, had been a friend to the West and an important client for military equipment in a country bordering the Soviet Union against whom he held a historical grievance in the loss of Azerbaijan during the Second World War. The Iranian revolution not only brought into sharp relief the distinctions between Shi'a and Sunni Islam, which most people had been unaware of, but also demonstrated the potential for unity in Islam against the West and the Soviet bloc alike. Events in Iran have affected other Islamic countries, where the Ayatollah Khomeini's reputation for piety has had an impact that potentially outweighs the distaste for some of the less palatable actions of his regime. During 1988-9 the controversy over Salman Rushdie's book, *The Satanic Verses*, demonstrated the capacity of Muslims in a wide variety of social and political situations to support such an extreme move as the condemning to death for blasphemy, in absentia, of a writer resident in the West.

Equally demonstrative of the pressure which Khomeini could apply to other Islamic countries was the decision taken in 1986 by King Fahd of Saudi Arabia to change the manner in which he is addressed from 'His Majesty' to 'The Custodian of the Holy Shrines', a move which was well received in Tehran (Hiro 1988: 216). Ruthven (1984: 356) suggests that, to some extent, this represents a reversal of the Saudi dynasty's formerly pro-Western emphasis on kingship above religious primacy. In an era when modern transport makes it possible for many more people to go on the *Hajj*, it also reflects Saudi determination to retain the guardianship of the Shrines. Iranian Shi'a criticism was renewed in July 1990 when more than fourteen hundred people were killed in a stampede in one of the approach tunnels to the foremost shrine at Mecca. Western incredulity at Islamic belief was also renewed when King Fahd said afterwards: 'It was fate. Had they not died there they would have died elsewhere at the same pre-destined moment.' Islamism was extended during the 1980s in a different sphere entirely when some of the wealthy Saudi Arabian banks were Islamicized and ceased to charge interest, in line with the teaching of the Qur'an. Instead, either they make a profit on paper transactions that effectively circumvent the prohibition or, as in the case of foreign aid, they take a stake in the venture financed by the loan.

If, as might reasonably be suggested, Iran is taken as a prototypical modern Islamic state on the grounds that it provides the best working example of what full-blown Islamism might look like, then the traditional principle of spiritual surveillance by the priesthood is the most significant outcome. This religion–state structure brings to mind the party–state composition of state socialist societies, but obviously there are important differences. Surveillance in the Soviet Union was based upon a political ideology conceived as a reaction to industrial capitalism, whilst that in Iran is based upon a version of a world religion that predates Western capitalism or socialism. Yet, as Fred Halliday (1988: 35–6) observes, the Iranian Revolution took place in a country far more developed than Russia in 1917 or China in 1949 and it was carried through by mass political confrontation rather than armed revolution. Furthermore, half of the population were in urban areas, there was a per capita income of $2,000 per annum and oil revenues were more than $20 billion per annum. Not surprisingly, commentators are not unanimous in their interpretation of this. Halliday stresses the rejection of modernism and materialism in the Iranian Revolution, whilst Keddie (1988: 15) argues that the rise of Islamist movements in general is not so much a 'traditional phenomenon or a return to the medieval' as a reaction to unpopular secularizing regimes. Whatever feelings have been aroused in the West, the Islamic revolution in Iran is directed at finding a pathway of development that is not only distinct from Western capitalism or Soviet state socialism but also consistent with revitalized Islamic teaching.

Turning finally to a completely different example of Islamic renewal, Colonel Qadhafi's *Green Book* of Libyan Socialist Islamic Revolution is alternatively titled *The Third Universal Theory*, and clearly implies an alternative to capitalism or socialism (Hiro 1988: 105–7). In Islamic terms the aim is to find the true pathway directed by the Prophet Muhammad, against a background of entrenched Western global systems.

Conclusion

A Re-examination of the Concepts: Modernization and Dependency in the Context of Inter-Societal Systems

Official Western policy towards global development after the Second World War was based on the premise that the West had gone through a process of modernization whilst the rest of the world was held back in the grip of traditional social forms. A sociological basis for this can found in the work of some of the founding fathers of the discipline. Emile Durkheim and Ferdinand Tonnies both distinguished between the pre-industrial and industrial worlds in terms of different forms of social solidarity, whilst Max Weber drew up his ideal types of social action and legitimated authority to accommodate generalized features of all societies, which can then be seen as skewed towards tradition in the old world and rationality in the new. These are dichotomous versions of a general concept of social evolution, through which societies are seen as progressing along a pathway of development or modernization from a traditional to a modern stage.

There are a number of clear examples of the evolutionary form, some of them from the nineteenth century as exemplified by the work of Auguste Comte and Herbert Spencer and others from more recent times such as that enshrined in the overarching theoretical synthesis of Talcott Parsons. But perhaps the best example of evolutionary modernization theory, because of its association with policy formation, is Walt Rostow's *The Stages of Economic Growth* (1960) which uses for a baseline the British Industrial Revolution as the archetypal case of economic development. These issues were raised in chapter 2 and later amplified in chapter 7 by reference to the plans for global reconstruction after the Second World War. The 'Eurocentric' nature of the underlying theories and concepts is indisputable but my aim here has been to make this clearer through the comparative approach adopted in part II by which the rise of Western civilization has been set against other historical and global developments.

Dependency theory, as propounded inter alia by Andre Gunder Frank, Samir Amin, Arghiri Emmanuel, etc., constitutes the denial of development, and consequently of modernization theory. Denial is on the grounds that Western development involved the creation of a capitalist world-economy which became a means to exploit non-Western countries, prevent them from developing and instead maintain them in an 'underdeveloped' (rather than undeveloped) condition. Immanuel Wallerstein emphasizes that this was a historical process, with its origins in the Renaissance and its culmination in the late nineteenth century, during which the European nations colonized large areas of the world. In this perspective, since Europeans took possession of colonies mainly for economic gain, the global economic profile was changed and an interdependent but unequal relationship established between colonizer and colonized. The core of the resulting 'capitalist world-economy' was, from the beginning, centred on north-western Europe, but it is important to note that some outposts of core activity were set up in the colonies from the time when, for instance, the sixteenth-century German banking house, the Fuggers, established a correspondent in Portuguese Goa (see chapter 6). By contrast, the periphery to the system has been wherever economic activities have taken place in forms subservient to the European core, because the concept of core and periphery seeks to avoid the simplistic geographical division between Europe and its colonies. Instead it sets a distinction, in terms of economic activity, that is roughly but not unproblematically equivalent to the traditional and modern societal dichotomy. The capitalist core is characterized by modern society, whilst the exploited periphery is handicapped by traditional institutions; in fact, many colonized territories became dualistic, containing enclaves of modern activity set against a background of traditional activity, which remained detached socially, politically and economically.

The main point of dependency theory is that the West, operating with a capitalist economic system, is seen as having modernized itself through the medium of enterprises and investments which, whether located in the West or in the colonies, fitted into that Western-dominated capitalist world-economy. The remaining sectors of the colonies were left to their own devices during the colonial episodes under the surveillance of the 'district commissioner' system or its equivalent, and since the end of colonialism these have been the areas particularly identified as economically deprived and therefore targeted for 'modernization' through various practical development schemes.

As described in part III, after the Second World War development policy was an element in the global plans for post-war reconstruction especially during the 1960s which the United Nations dubbed the first 'decade of development'. But Hamza Alavi and Teodor Shanin make the significant point that the dependency theorists' critical assault on modernization coincided with a widespread realization of failure in development plans and many development theorists became disillusioned, especially with modernization theory itself. Instead, they dedicated themselves to 'specific problems of particular societies, without making much effort to view them any longer within any broad analytical context' (1982: 3). Constitutional independence was seen generally to leave the former colonies in the position of attempting to modernize with forms of economic activity left over from colonialism. Core-type activities in the 'developing countries' tended to remain firmly under the control of Western companies, especially the transnational corporations, connected directly with the core of the capitalist world-economy. Peripheral-type activities were normally left under the developing countries' own control but were, in Amin's terms, 'disarticulated' from the capitalist world-economy, thus preventing any significant change in their economic fortunes.

Therefore, modernization theory and dependency theory are opposites, the one dedicated to economic and social development and the other to exposing reasons why this cannot take place within a Western-dominated capitalist world-economy. Each theory, however, is based upon an economistic concept, and any explanation of institutions other than the economy is taken as reducible to the terms of economy itself. Modernization theory posits that the application of the capitalist economic dynamic to the developing countries will result in their modernization and advancement along an imaginary route towards Western standards of living. Dependency theory is associated with the Marxist critique of capitalism, with its singular emphasis on class conflict derived from the contradiction between socialized production and private appropriation. Added to this, however, are the concepts of core and periphery which contain the extra contradiction between globally organized production and consumption that is disproportionately Western. This additional proposition has bestowed on dependency theory the epithet, 'neo-Marxist', but it does not detract from the fact that in dependency theory, as in orthodox Marxism, the development of economic institutions determines the form of other institutions in society. On these grounds of economistic bias, above all others, both modernization theory and dependency theory are found wanting.

Structuration theory

In taking up Anthony Giddens's structuration theory as a conceptual framework for social change, the alternative perspective presented here is that social, political and economic institutions, conceptualized as the structure of society, are in the passage of time all subject to routine reproduction by human beings and that human agency has the capacity to 'make a difference'. This is the essence of social change and it cannot be explained purely in terms of economic imperatives as in Marxist analysis. In the global context to which this book is dedicated, the overarching institutions of an inter-societal system have been categorized under the following framework as introduced in chapter 3 and developed through the ensuing chapters:

Symbolic orders/modes of discourse	Global information system
Political institutions	Nation-state system
Economic institutions	Capitalist world-economy
Law/modes of sanction	Global military order

(after Giddens 1985: 277)

These four global institutions are portrayed as such for the purpose of analysis but that which they subsume is clearly interdependent and overlapping. Above all, it is through them that we may perceive the connections between our day-to-day activities and the stark distinctions between the high-consumption living standards amongst people in the West and subsistence standards amongst people in the Third World. Firstly, we all participate in global communication if only passively as consumers and indeed that communication is characteristically mass communication which is unidirectional in form, collected in and broadcast from the West. There is in fact little capacity for feedback to the broadcasting agencies and overall little media production outside of the West. Secondly, we are all citizens of nation-states and have certain rights and obligations as a result. Our individual fortunes are to a great extent dependent upon the breadth of activities in the nation-state to which we hold citizenship. As mentioned earlier, to be a stateless person is to be in a very difficult position in the modern world. Thirdly, any examination of our immediate possessions will reveal that our purchases are derived from a global production network and thus may be connected directly with the capitalist world-economy. Fourthly, the maintenance and protection of all of these activities and the parts that we as individuals play in them has given rise to a global military order through which military force is the ultimate sanction in the defence of the normative aspects of our Western lives. People outside of the West clearly do not enjoy the same levels of protection.

In the widely used First World–Third World conceptualization of differences in living stardards within global institutions, there are complications in the definition of the intermediate Second World. Obviously it is an integral part of the terminology adopted after the Second World War but a precise form of delineation for all three 'worlds' has never been satisfactorily identified. As Worsley (1984: 310) points out, some Third World countries have aligned themselves with the First World and others with the Second World. The Second World has been commonly defined simply as the state socialist countries or the the Soviet bloc, but the Warsaw Pact military alliance has since disintegrated. In the functionalist terms of Wallerstein's world-system theory, the Second World formed part of a semi-periphery to provide a 'buffer zone' between core and peripheral countries. This semi-periphery embraced those Western countries such as Spain and Portugal which historically slipped from the core of the capitalist world-economy, together with the former European settler colonies of Australasia. Yet Spain and Portugal are nowadays full members of the European Community whilst Australia and New Zealand are OECD countries and undeniably enjoy Western standards of living. In more recent accounts those Third World countries which have exhibited significant capitalist economic development, the newly industrializing countries (NICs), have been in effect 'promoted' from the Third World to the semi-periphery (see Part IV). One of the results has been the Brandt Commission's (1980) portrayal of a world consisting merely of North and South, whereby a latitudinal line is notionally drawn around the globe and distorted to include Australasia within an industrialized northern hemisphere that embraces the Soviet Union and Eastern Europe. This leaves the developing countries all roughly located in the southern hemisphere, and as the Soviet Union and the Eastern European countries become part of the capitalist world-economy this may be the natural successor to the three 'worlds' of popular terminology.

Nevertheless, the Second World or semi-periphery is an important concept for dependency theory because of its role as a buffer-zone between core and periphery serving apparently to prevent the two from direct conflict over economic issues. It is conceptualized as a bridge between the 'haves' and 'have-nots' projecting to the latter a kind of potential escape route from deprivation that is, in fact, an illusion available only to a few countries which have enjoyed special relationships with the West. This point about special relationships would seem to be appropriate for the newly industrializing countries (NICs) of East Asia, i.e. Hong Kong, Singapore, South Korea and

Taiwan, for these have certainly enjoyed special attention from the West either as colonial entrepot centres or as capitalist ideological allies and recipients of military-oriented aid during the Cold War. As observed in chapter 11, these states have also benefited from their recent association with Japan industrially, and from a common historical and cultural background as 'post-Confucian' countries of the 'China periphery type' (see chapter 11). The Latin American newly industrializing countries of Mexico and Brazil were colonies of Spain and Portugal but have since been closely connected, culturally and economically if not politically, with the United States and the latter point is itself a reminder of the separate but interconnected nature of global institutions.

In terms of structuration theory, these generalizations of First, Second and Third Worlds are of limited validity. It is the variety of circumstances experienced in different parts of each of these 'worlds' during the development of the Western dominated inter-societal system that is of greater significance. Structuration theory hinges on the concept of the duality of structure whereby there is continuous interplay between immediate social interaction and institutional distanciation in time and space. In all nation-states, regardless of how they are labelled in terms of First, Second or Third Worlds, there are institutions through which society is reproduced. Firstly, there is communication and the transmission of knowledge through symbolic orders and modes of discourse. Some of these are indigenous to local cultures and others derived or imposed from external sources, including especially the pervasive global culture of Western society as illustrated, for instance, in Marshall McLuhan's (1964) analogy of a 'global village'. This conveys certain aspects of the modern world that are common to us all. Global products are familiar to us all, whatever the scale of our access to them and the part of the planet that we inhabit. Next, there is a complementary and overlapping set of political and economic institutions through which power over both people (authoritative power) and their environment (allocative power) is reproduced. The nation-state system is conceptualized as the dominant institutional framework of power over people and the capitalist world-economy as that of power over environmental resources. This is the essence of Western liberal democracy, the development of which became a justification for Western interference in other systems, projected as a model system for other parts of the world to emulate. The nation-state system of course impinges on the capitalist world-economy and vice versa, particularly in the sense in which the infrastructure of the nation-state supports the lives of people as socialized labour, whilst the products of that labour are appropriated as private property. Finally, there are normative institutions involving the reproduction through time and space of laws and modes of sanction. There are various levels of sanction in society including peer pressure in the context of social groups, cultural norms in a broader context, formal policing within the structure of the nation-state and at the global level international military interventions. In this respect, modern Western institutions are interspersed with traditional indigenous or local institutions but the ultimate sanction in support of normative elements is the global military order, as for instance in the numerous interventions of the USA in its familiar and widely accepted but, nevertheless, primarily self-styled 'global policing role'.

These social, political and economic institutions may be seen as both facilitative and restrictive for human beings in society. Modes of sanction or power or communication are constraining of people, but at the same time enable them to achieve things collectively, as suggested by such pioneering observers of Western society as Hobbes and Rousseau. Nevertheless, the enablement and constraint of the individual is not equally distributed and people benefit from social institutions to a greater or lesser degree according to their position in relation to such institutions, as interpreted initially in sociological terms by Durkheim, Marx and Weber. In order to arrive at a better understanding of the present, however, we should avoid abstract and deterministic models of social structure and change and instead use frameworks which trace the reproduction, through human agency, of social, political and economic institutions over time (the historical dimension) and space (the global dimension). That is, a synthesis delineating the reproduction of social, political and economic institutions through time and space is, I suggest, necessary to avoid economistically biased, evolutionary or ahistorical models, following the arguments set out in part I.

A very simple example of a category not properly interpreted in historical or comparative terms is the application of the term newly industrializing countries (NICs) to the so called 'four little tigers' of East Asia and to Brazil and Mexico in Latin America as well. Quite clearly the historical and cultural background of the former, with their proximity to China and Japan, is very different to the latter, with their proximity to the USA. As in other comparable cases this renders the indiscriminate use of an overarching term inadvisable, and the inferences that may be drawn from it, unreliable. Similar criticism may be applied to Wallerstein's terms core and periphery in relation to the capitalist world-economy. There needs to be a framework capable of accommodating economic interdependence, because this undoubtedly exists on a global scale and it involves not only capitalist countries but also, to a growing extent, the state socialist countries, given the changes in Eastern Europe that began in the late 1980s. It is helpful however to employ the concept of the capitalist world-economy in conjunction with those of nation-state system, global military order and global information system. This composite framework facilitates distinctions between economic interdependence, political separation, military alliance and cultural exchange as hallmarks of an inter-societal system which best depicts the contemporary world situation. None of these dimensions is reducible to the others, and to single out any one as automatically more important than the others is an oversimplification. Nation-state governments cannot manage their internal economies without reference to world markets, nor can they maintain political separation without reference to the global military order and these conditions can be illustrated, as follows, in relation to global institutions as already identified:

Global institution	Form of relationship
Global information system	cultural exchange
Capitalist world-economy	economic interdependence
Nation-state system	political separation
Global military order	military alliances

(after Giddens 1985: 277)

One aspect of the links between these systems that was emphasized especially in parts II and III is the industrialized production of weapons. As a major feature of the global situation since the Second World War, the NATO–Warsaw Pact military divide has had an effect upon the global economy. The mainspring of economic growth has been the industrial mass production of all kind of goods, including military weapons. Advanced technology has enabled the military establishments of the two superpowers to take the world to the very brink of global destruction, and no part of the world is exempt from the scope of nuclear weapons. Equally, industrial technology has facilitated the spread of sophisticated small and intermediate weapons which are mass produced and distributed relatively easily. Moreover, whilst the technology for nuclear warheads and intercontinental ballistic missiles is difficult and expensive to develop, virtually every nation-state and many oppositional nationalist movements have found its possible to obtain other types of sophisticated weaponry. When Kuwait was annexed in August 1990, the combined forces of several advanced industrial countries were judged necessary to confront the accumulated military power of Iraq under Saddam Hussein. In fact, military expenditure has formed an enormous proportion of overall expenditure amongst the nation-states of the world.

Military expenditure has had a high priority not only in nation-states' internal budgets but also in their aid programmes to less developed countries. In chapter 9, the various shortcomings of development aid were outlined and amongst these is the high priority accorded to military expenditure. The reason for this has lain in the apparent necessity for nation-state governments to secure their political authority with military power, against the background of overarching policies from the USA and the USSR, each maintaining a network of military allies across the globe. Additionally, there is the determination of the advanced industrial nations, and some less advanced ones, to enhance their exports with contracts for military weaponry. Linked to this are the the high-technology manufacturing capabilities of the transnational corporations which dominate the core of the world's productive resources. Industrial enterprise, technological development and financial expenditure devoted to military weapons have been firmly linked to the general progress of these fundamental aspects of economy, in the West and in the state socialist countries too. The most recent phase of NATO–Warsaw Pact competition in arms production during the 1980s saw the creation of extra tiers of delivery systems for nuclear weapons largely to force negotiation between the USA and the USSR. The result has been that during the ensuing stage of de-escalation and arms limitation the starting point has been higher than ever before in terms of both quality and quantity of weaponry.

Structuration theory does embrace the Marxist principle that in the system integration of modern society there is contradiction whereby industrial production is socialized (organized on a societal basis) whilst the appropriation of the profit is privatized (subject to 'free enterprise'). But, production organized in this way is seen not only as a form of domination but also as an enormous enabling factor for society through the levels of production that can be achieved in the general interest of lowering costs and broadening access to consumption. Nevertheless, the appropriation of profit is a form of exploitative domination harnessed to sectional interests. This much derives from orthodox analysis of the class system, but the concept is extended to draw also from dependency theory and world system theory. This involves the additional contradiction whereby industrial production has been globalized, but mainly for Western consumption. That is, production is organized through a new international division of labour involving global production lines and, in part, cheap labour from the Third World, as described in chapters 9 and 10, with the greater portion of that production being consumed by people in advanced industrial countries. Implicit in this is the proposition that labour utilized in the Third World is priced low not only because of expectations associated with existing low standards of living but also because it is supplied without the welfare costs that have become a part of socialized labour in the West. Therefore, whilst global production is an extension of socialized production which could be an enormous enabling factor in the general interest, the West's disproportionately high consumption is a form of appropriation that constitutes exploitative domination for sectional interests.

Inter-societal systems

However, Marxist class analysis and the emphasis in dependency theory on the capitalist world-economy, together, are not enough to explain social change adequately and it is appropriate here to underline what was set out in chapter 3. Rather than as evolutionary progress, or even as a dualistic system of Western modernization and peripheral dependency, it is preferable to conceptualize global change in terms of inter-societal systems (see figure 4 in chapter 3). In the history of human beings on this planet, something like seven thousand years ago class-divided societies were organized amidst the tribal societies which had existed for very much longer. They are termed thus because they involved the separation of a minority urban class within the city from a more numerous rural class outside of it.

The crucial point is that class-divided societies involving a form of symbiosis between city and countryside did not supersede tribal societies but existed alongside them in what is termed here an inter-societal system. The use of the term symbiosis denotes an interdependent relationship between the two classes, but culturally the urban class is as far removed from the rural class as it is from tribal society. By the fifteenth century, European forms of class-divided societies, organized as separate kingdoms and city-states and not as unitary hierarchical empire as in other cases, developed capacities for maritime expansionism and gradually came to dominate other class-divided societies and tribal societies around the globe, to form a further example of an inter-societal system. There are considerable time–space implications to this, because the European colonial episodes took place over several centuries and some colonies gained their independence before others were seized. The Latin American countries, for instance, became constitutionally independent during the early nineteenth century before Europe had begun to take possession of the interior of Africa. Coincidentally with these colonial episodes, the form of European society itself changed significantly with the extension of its politico-military, economic and cultural power. By the twentieth century, 'Western' institutions had become global in extent to form the first truly global culture whilst the liberal–democratic nation-state in the polity (public sector) and industrialized production in the economy (private sector) had transformed Western society into the class (capitalist) form. That is, socially organized and state-surveilled but privately owned industrial production was extended to such an extent that class was no longer a matter of the physical city–countryside division. Instead, it became an integral part of all social organization. In the industrialized societies, by definition, virtually everyone is involved in some way with socialized production and/or private appropriation, but in the late twentieth century that involvement is much more complex than Marx envisaged from his nineteenth-century standpoint. Now, the individual is linked through the day-to-day reproduction of a wide range of institutions to a contemporary inter-societal system which, to amplify the frameworks set out earlier in this concluding chapter, involves:

1　Widely broadcast, and therefore highly generalized, communications in a global information system which reinforces the dominant Western culture.
2　Models of citizenship involving equality before the law, representative democracy and welfare rights, legitimated by the existence of nation-states in a nation-state system (with due acknowledgment to actual differences between model and material forms which have formed the substance of social science investigation).
3　Production through a new international division of labour and allocation through the capitalist world-economy.
4　Normative patterns protected through layers of sanction including informal group pressures, cultural norms and formal policing, but culminating in the global military order.

More recently the hegemony of the class (capitalist) societies in the contemporary inter-societal system was challenged by the state socialist societies with their alternative approach to the organization of production. After the Second World War, this broadened into the superpower confrontation of the post-war global military order and, with the end of European colonialism, these two predominantly military alliances of advanced industrial societies have co-existed with the so-called developing countries which have been encouraged to modernize. The First World–Second World–Third World framework cannot be ignored, because it has been so widely used, but is nevertheless, unsatisfactory in a number of ways. For instance, it is inadequate in the sense that some Third World countries have accepted the capitalist pathway to development, whilst others have rejected it and opted for socialism. Yet others, rejecting both, have sought to adapt modern institutions to the teachings of Islam, as described in chapter 12. Within the Third World especially, surviving examples of class-divided and tribal social structure remain dotted around the globe, but they have been marginalized by Western institutions and exist uneasily in the context of the twentieth-century inter-societal system. In these overall arrangements, the nation-state is clearly the model societal form, but the global communication system (mass communications) ensures that culture is exchanged and assimilated widely. The mass-communication technology is based mainly in the West, and so the preponderence of broadcast material originates from and is produced as Western culture.

Perhaps the most significant outcome is that all societies exist in the same set of global systems which guarantees none of them continuing modernization nor dependency. Any categorization, including that based upon three 'worlds', is in the long term transitory. Since the Second World War there has been both political and military conflict between capitalist and state socialist nation-states, but the primary economic system undoubtedly has been and continues to be the capitalist world-economy. Over a longer period, however, this economic system has had its focus changed from time to time, with Britain enjoying hegemonic dominance in the nineteenth century and losing it to the USA in the twentieth century. Now some observers see Japan in conjunction with other East Asian 'newly industrializing countries' aspiring to hegemony, when previously they would have been designated as developing countries. It was described in part IV how, during the last quarter of the twentieth century, even the United States has incurred a deficit on its balance of payments and has become a large-scale debtor to Japan. As part of this process, the new international division of labour has involved the abandonment of some industrial production in the' West and its replacement with industrial production in 'newly industrializing countries'. Additionally, the source of much of the West's and Japan's energy supplies, Middle East oil, has become subject to renewed forms of Islamic society and government, as described in chapter 12. This is a revival of much older contentions between Europe and Islam over religious belief and the supply of commodities which was one of the starting points to the historical analysis, in part II.

During the last few months of 1989 the *perestroika* and *glasnost* movements that have been a feature of the Soviet Union under the leadership of Mikhail Gorbachev were extended to its Eastern European statellites to even greater effect. Hitherto heavily entrenched regimes were swept aside virtually overnight in favour of multi-party systems and the market economy. That supreme symbol of the Cold War, the Berlin Wall, was officially breached and subsequently demolished. Above all the party–state system, which was described in chapter 8 as the cornerstone of state socialist society, collapsed contrary to all the expectations of Western observers. As these societies, having hitherto forsaken centralized planning, open up completely to capitalist exchange, they will provide new consumer markets for Western and Japanese production and, coincidentally, new production sites and labour forces for the transnational corporations. It is difficult to see this not having a further profound effect on the new international division of labour and the definition of newly industrializing countries towards the end of the twentieth century.

There is no automatic outcome to these events, which are of a social and political as well as an economic nature. In the terms of the development debate, they may result in modernization or dependency for the territories involved. It is the weakness of existing theories, however, that they do imply preordained eventualities. Modernization theory, in all its variations, bases economic development upon the premise of a capitalist formula derived from the original British industrial revolution, as outlined in chapter 2. Dependency theory, in all its forms, including world-system theory, views all development as one-sided in favour of the West, in a situation that can only be reversed by socialist revolution. In this respect 'neo-Marxism' is no different from orthodox Marxism. This represents a need for new concepts which can be reached, I propose, through the medium of structuration theory. Its conceptual framework conjoins social interaction with institutional analysis and engages with social, political and economic systems in their fullest time and space contexts.

References

Abel, E. 1969: *The Missiles of October: the story of the Cuban Missile Crisis.* London: MacGibbon & Kee.

Abercrombie, N., Hill, S. and Turner, B. S. 1980: *The Dominant Ideology Thesis.* London: Allen & Unwin.

Alavi, H. and Shanin, T. 1982: *Introduction to the Sociology of 'Developing Societies'.* London: Macmillan.

Ali, T. 1975: Pakistan and Bangla Desh: results and prospects. In R. Blackburn (ed.), *Explosion in a Sub-Continent: India, Pakistan, Bangla Desh and Ceylon,* Harmondsworth: Penguin, 293–347.

Amin, S. 1974: *Accumulation on a World Scale: a critique of the theory of underdevelopment* (2 vols). New York: Monthly Review Press.

Anderson, P. 1979: The absolutist state in the West. In P. Anderson (ed.), *Lineages of the Absolutist State,* London: New Left Books.

Ashworth, W. 1975: *A Short History of the International Economy since 1850.* London: Longman.

Atkinson, D. 1971: *Orthodox Consensus and Radical Alternative: a Study in Sociological Theory.* London: Heinemann.

Bailey, S. D. 1989: *The United Nations: a short political guide.* London: Macmillan.

Baran, P. 1957: *The Political Economy of Growth.* New York: Monthly Review Press.

Barnett, C. 1972: *The Collapse of British Power.* New York: William Morrow.

Barratt Brown, M. 1982: Developing societies as part of an international political economy. In H. Alavi and T. Shanin (eds), *Introduction to the Sociology of 'Developing Societies',* London: Macmillan, 153–71.

Bauer, P. 1984: *Reality and Rhetoric: studies in the economics of development.* London: Weidenfeld & Nicholson.

Beazley, C. R. 1968: *Prince Henry the Navigator: The hero of Portugal and modern discovery 1394–1460 AD.* London: Frank Cass.

Bell, D. 1960: *The End of Ideology.* Glencoe, Ill.: Free Press.

Bell, D. 1973: *The Coming of Post-Industrial Society: a venture in social forecasting*. London: Heinemann.

Bendix, R. 1967: Tradition and modernity reconsidered. *Comparative Studies in Society and History*, 9(3), 292–346.

Berger, P. L. 1987: *The Capitalist Revolution: fifty propositions about prosperity, equality, and liberty*. Aldershot: Wildwood House.

Bethell, L. (ed.) 1987: *Colonial Spanish America*. Cambridge: Cambridge University Press.

Bienefeld, M. 1981: Dependency and the Newly Industrializing Countries (NICs): towards a reappraisal. In D. Seers (ed.) *Dependency Theory: a critical reassessment*, London: Frances Pinter, 79–96.

Booth, D. 1985: Marxism and development sociology: interpreting the impasse. *World Development*, 13(7), 761–87.

Boxer, C. R. 1973: *The Dutch Seaborne Empire, 1600–1800*. Harmondsworth: Penguin.

Brandt Commission 1980: *North–South: a programme for survival*. London: Pan Books.

Braudel, F. 1981: *Civilization and Capitalism 15th to 18th Century: Vol. 1 The Structures of Everyday Life*. London: Collins.

Braudel, F. 1982: *Vol. 2 The Wheels of Commerce*. London: Collins.

Braudel, F. 1984: *Vol. 3 The Perspective of the World*. London: Collins.

Braverman, H. 1974: *Labor and Monopoly Capital: the degradation of work in the twentieth century*. New York: Monthly Review Press.

Bray, F. 1986: *The Rice Economies: technology and development in Asian Societies*. Oxford: Basil Blackwell.

Brett, E. A. 1985: *The World Economy since the War: the politics of uneven development*. London: Macmillan.

Burke, P. 1986: *The Italian Renaissance: culture and society in Italy*. Cambridge: Polity Press.

Campbell, A., Keen, C., Norman, G. and Oakeshott, R. 1978: *Worker-Owners: the Mondragon achievement*. London: Anglo-German Foundation.

Carciofi, R. 1983: Cuba in the seventies. In G. White, R. Murray and C. White (eds), *Revolutionary Socialist Development in the Third World*, Brighton: Wheatsheaf Books, 193–233.

Chaudhuri, K. N. 1978: *The Trading World of Asia and the English East India Company, 1660–1760*. Cambridge: Cambridge University Press.

Clegg, S. R., Higgins, W. and Spybey, T. 1990: 'Post-Confucianism', social democracy and economic culture. In S. R. Clegg and S. G. Redding (eds), *Capitalism in Contrasting Cultures*, Berlin: de Gruyter, 31–78.

Corbridge, S. 1990: Post-Marxism and development studies: beyond the impasse. *World Development*, 18(5) 623–39.

Coser, L. A. 1979: American trends. In T. Bottomore and R. Nisbet (eds), *A History of Sociological Analysis*, London: Heinemann, 287–320.

Dahrendorf, R. 1959: *Class and Class Conflict in Industrial Society*. London: Routledge & Kegan Paul.

Davidson, B. 1984: *The Story of Africa*. London: Mitchell Beazley.

Davis, H. and Scase, R. 1985: *Western Capitalism and State Socialism: an introduction*. Oxford: Basil Blackwell.

Dawson, R. (ed.) 1964: *The Legacy of China*. Oxford: Oxford University Press.

Denley, P. 1988: The Mediterranean in the age of the Renaissance, 1200–1500. In G. Holmes (ed.), *The Oxford Illustrated History of the Middle Ages*, Oxford: Oxford University Press, 235–96.

Deutsch, K. 1969: *Nationalism and Its Alternatives*. New York; Knopf.

Dimbleby, D. and Reynolds, D. 1988: *An Ocean Apart: the relationship between Britain and America in the twentieth century*. London: Hodder & Stoughton.

Dinham, B. and Hines, C. 1983: *Agribusiness in Africa: a study of the impact of big business on Africa's food and agricultural production*. London: Earth Resources Research Ltd.

Djilas, M. 1966: *The New Class: an analysis of the communist system*. London: Allen & Unwin.

Doeringer, P. and Piore, M. 1971: *Internal Labour Markets and Man-Power Analysis*. Lexington, Mass.: D. C. Heath, Lexington Books.

Donahue, J. M. 1986: *The Nicaraguan Revolution in Health*. South Hadley: Bergin & Harvey.

Duroselle, J.-B. 1990: *Europe: a history of its peoples*. London: Viking.

Eccleston, B. 1989: *State and Society in Post-War Japan*. Cambridge: Polity Press.

Edwards, R. 1979: *Contested Terrain: the transformation of the workplace in the twentieth century*. London: Heinemann.

Eisenstadt, S. N. 1968: *Comparative Perspectives on Social Change*. Boston, Mass.: Little, Brown & Co.

Emmanuel, A. 1972: *Unequal Exchange: a study in the imperialism of trade*. New York: Monthly Review Press.

Etzioni-Halevy, E. 1981: *Social Change: the advent and maturation of modern society*. London: Routledge & Kegan Paul.

Foucault, M. 1977: *Discipline and Punish*. London: Allen Lane.

Frank, A. G. 1966: The development of underdevelopment. *Monthly Review*, 18(4) 23–8.

Frank, A. G. 1967: *Capitalism and Underdevelopment in Latin America*. New York: Monthly Review Press.

Frobel, F., Heinrichs, J. and Kreye, O. 1980: *The New International Division of Labour*. Cambridge: Cambridge University Press.

Fromkin, D. 1991: *A Peace to End All Peace: creating the modern Middle East*. Harmondsworth: Penguin.

Fuentes, A. and Ehrenreich, B. 1987: Women in the global factory. In R. Peet (ed.), *International Capitalism and Industrial Restructuring: a critical analysis*, Boston, Mass.: Unwin Hyman, 201–15.

Gamble, A. and Walton, P. 1976: *Capitalism in Crisis: inflation and the state*. London: Macmillan.

Gayle, D. J. 1986: *The Small Developing State: comparing political economies in Costa Rica, Singapore and Jamaica*. Aldershot: Gower.

Geertz, C. 1963: *Old Societies and New States*. New York: Collier-Methuen.

Gellner, E. 1983: *Nations and Nationalism*. Oxford: Basil Blackwell.

George, S. 1986: *How the Other Half Dies* (revised edn). Harmondsworth: Penguin.

Giddens, A. 1976: *New Rules of Sociological Method: a positive critique of interpretative sociologies*. London: Hutchinson.

Giddens, A. 1979: *Central Problems in Social Theory: action, structure and contradiction in social analysis*. London: Macmillan.

Giddens, A. 1981: *A Contemporary Critique of Historical Materialism: Vol. 1 Power, Property and the State*. London: Macmillan.

Giddens, A. 1984: *The Constitution of Society: outline of the theory of structuration*. Cambridge: Polity Press.

Giddens, A. 1985: *The Nation-State and Violence: Vol 2 of a Contemporary Critique of Historical Materialism*. Cambridge: Polity Press.

Goffman, E. 1961: *Asylums*. New York: Anchor Books.

Goldthorpe, J. H. 1978: The current inflation: towards a sociological account. In F. Hirsch and J. H. Goldthorpe (eds), *The Political Economy of Inflation*, Oxford: Martin Robertson, 186–216.

Gordon, A. 1985: *The Evolution of Labour Relations in Japan*. Cambridge, Mass.: Harvard University Press.

Gould, J. D. 1972: *Economic Growth in History*. London: Methuen.

Gouldner, A. W. 1971: *The Coming Crisis of Western Sociology*. London: Heinemann.

Hall, J. A. 1986: *Powers and Liberties: the causes and consequences of the rise of the West*. Harmondsworth: Penguin.

Halliday, F. 1988: The Iranian revolution: uneven development and religious populism. In F. Halliday and H. Alavi (eds), *State and Ideology in the Middle East and Pakistan*, London: Macmillan, 31–63.

Harris, N. 1987: *The End of the Third World*. Harmondsworth: Penguin.

Harrison, D. 1988: *The Sociology of Modernization and Development*. London: Unwin Hyman.

Haug, W. F. 1986: *Critique of Commodity Aesthetics: appearance, sexuality and advertising in capitalist society*. Cambridge: Polity Press.

Hayter, T. 1981: *The Creation of World Poverty: an alternative view to the Brandt Report*. London: Pluto Press.

Hayter, T. and Watson, C. 1985: *Aid: rhetoric and reality*. London: Pluto Press.

Henderson, J. 1989: *The Globalization of High Technology Production: society, space and semi-conductors in the re-structuring of the modern world*. London: Routledge.

Herndon, B. 1970: *Ford*. London: Cassell.

Higgins, T. 1957: *Winston Churchill and the Second Front, 1940–43*. Oxford: Oxford University Press.

Hill, C. 1972: *The World Turned Upside Down*. London: Temple Smith.

Hiro, D. 1988: *Islamic Fundamentalism*. London: Paladin.

Hohenberg, P. M. and Lees, L. H. 1985: *The Making of Urban Europe 1000–1950*. Cambridge, Mass.: Harvard University Press.

Hoogvelt, A. M. M. 1978: *The Sociology of Developing Societies* (2nd edn). London: Macmillan.

Hoogvelt, A. M. M. 1982: *The Third World in Global Development*. London: Macmillan.

Hoselitz, B. F. 1960: *Sociological Aspects of Economic Growth*. New York: Free Press.

Husaini, S. W. A. 1980: *Islamic Environmental Systems Engineering: a systems study of environmental engineering, and the law, politics, education, economics and sociology of science and culture of Islam*. London: Macmillan.

James, E. 1988: The northern world in the Dark Ages, 400–900. In G. Holmes (ed.), *The Oxford Illustrated History of Medieval Europe*, Oxford: Oxford University Press, 63–114.

Jones, T. 1976: *Ghana's First Republic, 1960–1966: the pursuit of the political kingdom*. London: Methuen.

Junkerman, J. 1987: Blue-sky management: the Kawasaki story. In R. Peet (ed.), *International Capitalism and Industrial Restructuring*, Boston, Mass.: Allen & Unwin, 131–44.

Kahn, H. 1979: *World Economic Development: 1979 and Beyond*. London: Croom Helm.

Karst, K. 1989: *Belonging to America: equal citizenship and the constitution*. New Haven, Conn.: Yale University Press.

Keddie, N. R. 1988: Ideology, society and the state in post-colonial muslim societies. In F. Halliday and H. Alavi (eds), *State and Ideology in the Middle East and Pakistan*, London: Macmillan, 9–30.

Kennedy, P. 1988: *The Rise and Fall of the Great Powers*. London: Unwin Hyman.

Kerr, C., Dunlop, J. T., Harbison, F. and Myers, C. A. 1960: *Industrialism and Industrial Man*. Cambridge Mass.: Harvard University Press.

Ketcham, R. 1987: *Individualism and Public Life: a modern dilemma*. Oxford: Basil Blackwell.

Kidron, M. and Segal, R. 1981: *The State of the World Atlas*. London: Pan Books.

Laclau, E. 1971: Feudalism and capitalism in Latin America. *New Left Review*, 67 (May–June), 19–38.

Lamb, G. 1981: Rapid capitalist development models: a new politics of dependence? In D. Seers (ed.), *Dependency Theory: a critical reassessment*, London: Frances Pinter, 97–108.

Lane, D. 1971: *The End of Inequality?: stratification under state socialism*. Harmondsworth: Penguin.

Lane, D. 1978: *Politics and Society in the USSR* (2nd edn). Oxford: Martin Robertson.

Lane, D. and O'Dell, F. 1978: *The Soviet Industrial Worker: social class, education and control*. Oxford: Martin Robertson.

Lee, C.-C. 1980: *Media Imperialism Reconsidered: the homogenizing of television culture*. Beverly Hills, Calif.: Sage.

Le Goff, J. 1988: *Medieval Civilization 400–1500*. Oxford: Basil Blackwell.

Lenski, G. and Lenski, J. 1978: *Human Societies* (3rd edn). New York: McGraw-Hill.

Littler, C. 1982: De-skilling and changing structures of control. In S. Wood (ed.), *The Degradation of Work? Skill, de-skilling and the labour process*, London: Hutchinson, 122–45.

Lockwood, D. 1964: Social integration and system integration. In George Z. Zollschan and W. Hirsch (eds), *Exploration in Social Change*, London: Routledge & Kegan Paul.

Lopez, R. S. 1963: The crossroad within the wall. In O. Handlin and J. Burchard (eds), *The Historian and the City*, Cambridge, Mass.: MIT Press, 27–43.

McLelland, D. 1973: *The Achieving Society*. New York: Van Nostrand.

McLuhan, M. 1964: *Understanding Media*. London: Routledge & Kegan Paul.

Mann, M. 1986: *The Sources of Social Power: Vol 1 A History of Power from the Beginning to AD 1760*. Cambridge: Cambridge University Press.

Mansfield, P. 1985: *The Arabs* (3rd edn). Harmondsworth, Penguin.

Marcuse, H. 1964: *One Dimensional Man*. London: Routledge & Kegan Paul.

Marshall, T. H. 1950: *Citizenship and Social Class and Other Essays*. Cambridge: Cambridge University Press.

Mathias, P. 1969: *The First Industrial Nation: an economic history of Britain, 1700–1914*. London: Methuen.

Mitter, S. 1986: *Common Fate, Common Bond: women in the global economy*. London: Pluto Press.

Murakami, Y. 1984: *Ie* society as a pattern of civilization. *Journal of Japanese Studies*, 10(2), 281–363.

Murakami, Y. 1986: Technology in transition: two perspectives on industrial policy. In H. Patrick (ed.), *Japan's High Technology Industries: lessons and limitations of industrial policy*, Seattle: University of Washington Press, 211–41.

Nations, R. 1975: The economic structure of Pakistan and Bangla Desh. In R. Blackburn (ed.), *Explosion in a Sub-Continent: India, Pakistan, Bangla Desh and Ceylon*, Harmondsworth: Penguin, 252–92.

Nawwab, I. I., Speers, P. C. and Hoye, P. F. (eds). 1980: *Aramco and Its World*. Washington DC: Aramco.

Needham, J. 1956: Mathematics and science in China and the West. *Science and Society*, 20, 320–43.

Nkrumah, K. 1965: *Neo-Colonialism: the last stage of imperialism*. London: Thomas Nelson.

Oliver, R. and Fage, J. D. 1988: *A Short History of Africa* (6th edn). Harmondsworth: Penguin.

Overseas Development Institute (ODI) 1990: *Recent Initiatives on Developing Country Debt* (pamphlet). London: ODI.

Phizacklea, A. 1990: *Unpacking the Fashion Industry: gender, racism and class in production*. London: Routledge & Kegan Paul.

Poggi, G. 1978: *The Development of the Modern State: a sociological introduction*. London: Hutchinson.

Rizzi, B. 1985: *The Bureaucratization of the World: the USSR: bureaucratic collectivism*. London: Tavistock.

Roberts, J. 1985: *The Triumph of the West*. London: BBC Publications.

Rocher, G. 1974: *Talcott Parsons and American Sociology*. London: Nelson.

Rolt, L. T. C. 1970: *Isambard Kingdom Brunel*. Harmondsworth: Penguin.

Ross, D. 1991: *The Origins of American Social Science.* Cambridge: Cambridge University Press

Rostow, W. W. 1960: *The Stages of Economic Growth: a non-communist manifesto.* Cambridge: Cambridge University Press.

Rothschild, J. 1989: *Return to Diversity: a political history of East Central Europe since World War II.* Oxford: Oxford University Press.

Rowling, N. 1987: *Commodities: how the world was taken to market.* London: Free Association Books.

Roxborough, I. 1979: *Theories of Underdevelopment.* London: Macmillan.

Ruthven, M. 1984: *Islam in the World.* Harmondsworth: Penguin.

Sahlins, M. 1972: *Stone Age Economics.* Chicago: Aldine.

Scott, J. 1979: *Corporations, Classes and Capitalism.* London: Hutchinson.

Shwadran, B. 1973: *The Middle East Oil and the Great Powers.* New York: Wiley.

Skocpol, T. 1979: *States and Social Revolutions: comparative analysis of France, Russia and China.* Cambridge: Cambridge University Press.

Smelser, N. 1959: *Social Change in the Industrial Revolution.* London: Routledge & Kegan Paul.

Smith, A. D. 1983: *State and Nation in the Third World.* Brighton: Wheatsheaf Books.

Smith, A. D. 1986: *The Ethnic Origins of Nations.* Oxford: Basil Blackwell.

Spencer, H. 1873: *The Study of Sociology.* London: Kegan Paul, Trench & Co.

Spybey, T. 1984: Traditional and professional frames of meaning for managers. *Sociology*, 18(4), 550–62.

Steel, R. 1977: *Pax Americana* (revised edn). Harmondsworth: Penguin.

Strasser, H. and Randall, S. C. 1981: *An Introduction to Theories of Social Change.* London: Routledge & Kegan Paul.

Sugimoto, Y. 1986: The manipulative basis of 'consensus' in Japan. In G. McCormack and Y. Sugimoto (eds), *Democracy in Contemporary Japan*, Sydney: Hale & Iremonger, 65–75.

Sugimoto, Y. and Mouer, R. 1985: *Images of Japanese Society.* London: Routledge & Kegan Paul.

Sweezy, P., Dobb, M., Takahashi, K., Hilton, R., Hill, C., Lefebvre, G., Procacci, G., Hobsbawm, E. and Merrington, J. 1976: *The Transition from Feudalism to Capitalism.* London: Verso.

Thompson, P. 1983: *The Nature of Work.* London: Macmillan.

Tilly, C. 1975: Reflections on the history of European state-making. In C. Tilly (ed.), *The Formation of National States in Western Europe*, Princeton, NJ: Princeton University Press.

Touraine, A. 1974: *The Post-Industrial Society.* London: Wildwood House.

Vale, M. 1988: The civilization of courts and cities in the north, 1200–1500. In G. Holmes (ed.), *The Oxford Illustrated History of the Middle Ages*, Oxford: Oxford University Press, 297–351.

Wallerstein, I. 1974: *The Modern World System.* New York: Academic Press.

Wallerstein, I. 1979: *The Capitalist World-Economy.* Cambridge: Cambridge University Press.

Wallerstein, I. 1982: Crisis as transition. In S. Amin, G. Arrighi, A. G. Frank and I. Wallerstein (eds), *Dynamics of Global Crisis*, London: Macmillan, 11–54.

Wallerstein, I. 1984: *The Politics of the World-Economy: the states, the movements and the civilizations*. Cambridge: Cambridge University Press.

Warren, B. 1980: *Imperialism: pioneer of capitalism*. London: Verso.

Weber, M. 1978: *Economy and Society* (2 vols). Berkeley, Cal.: University of California Press.

Weiner, M. J. 1981: *English Culture and the Decline of the Industrial Spirit, 1850–1980*. Cambridge: Cambridge University Press.

Westoby, A. 1981: *Communism since World War II*. Brighton: Harvester Press.

Whitton, D. 1988: The society of northern Europe in the High Middle Ages, 900–1200. In G. Holmes (ed.), *The Oxford Illustrated History of the Middle Ages*, Oxford: Oxford University Press, 115–74.

Wilson, C. 1965: *England's Apprenticeship, 1603–1763*. London: Longman.

Wittfogel, K. 1957: *Oriental Despotism: a comparative study of total power*. New Haven, Conn.: Yale University Press.

World Bank 1987: *World Bank Development Report 1987*. Oxford: Oxford University Press.

Worsley, P. 1984: *The Three Worlds: culture and world development*. London: Weidenfeld & Nicholson.

Wu, Y.-L. 1985: *Becoming an Industrialized Nation: ROC's development on Taiwan*. New York: Praeger.

Yapp, M. E. 1991: *The Near East since the First World War*. Harlow: Longman

Zaller, R. 1984: *Europe in Transition, 1660–1815*. Lanham, Mar., University Press of America.

Index